RESISTANCE
FALL OF

Introduction • p2

Basic Training • p4

Intel • p10

The Missions • p24

- Operation: Delivery 26
- A Lone Survivor 34
- Spires 42
- Fates Worse Than Death 46
- Conversion 53
- Hunted Down 57
- Path of Least Resistance 64
- The Cathedral 70
- Outgunned 78
- Into the Fire 82
- Conduits 86
- Viper's Nest 93
- No Way Out 97
- Secrets 102
- Angel 106
- Search and Rescue 111
- Common Ground 114
- A Disturbing Discovery 120
- Devil at the Door 125
- Evacuation 129
- Parting Ways 134
- Into the Depths 136
- In a Darker Place 141
- A Desperate Gamble 144
- Ice and Iron 148
- Burning Bridges 153
- On the Ice 158
- Giant Slayer 162
- Angel's Lair 165
- Last Hope 170

Multiplayer • p176

Top Secret • p201

INTRODUCTION

Getting to create a strategy guide for a PlayStation 3 launch title is a huge treat. Getting to create a strategy guide for a Playstation 3 launch title from developer Insomniac Games is like winning the lottery, finding your lost wallet, *and* learning that eating chocolate cake will cause you to lose weight. Well, for me anyway. It's been my pleasure to work alongside these talented designers, animators, code crunchers, etc., for over the last 10-plus years, and to experience such an amazing, high-intensity and high-quality game right out of the gate speaks volumes to their talent, expertise, and technical/gaming know-how. Anyway, enough with the praise—on to the strategy guide you hold in your hands!

We've taken great pains to give you the most comprehensive strategies for *Resistance: Fall of Man* and hopefully you will agree. With a complete single-player walkthrough and plenty of multiplayer strategies, you can use this guide as a constant companion while delving deep into the alternate, yet eerily familiar, reality of the game. In addition, all of Resistance's secrets are revealed, including Insomniac's trademark "Skill Points." If you want to know more, just flip to the back of the book. There is one disclaimer to note before jumping into battle: The single-player portion of this guide was written based upon the "Normal" difficulty setting. When playing on "Hard" and "Superhuman" mode, more enemies populate the levels, thus potentially changing some of the strategy.

Chimera Origin Point
SIBE
C3
C2
C1
Estimated Chimeran Spread
55 C 160,046 attached
0
500
1000
METERS

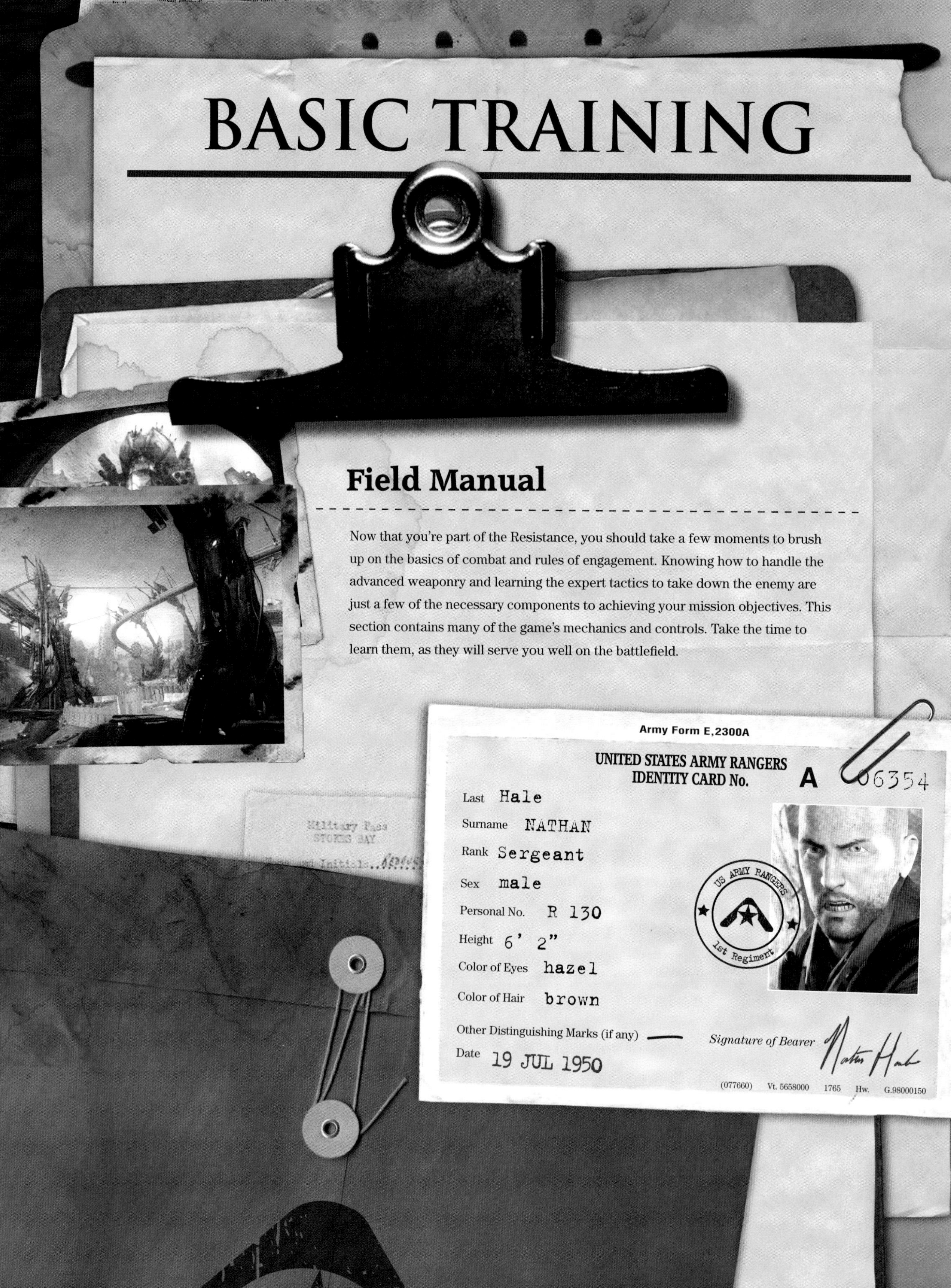

BASIC TRAINING

Field Manual

Now that you're part of the Resistance, you should take a few moments to brush up on the basics of combat and rules of engagement. Knowing how to handle the advanced weaponry and learning the expert tactics to take down the enemy are just a few of the necessary components to achieving your mission objectives. This section contains many of the game's mechanics and controls. Take the time to learn them, as they will serve you well on the battlefield.

Control Layout (Default Configuration)

ACTION CONTROLS

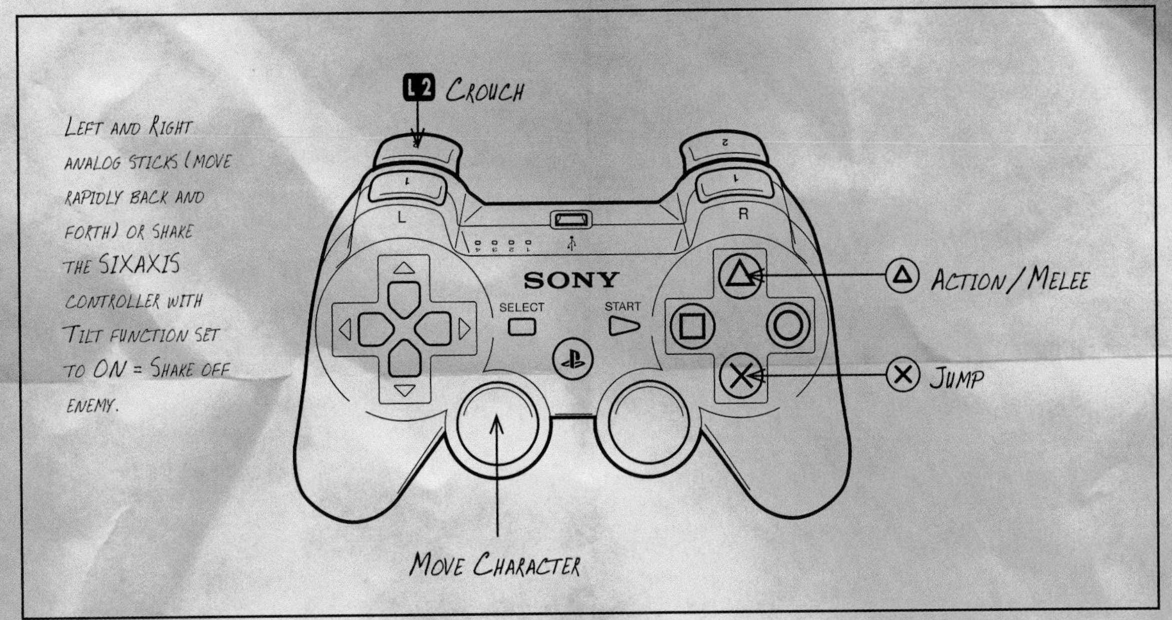

WEAPON CONTROLS

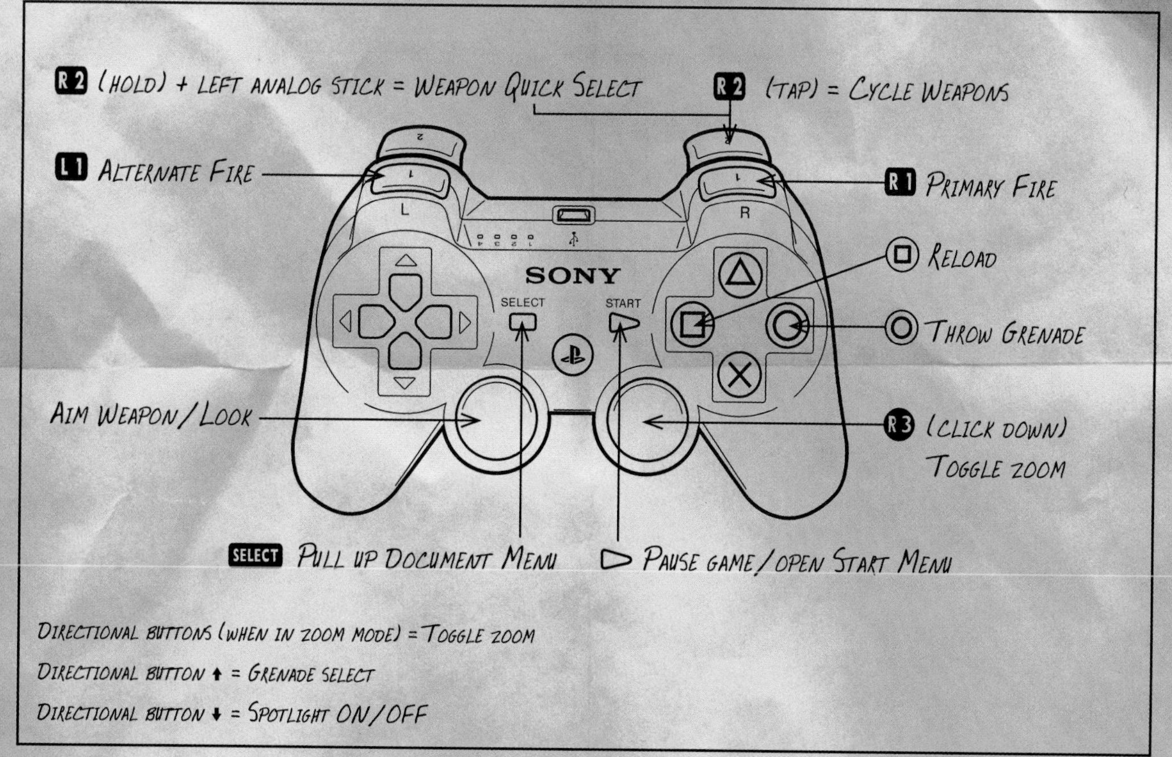

Directional buttons (when in zoom mode) = Toggle zoom
Directional button ↑ = Grenade select
Directional button ↓ = Spotlight ON/OFF

GAME MODES

At the Main Menu, choose from Campaign, Cooperative, Multiplayer and Options. Campaign is where you play through the *Resistance: Fall of Man* single-player story mode. Cooperative allows you to play through the single-player story mode cooperatively with a friend via split screen. With Multiplayer, you can either play offline with four player split-screen competitive play or connect to the Internet to play online. Note: For online play, you must be connected via broadband service (either DSL, cable modem or higher speeds).

When you select the Campaign Mode from the Main Menu, you can begin a New Game, Continue your saved game, or choose a previously played level.

THE SINGLE-PLAYER GAME SCREEN

Damage Arrow: The Damage Arrow appears when you take damage from enemy fire. It also displays the direction from which you are being attacked.

Crosshairs/Weapon Reticle: Use the crosshairs or other sights to aim weapons. The crosshairs will turn red when they overlap an enemy.

Grenade Indicator: This icon appears when a tossed grenade lands nearby. The Grenade Indicator displays the proximity of a tossed grenade, its type, and general location (not shown).

Health Meter: This meter displays your health status. The Health Meter is comprised of four health bars. When all health bars are depleted, your character will die. Use Sym-Bacs to restore your Health Meter. Note: Early in the game, your character will develop the ability to regenerate one health bar as long as he isn't taking damage.

Weapon HUD: This window displays information about your currently equipped weapon. The top bar displays the amount of ammo currently loaded, while the number to the right displays the total amount of ammo available for that weapon. The bottom bar displays information about your weapon's alternate fire, including the amount of ammo available or its effect. The number to the right displays the type of grenade currently equipped and the number left in your inventory.

THE PAUSE MENU

Press ► to pause the game and display the Pause Menu. Adjust your Options, view collected Intel, access Extras (which includes rewards earned, secret Skill Point challenges, and previously viewed movies), and return to the game. Note that accessing the Pause Menu during online gameplay will not pause the game.

COOPERATIVE MODE

You can play cooperatively through the *Resistance: Fall of Man* single-player story mode with a friend via split-screen. In Cooperative Mode, your buddy will accompany you through the game as a secondary character. As with Single-Player Mode, you can choose to load a previously saved game or select from any levels you've already completed.

COMBAT TRAINING

Nothing can prepare you for the mission for which you are about to embark, however, there are some basics that you can adhere to that may ultimately mean the difference between life and death. Take a few moments to study up before heading out onto the battlefield.

WEAPON SELECTION

Resistance: Fall of Man features a unique Weapon Quick Select System that lets you access your current weapon inventory to quickly choose a weapon. When it is open, the information in the center of the Quick Select Menu displays the name of your currently highlighted weapon, the amount of ammunition currently loaded, the total amount of ammo available for that weapon, and the amount of ammo available for the weapon's alternate fire.

To use the Weapon Quick Select System:

- ★ Press and hold R2 to pause the game and pull up the Quick Select Menu.
- ★ Use the left analog stick to select a weapon.
- ★ Release R2 to equip the weapon and close the Quick Select Menu.
- ★ When holding more than eight weapons (only available on the second playthrough), you can toggle between a second Quick Select Menu by holding R2 and tapping ●.
- ★ You can also reconfigure the order/arrangement of your weapons in the Quick Select Menu. To swap a weapon with another, highlight it and press ⊗. Next, use the left analog stick to select the slot you want to place it in and press ⊗ a second time.
- ★ In addition to the Weapon Quick Select System, you can cycle through your available weapons any time by tapping R2.

WEAPONS AND ITEMS

SECONDARY FUNCTIONS

Each weapon has a unique secondary fire option that can provide an edge in battle. To use a weapon's alternate fire, press R1. To learn about your weapon's alternate fire function, highlight it in the Weapon Quick Select Menu (the information is displayed underneath the Weapon Quick Select Menu), or pause the game and select the weapon document from the Intel Menu whenever a new weapon is acquired.

WEAPON ZOOM

Almost every weapon has a zoom feature that enables you to look through its sights for more precise aiming. To use the zoom feature, press down on the right analog stick (R3). To return to a normal view, press R3 a second time.

GRENADES

There are four grenade types in the game, each with its own devastating results. Press ◉ to toss a grenade. Press the directional button Up to cycle through the available grenades in your inventory.

SYM-BAC SERUM

Developed using alien technology, these glowing yellow canisters can restore your health. One canister of Sym-Bac serum replenishes one health bar.

AMMUNITION

Pick up and refill ammunition for your weapons by grabbing ammo packs and fallen weaponry.

INTEL/LORE ITEMS

As you play through the game, you will find special Intel Items in the form of documents, dossiers and journals that reveal more information on the game's back story. To view the Intel Items, press START to access the Pause Menu and then select INTEL.

SKILL POINTS

You can earn Skill Points by completing secret challenges. Earning Skill Points unlocks a variety of cheats that can be accessed by pressing START to access the Pause Menu and then selecting EXTRAS. To view the list of Skill Points and learn how to achieve them, refer to the "Top Secret" section in this guide.

HERO MOMENTS

If an ally gets pinned down or attacked by an enemy, you have a few brief moments to save him before he dies. Saving allies during these "Hero moments" allows them to continue fighting by your side and stack the odds in your favor.

VEHICLES

In addition to being on foot, you have an opportunity to commandeer alternate means of transportation. When you find a vehicle, approach it and press ▲ to get inside. All vehicles have passenger seats/alternate weaponry that allow a second player (via cooperative play) to hop in and use. Even when playing alone, you can switch to the passenger seat by pressing ◉. For more information and descriptions on these vehicles, turn to the "Intel" section in this guide.

VEHICLE CONTROLS

M-12 Sabertooth Tank
△ = Enter/exit vehicle
Left analog stick = Move
Right analog stick = Camera
R1 = Fire cannon
L1 = Fire machine gun
○ = Switch to turret
Right analog stick (passenger) = Aim
R1 button (passenger) = Fire machine gun

LU-P Lynx All Purpose Vehicle
△ = Enter/exit vehicle
Left analog stick = Steer
Right analog stick = Camera
✕ or R2 = Accelerate
□ or L1 = Brake
□ (hold) or L2 (hold) = Reverse
○ = Switch to passenger seat
Right analog stick (passenger) = Aim
R1 (passenger) = Fire

Chimeran Stalker
△ = Enter/exit vehicle
Left analog stick = Move
Right analog stick = Aim/pitch
R1 = Fire machine gun
L1 = Fire missile
○ = Switch to Gunner seat
Right analog stick (passenger) = Aim
R1 (passenger) = Fire machine gun

INTEL

NO. 378-x-1

Weapons

If we're to win the fight against the Chimera, we know we need to utilize and develop the best weapons technology will allow. We had the top scientists in the world work in secret to reverse engineer many of the Chimera's weaponry. Intelligence reports of never-before seen weapons on the battlefield that are neither British-made nor from the Chimera, lead some to believe there are potentially other agencies involved. We're trying to establish a connection between these weapons and the mysterious soldiers.

Cycling Weapons

The order in which you cycle through your weapons is reflective of your QS wheel order. Mastering your QS wheel order grants you a massive advantage and the ability to react more quickly to all situations.

HUMAN WEAPONS TECHNOLOGY

BRITISH INTELLIGENCE AGENCY
TACTICAL REPORT:

Description

The M5A2 Folsom Carbine is the standard-issue rifle of the US Army Rangers. The Folsom is nicknamed "the paddle" for its wide wooden stock and ability to "spank" an enemy. The M5A2 uses the same .303 rounds as the British Rifle, No. 6 Mk 6. Press L1 to fire the underslung M200 40mm Grenade Launcher. The M200 uses high-explosive grenades, which can immediately multiply the firepower available to an individual soldier.

M5A2 CARBINE

Description

The British Army uses the Rossmore 236 Combat Shotgun for base defense and urban warfare. Known for its potent stopping power, it is especially effective in close-quarters engagements. Since the Chimeran invasion, soldiers have found the shotgun very adept at dispatching Howlers. Press L1 to discharge both barrels. This method is less efficient than firing the barrels individually, but using it effectively can sometimes mean the difference between life and death.

ROSSMORE 236

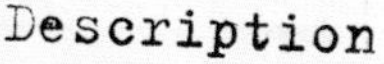

Description

The L23 Fareye is the weapon of choice for British Royal Marine Commando sniper teams. The rifle chambers a .303 Mk 10 round with a muzzle velocity of nearly 3400ft/s. Click R3 to use the scope, and press the directional buttons Down and Up to zoom the scope in and out. Press the directional buttons Left and Right to quickly switch between pre-set magnification levels. As a secondary feature of the Fareye, you can hold L1 to focus concentration. This creates the sensation of slowing down time, thus eliminating all outside distractions.

L23 FAREYE

XR-005 HAILSTORM—HUMAN?

Description

Presumably of US origin, the XR-005 "Hailstorm" is not found on any known order of battle. The weapon fires subsonic bolts that are designed to ricochet off hard surfaces. Shots will continue to travel until they find a soft target or are exhausted. Kills outside the line of sight are possible with banked shots, too. Press L1 to launch the remainder of the Hailstorm's clip. This creates an Auto-turret as the clip fires its bolts at nearby targets. The recoil from the bolts even makes the clip hang in mid-air.

XR-003 SAPPER—HUMAN?

Description

British Intelligence believes that the XR-003 "Sapper" mine launcher is a product of secret US weapons programs. Press L1 to fire a stream of organic cluster mines. Each mine is encased in a living cell similar to those used by the Widowmaker. The mines stick to most surfaces, including each other. You can use the Sapper in combat to set large cluster mine traps for ambushing Chimera. Aim at a mine and press L1 to detonate the targeted mine; press and hold L1 to detonate all mines in the vicinity.

L209 LAARK

Description

The L209 LAARK (Light Anti-Armor Rocket) was originally designed for use against Russian armored divisions. Since the Chimeran invasion, though, it has been successful against the Stalker and other heavy vehicles. Once fired, LAARK rockets are capable of user-guided maneuverability. Hold down L1 to slow down the rocket and reorient it in flight. Aiming the reticle at any desired target steers the rocket in the designated direction. The higher the pressure on L1, the slower the rocket goes. Hold down R1 after firing to release auto-guided sub munitions.

Description

The L11-2 Dragon's ability to damage numerous targets simultaneously with a single sweep overshadows its short range. Press R1 to release an atomized chemical agent that is catalyzed to produce a stream of caustic vapor. Hold L1 to create a cloud of uncatalyzed vapor, and release L1 to catalyze and launch the cloud. This is useful for area-denial, as the cloud remains deadly until its chemical reaction is completely exhausted.

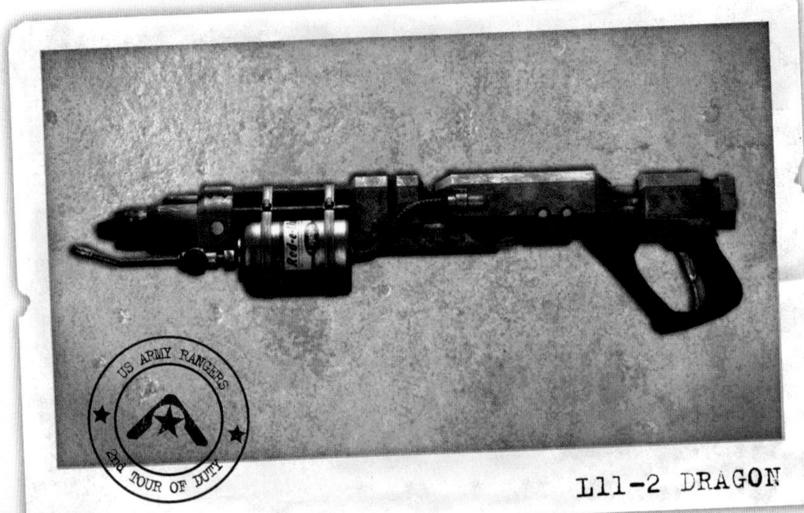

L11-2 DRAGON

BRITISH INTELLIGENCE AGENCY TACTICAL REPORT:

CHIMERAN WEAPONS TECHNOLOGY

Description

The Bullseye is the Chimeran main battle rifle. It has a rapid cyclic rate and a high damage capability. Press L1 to fire a Homing Tag. Once a foe is marked, the tag draws the Bullseye's primary fire. Skillful placement of the tag allows you to place entire magazines of ammunition on a target from the safety of cover.

BULLSEYE

AUGER

Description

The Auger rifle fires blasts of transient radiation that tunnels through solid matter. The blasts increase in power with each object they pass through. Although the Auger has a relatively small ammunition capacity, the fact that it ignores cover means every blast is potentially lethal. Press L1 to deploy a Force Barrier. This barrier alters the Auger's energy blast to create a shield that is impervious to all weapon-fire except that from the Auger. Enemies will incur damage if they touch the barrier.

BULLSEYE MARK II

Description

The Bullseye Mark II is an upgraded version of the Chimeran service rifle. It has the same functionality as the standard model, but uses a supercharged power cell to develop significantly more firepower. Slugs fired from the Mark II create massive, permanent holes in its victims. Those not killed outright receive wounds that do not readily close. Fatal blood loss is inevitable without immediate medical attention. It is for this reason the Mark II is referred to simply as "blue death."

Description

The Chimeran Reaper carbine is designed for the hit-and-run attacks of the Slipskull skirmishers. Its light weight and collapsing frame keeps the creature's hands free until the weapon is needed. The Slipskulls' independently focusing eyes give it the distinct advantage of wielding two Reapers at once. Hold the reticle over an enemy to engage Target Acquisition. When the reticule turns red, press and hold R1 or L1 to track an enemy within the field of view. Each Reaper can track a separate enemy.

REAPERS

ARC CHARGER

Description

The Arc Charger fires a blast of energy that briefly clings to organic tissue, while additional blasts increase the intensity of the energy. Press R1 to trigge the energy to arc to nearby targets. Upon striking additional targets, press L1 to arc the energy again. The energy's power increases with each successive arc, as does its ability to strike new targets. With the proper timing, you can attack many targets at once. The Arc Charger is particularly devastating against multiple enemies where it can develop maximum intensity.

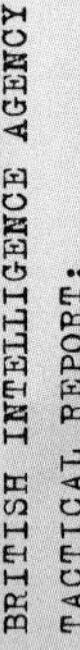

SPLITTER

Description

The Splitter is an advanced Chimeran weapon. Its potential for collateral damage makes it uncommon outside the most hotly contested battlefronts of the Chimeran invasion. Press R1 to fire a packet of high-velocity, explosive rounds. Press L1 to split the rounds multiple times, and press and hold L1 to increase the distance between the split rounds. This can potentially create a literal wall of gunfire to cut down an entire squad of opposition.

GRENADES

FRAG GRENADE—HUMAN

Description

The No 22 Fragmentation Grenade is a standard issue, anti-personnel munition used throughout the British armed forces. The grenade has an exposed fuse that releases irritating smoke prior to detonation. Although not hazardous in the quantities produced, it does discourage a target from picking up and throwing back the grenade. The Fragmentation Grenade is ideal for assaulting entrenched enemy positions or attacking around corners.

GRENADES

AIR-FUEL GRENADE—HUMAN

Description

The No 42 Air-Fuel Grenade is used to combat Chimera in the tight spaces commonly found in urban conflicts. A thrown grenade adheres to most surfaces and immediately releases a cloud of flammable vapor. Once deployed, the cloud ignites and creates a massive explosion. The resulting heat and pressure wave causes vast injuries to anything caught in the blast. With their reliance on external cooling systems, Chimera are especially susceptible to this kind of damage.

HEDGEHOG—CHIMERAN

Description

The Hedgehog Grenade is a Chimeran anti-personnel mention that is thrown like an ordinary hand grenade. Upon landing, it springs up and expands into a spiny cluster. At its "kill height," the Hedgehog fires spines in all directions with enough force to pin targets against nearby walls. The effect is especially deadly in confined quarters.

BACKLASH GRENADE—HUMAN? (2ND TOUR OF DUTY)

Description

The Backlash Grenade is a relatively new weapon on the battlefield. It is an extremely rare munition believed to be of human construction, although the origin of its technology is unknown. This grenade projects a spherical shield that damages any Chimeran creature caught within its blast radius. The shield also reflects most Chimeran weapons fire, effectively turning a Chimeran creature's own weapon against it.

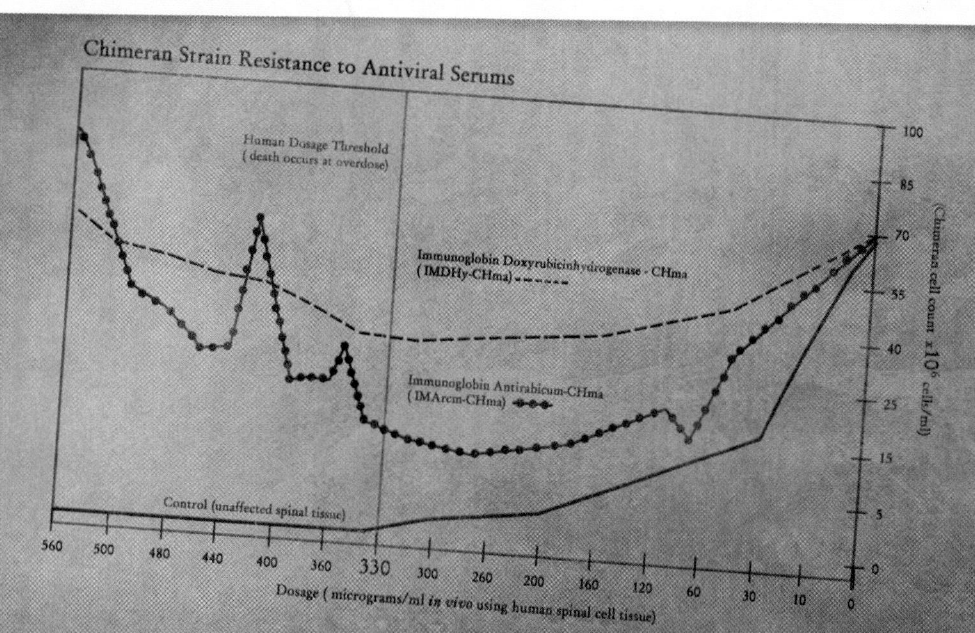

The Chimera

No one in the United Kingdom saw them coming. The events that led up to the Chimeran infiltration of Russia and then the rest of the Europe are still being pieced together and unraveled. Although we've abandoned the cities and retreated to military bases and outposts, we still have plenty of fight left in us. The key to defeating this horrific enemy is to know them inside and out. We must remember our brave field officers who risked life and limb to get this information. Many of them are no longer with us, and the ones who are will never be the same.

CHIMERAN STUDY - TOP SECRET

HYBRID

Description

Hybrids are the foot soldiers of the Chimeran army. They are a savage, keen and tenacious foe. Hybrids quickly learn the methods of their adversaries as evidenced by their expertise in British Army tactics. Beyond their adaptive nature, the most obvious Hybrid attribute is their sheer numbers. Hybrids have overwhelmed humans on every battlefield since the Chimeran invasion first reached Britain.

CRAWLER

Description

Crawlers are small, beetle-like creatures used to spread the Chimeran infection. Capable of limited flight, Spire missles most often deliver them to the battlefield. Upon finding victims, Crawlers penetrate their bodies, usually through the mouth and nose and inject the Chimeran virus. The infected host falls into a coma as the virus begins the inexorable conversion of the host into a Chimeran creature.

LEAPER

Description

Crawlers that fail to infect a host eventually evolve into Leapers. They first seek out sustenance, such as human or animal corpses. After gorging themselves, they develop a protective pupae, referred to as a Leaper Pod. They eventually spawn from their pods upon maturation. The voracious young Leapers attack opponents with teeth and claws.

MENIAL

Description

Unlike other Chimera intended for combat, the Menial strain are used as a tool for basic labor. Menials generally ignore other Chimera as they mindlessly handle their duties. Seldom encountered in combat, they are unarmed and appear sluggish and non-aggressive. Like all Chimera, though, these foes are quite dangerous, especially when cornered.

COCOON

Description

Upon their delivery to conversion centers, Chimera infection victims are enveloped in cocoons. Within each cocoon, a human body is broken down and recombined into a strain of Chimera. It is theorized that multiple human bodies are required for the larger strains. External measures must be taken to keep the cocoons from overheating. This outside intervention suggests that the conversion process is not performed in ideal circumstances. It is unknown if there is a more natural way for the Chimera to reproduce.

CARRIER

Description

Carriers collect infected humans from the battlefield after a Crawler attack and ferry their catch to the nearest conversion center. As these infected bodies are also the Carrier's food source, not all of them survive to be converted. Early in the Chimeran invasion of Britain, Carriers formed caravans hundreds of miles long. It is unknown if the Carriers have found a new role now that fewer victims are available for conversion.

HOWLER

Description

Howlers are a large, quadruped strain of Chimera. Their rudimentary vocalizations are believed to provide the beasts with some level of communication. People can hear their calls for miles; this sound alone has a chilling effect on those familiar with the source. Howlers have a leathery hide that shrugs off most light-arms fire, but combat shotguns at close range are highly effective.

STEELHEAD

Description

Clever, calculating and extremely powerful, Steelheads are a superior variant of the Hybrid strain. Because of their heavy armor, they are often at the forefront of battle. They willingly endure any punishment to advance the Chimeran invasion. Steelheads wield the Auger rifle, a weapon that tunnels through walls. This makes their relentless attacks virtually unstoppable.

TITAN

Description

The Titan strain represents the limit of Chimeran evolution of the human form. These foes are extremely strong and wield weapons that are commonly found on vehicles, such as Stalker heavy siege pods. Titans do not wear any form of body armor; their calloused hides are sufficiently thick to protect them in the fiercest firefights.

SLIPSKULL

Description

Slipskulls are cunning opportunists who prefer to take pot-shots and make blind-siding attacks rather than face their opponents. With their speed and stealth, they excel as scouts and ambushers. When fighting a Slipskull, immediately engage it to prevent it from summoning Chimeran reinforcements. Explosives are the recommended response in such situations. Hybrid Bullseye rifles and the Slipskull's own Reaper carbines are also suitable.

LEAPER POD

Description

Leapers are spawned from membranous sacs known as Leaper Pods. These pods are supposedly deposited by other Chimeran strains, possibly Widowmakers. Spawning is triggered by local vibrations and the pods function as living mines. Always observe caution when traveling in Chimeran-held territory, as early detection of Leaper Pods has the potential to save lives. Use explosives, such as grenades and rockets) to destroy the pods before they release the Leapers within.

GRAY JACK

Description

Gray Jacks are decrepit Hybrids that have nearly outgrown their bodies. As they approach death, their cooling units become over-taxed and their rampant metabolism steadily cooks them from the inside out. The resulting necrosis gives Gray Jacks an odor of decaying flesh. Although unarmed and seemingly frail, their long reach is potentially deadly.

HARDFANG

Description

Hardfangs are similar to Hybrids, although these foes are tougher and crueler. Their conversion process has been skewed to heighten their aggressiveness and eliminate all self-preservation instinct. They rush deep into the fray to use the Arc Charger weapon and strike multiple targets. Royal Marine Commandos often use a designated marksman to dispatch Hardfangs before they can become a threat.

ROLLER

Description

Rollers are adult Leapers that have developed a faster, trundling locomotion. As they near the end of their life cycle, internal decomposition results in venting of a corrosive spray. Rollers use this as an opening attack, blinding their prey before closing in to strike with their claws and teeth.

WIDOWMAKER

Description

The appearance of a Widowmaker on the battlefield requires immediate engagement by all soldiers. Widowmakers attack with their barbed fore-talons or by spewing explosive globules. These foes also have a rallying effect on other Chimeran strains, irreversibly turning the tide of a battle. Attack with high explosives or a vehicle-mounted weapon to dispose of them.

ADVANCED HYBRID

Description

Advanced Hybrids are the fanatical defenders of the Chimeran Towers. Every aspect of their physiology has been tuned to grant them extreme levels of performance. They are outfitted with specialized cooling units to ensure their core body temperature doesn't climb too high during combat. Incredibly tough, Advanced Hybrids can tear apart any intruders they encounter.

ANGEL

Description

Until only recently, Angels were only a mystery. They are believed to be the most advanced Chimeran strain currently operating in Britain. Angels are usually found near Chimeran strongholds, although there have been some battlefield sightings. Initial observations indicate that Angels exert a command influence over other Chimeran strains. The extent of this connection is unclear. As leadership units, Angels don't directly participate in combat. The extent of their offensive capabilities is unknown.

Vehicles

The fight against the Chimera required a huge mobilization, the likes of which the British military had never undertaken. In addition to our ground forces, we utilized our land and air forces to the fullest—even making use of Chimeran technology once it was acquired.

U/AV-17 HAWK—HUMAN

598743-62598

Description

The U/AV-17 Hawk is a US VTL combat transport for personnel and light armor. When delivering soldiers, the Hawk swivels its rotors to direct downwash away from the jump doors. This enables soldiers to fast-rope down while under the cover of the .30 caliber door guns. Once its cargo is away, the Hawk's versatility means it can loiter to offer tactical support or quickly return to reload for another deployment.

AGENCY

Description

The British P-1117 Kingfisher is derived from an early iteration of the American U/AV-17. The Kingfisher is exceedingly capable at inserting soldiers into combat situations. Unfortunately, the Chimera have responded to this ability with the Stalker AA platform. At present, all remaining Kingfishers are in the service of British Intelligence. Now, however, they are mainly relegated to the role of aerial reconnaissance and combat coordination.

P-1117 KINGFISHER—HUMAN

Description

The M-12 Sabertooth is the US light battle tank. The main turret supports an 80mm rifled tank cannon and a 20mm Gatling gun. A .50 caliber anti-personnel machine gun is mounted on a coaxial turret. A notable element of the tank's design is its ability to be carried for short distances by VTOL transport. Sabertooth brigades are commonly flown in for the final leg of an attack, known as "the pounce."

M-12 SABERTOOTH—HUMAN

LU-P LYNX—HUMAN

Description

The LU-P Lynx is a British Army, all-terrain, light-utility vehicle used for long-range patrols. Although unarmored, the Lynx is extremely crash-worthy due to its reinforced chassis. It has four-wheel drive and a deceptively wide track, which keeps it from tipping over in tight turns. The Lynx is outfitted with a 360-degree, shock-dampened turret equipped with an L-650 12.7mm general purpose machine gun.

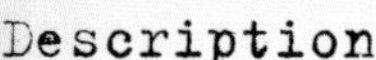

Description

Chimeran Dropships, known as "buzzards," are armed shuttles that provide limited air-support. Advanced propulsion units create dramatic lift, enabling them to be better armored than equivalent human aircraft. Dropships bring Chimera troops into battle via external transport containers. Each transport holds multiple Chimeran squads for maximum tactical flexibility. The containers can be dropped from low altitude directly into battle.

Description

The Stalker is a Chimeran heavy weapons platform. Equipped with an AA autocannon, a missile pod and an anti-personnel gun, a single Stalker can make friendly air support over a battlefield impossible. Their multi-legged locomotion gives them superior maneuverability over all types of terrain. Stalkers are heavily armored against a catastrophic kill. The vehicle's only known vulnerability is the partially exposed Power Core on the rear of its hull.

STALKER—CHIMERAN

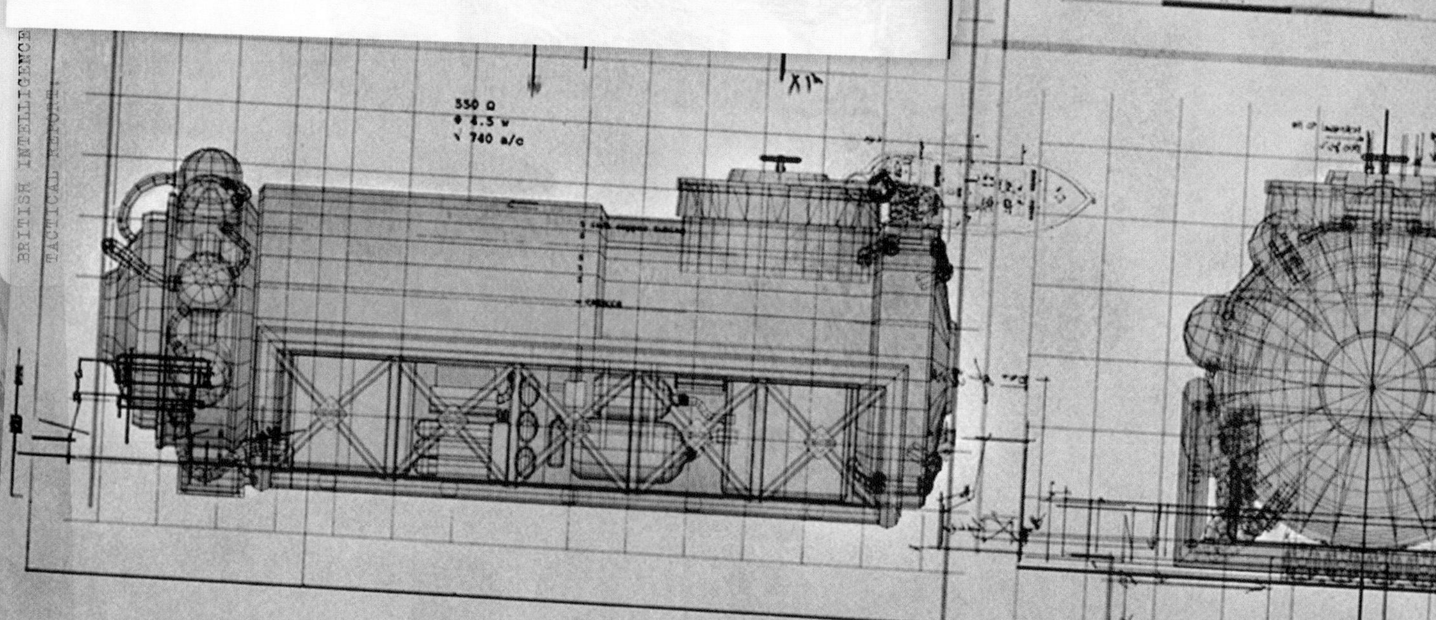

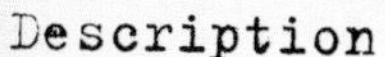

III. Intel
VEHICLES

Description

The Burrower is an armored transport capable of inserting Chimera directly into battle at a moment's notice. Although unarmed, the Burrower inflicts terrific damage with the excavating teeth on its "face." Outside of combat, Burrowers are used to develop Chimeran infrastructure. They have carved a network of tunnels throughout Britain to accommodate supply lines. The tunnels also serve to protect the power conduits found near Chimeran structures.

Throrax

Wing Expanded

Abdomen

Top View

BURROWER—CHIMERAN

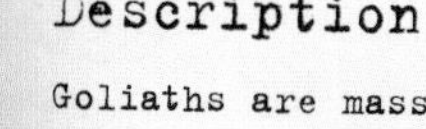

Description

Goliaths are massive walking siege batteries that the Chimera use to subjugate entire cities. They employ concussion mortar batteries to soften up the opposition. Entire companies have broken under mortar barrages and simply run for their lives. This exposes them to the Goliath's most fearsome weapon—the Spire. Spires are biological warfare missiles that deliver payloads of Chimeran Crawlers. A single Spire can infect thousands, and Goliaths never use just one.

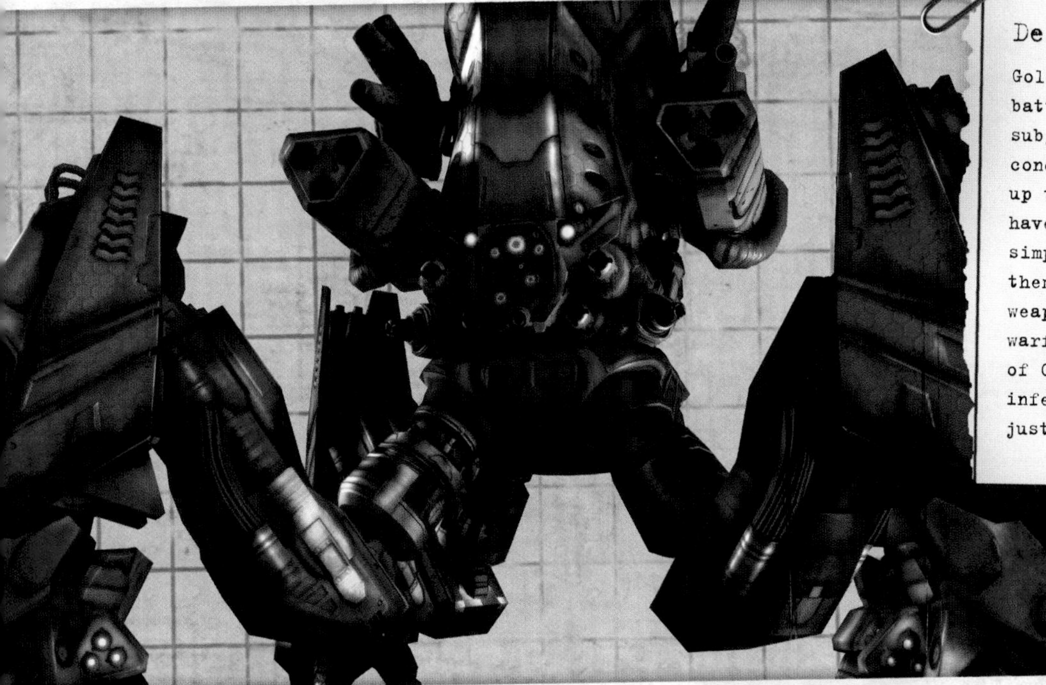

GOLIATH—CHIMERAN

SCALE: 1/38

REV. 3.7.1 jUNE

EXTRA! DAILY NEWS EXTRA!

I.8

FRIDAY, NOVEMBER 17, 1939

SCEA

TRAGEDY STRIKES!

125 RUSSIAN REFUGEES DIE IN FINLAND AFTER INEXPLICABLY SEEKING ASYLUM; NO RESPONSE FROM ST. PETERSBURG

By Edwin Bennet

IMATRA - Tensions mount on the Finnish-Russian border as tragedy strikes the town of Imatra on the Karelian Isthmus, located 143 miles southeast of Helsinki.

A local police station was overrun by haggard Russian citizens in the late morning. By noon, 125 Russians were dead and dozens more injured by the Finnish police. The Finnish government immediately issued formal apologies to the Russian government. However, contact with St. Petersburg has been non-existent.

Early reports indicate the refugees arrived on both foot and via caravan. According to the local constabulary, the refugees arrived completely unannounced. "We had no idea what was going on when they first arrived," says Officer Fredrik Laine. "We received reports of a mob coming into town from the southeast. We feared it was some kind of invasion. Before we could fully mobilize they were at the station."

The refugees were dirty, bloodied, and tired. They stormed the doors of the police station and begged for asylum. The confused officers responded in the negative. "We simply didn't have any room for them all," said Officer Laine. "They were loud and panicked. We heard screams from the back of the crowd, so we dispatched a number of officers to go investigate while we attempted to negotiate with the men at the front."

Bedlam quickly ensued as the scene turned riotous. The police officers, fearing that the crowd was preparing to attack, drew their weapons and discharged at least one pistol shot into the air in the hope of gaining control of the situation. The frightened and angry refugees interpreted this as a hostile act and turned belligerent. Eyewitnesses indicate that the younger men in the group acted first and rushed the officers in an attempt to get weapons of their own. They were ordered to stand down, but refused to comply. The Finnish police opened fire into the air above the crowd once again.

The crowd burst. Those who attempted to run away trampled dozens of their brethren in the process. Those who turned to fight did so with vigor while the bewildered police tried to maintain some measure of calm and normalcy. The order was given to shoot to disable, not kill, though the police incurred some regrettable casualties.

A tenuous calm was eventually established while doctors tended to the wounded. Translators, medical workers, and government officials descended upon Imatra in equal amounts in the face of this international incident. The translators established that the refugees meant no harm, but merely wanted to escape their mother country for as-yet unknown reasons. Many of their number were weakened or died before they reached the Finnish border due to the biting cold. The survivors were given temporary shelter and blankets while authorities attempted to locate appropriate lodging.

Tensions mount on the Finnish-Russian border as tragedy strikes the town of Imatra on the Karelian Isthmus, located 143 miles southeast of Helsinki.

The Finnish government immediately prepared a formal statement and extended an official apology to the Tsar. However, St. Petersburg has not responded. Neither radioed transmissions or couriered messages from Helsinki was acknowledged, much less returned.

The Tsar's silence has caused no small amount of worry amongst Europe as a whole, as many remember the brutal execution of twelve Frenchmen by the Tsar in 1921. The so-called Red Curtain remains a reminder of Russia's isolationist practices.

Is this wave of refugees a precursor to some new aggressive act by Russia? Rumors abound throughout Europe, particularly in Finland and the other countries bordering Russia. There have already been reports of a defense coalition being formed amongst these perhaps endangered countries, though we have been unable to confirm anything regarding these rumors as of press time.

... and infiltration led Russia to close its ... that its size rivals China's Great Wall.

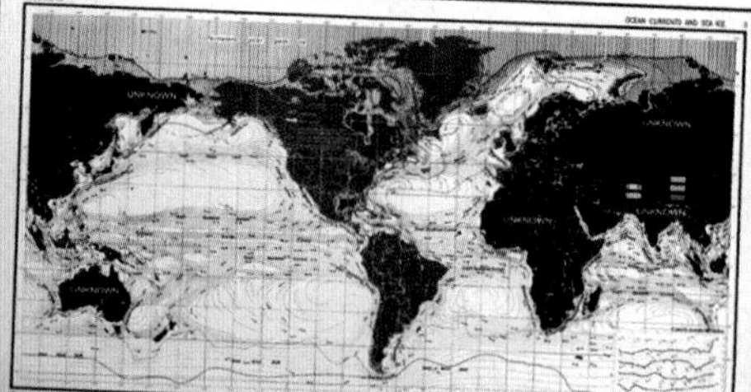

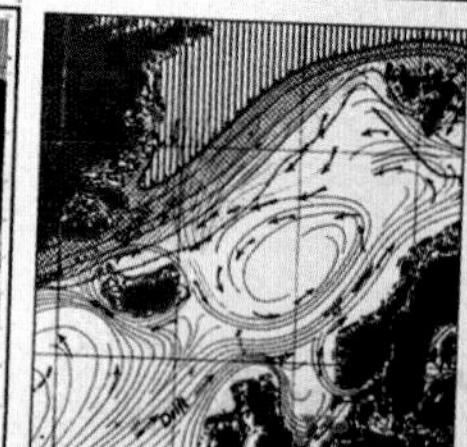

CURIOUS WEATHER

A report citing the curious weather patterns that have emerged in the last fifteen years was released by a leading group of scientists in the country's premier scientific journals.

While Meteorologists still have no clue as to the exact origins of the crippling cold that struck Sweden and killed a confirmed 138 people last winter, these scientists speculate that what occurred in Sweden was just the latest in a curious string of odd weather all over the globe. They suggest something larger on a global weather scale may be occurring. The report mentions how 1923 became known as "Nineteen Hundred and Fish" amongst the fishermen of Newfoundland. Fishing was extremely productive during that year. This success was mostly attributed to the strange shifts in the East Greenland Current. The report posed some of the following questions: Could these be simply natural climate variations or the result of something else? Perhaps a far greater threat to society than previously thought?

These scientists have reached the disturbing conclusion that this global climate change may be triggering a self-perpetuating climate time bomb. The scientists who published the report can't be reached for comment though and haven't been heard from since the report was released. Their last confirmed whereabouts put them in the Nordic countries near the Russian borders doing follow-up research.

FROM THE CRIME DESK

A daring bank robbery struck our fair city yesterday right at close of business. Three armed men and possibly one female accomplice entered First National Bank on the corner of 1st and Ballad Avenue brandishing weapons. Sources suggest that they stole the unprecedented amount of over eighty thousand dollars! They escaped in what eyewitnesses identified as one of the ...

MAN ON THE STREET

Greetings, readers! I am Edwin Bennet, and I'm honored to be welcomed onto the staff here at the Daily News. The editor-in-chief has done me the enormous service of giving me an editorial column where I can share my views on current events, Brockway, and what the man on the street is taking about.

XTRA! DAILY NEWS EXTRA!

SCEA

JULY 11, 1951

THE FALL OF MAN

1898

APRIL

ewspapers report of atrocities med against revolutionaries g to free Cuba from Spanish When the USS Maine is sunk in a harbor, American sentiment strongly towards intervention. tant to get involved, but eager to face, President William McKinley s a secret emissary to deliver timatum to Spain: grant Cuba endence or face US military

1933

J. Robert Oppenheimer graduates from Harvard with a Ph.D. in theoretical physics.

Albert Einstein concludes his term as guest professor at Princeton University and returns to Europe to a position at the University of Zurich, in Switzerland.

1935

US President Franklin D. Roosevelt creates the Works Progress

THE GAUNTLET

Operation: Deliverance

York, England
11 July 1951—06:13 GMT

MISSION OVERVIEW

The Chimeran threat began in Russia. The origin of the virus is unknown, but its effects were devastating and swift. It began in the 1920s with reports of biological experiments from inside Russia. Then reports of villages destroyed overnight, followed by entire cities. The Chimera stayed sealed within Russia for over a decade. In 1949, they launched an attack that overwhelmed all of Europe in a matter of weeks. In March of 1950, the Chimera burrowed under the Channel. Survivors abandoned the cities and retreated to military bases and outposts.

As part of an American assault team, Sergeant Nathan Hale was tasked with rendezvousing with the British resistance, as well as escorting a secret weapon back to the States. However, things did not go as planned. What follows are the known events from July 11th to July 14th, the day Sergeant Hale was last seen alive.

HERN COMMAND
LASSIFIED

FIELD REPORT

Enemy Intel
Hybrid

Hardware
M5A2 Carbine
Bullseye

Mission Objective

★ Get out of the street.

★ Get to the bus depot.

York: Mission 1

START

	A
	I

FIRST ENCOUNTERS

★ Get Out of the Street

The moment Hale and his men set foot on solid ground, things go from bad to worse. The Chimera assault is in full force and York is in ruins. Over the roar of enemy fire and deafening explosions overhead, Hale's Captain orders him to follow the other men and provide support. Have your gun at the ready, as it won't take more than a millisecond to meet the enemy—a pack of vile and vicious Chimera Hybrids!

M5A2 Carbine

WEAPON INTELLIGENCE

The M5A2 Folsom Carbine is the standard-issue rifle of the US Army Rangers. The Folsom is nicknamed "the paddle" for its wide wooden stock and ability to "spank" the enemy. The M5A2 uses the same .303 round as the British Rifle, No. 6 Mk 6.

Press the L1 button to fire the underslug M2000 40mm Grenade Launcher. The M200 uses high-explosive grenades, which can immediately multiply the firepower available to an individual soldier. You can reload the weapon by pressing ■.

Catch up with the other soldiers and engage the enemy in battle. Hale's allies will take the brunt of the first assault, but that doesn't mean you should let them do all the work.

HERO MOMENT!

During your tour of duty, an enemy will pin down or attack an ally. When this occurs, you only have a few seconds to save him. Saving allies during these "hero moments" enables them to continue fighting by Hale's side and stack the odds in your favor.

Most likely, the Hybrids will have one of your men pinned down, going in for the kill. Keep an eye on your comrades and quickly save them before it's too late.

Continue to follow the allies down the street. Another ferocious pack of Hybrids awaits at the end of the street near the blockade. Quickly take cover and do your best to pick them off.

Not only are the Chimera ruthless and relentless, they are also amazing sharpshooters. They can pinpoint and target their enemies with ease from great distances. The only way Hale can survive this "gauntlet" is to continually find and use cover. Make good use of solid objects in the environment (such as corners, doorways, rubble, blockades, etc.) and duck behind them, then pop out and return fire when things cool off.

The Chimera Hybrid

Hybrids are the foot soldiers of the Chimeran army. Although these foes are quite savage, they are also keen and tenacious. Hybrids quickly learn the methods of their adversaries; in fact, they already display expertise in British Army tactics! Beyond their adaptive nature, the most obvious attribute of Hybrids is their sheer numbers. Hybrids have overwhelmed humans on every battlefield since the Chimeran invasion first reached Britain.

When the immediate threat has been eliminated, cautiously follow the path around the building to the right. At the end of the path, two burning soldiers emerge from the wreckage of a downed U/AV-17 Hawk. It's a gruesome sight, and one you'll not soon forget.

Unfortunately, there isn't time to grieve for your fallen comrades, as another Hybrid comes barreling down the street toward Hale at full force. Either take cover and return fire, or use the butt of your Carbine to slam the creature in the head.

MELEE ATTACK

When a Chimera gets too close for comfort, execute a swift melee attack to knock it back or kill it. Press ⓐ with any equipped weapon to initiate this quick and oftentimes lethal close-range attack.

Continue to follow the path along the street between all of the debris. Up ahead, a U/AV-17 Hawk hovers overhead as more allies fast-rope down from its hold to join the fight.

CLASSIFIED

NORTHERN COMMAND

Containment Facility

Vehicle Intelligence-The U/AV-17 Hawk

The U/AV-17 is a US VTOL combat transport for personnel and light armor. When delivering soldiers, the Hawk swivels its rotors to direct downwash away from the jump doors. This enables soldiers to fast-rope down while under cover of the .30 caliber door guns. Once its cargo is dropped off, the Hawk's versatility enables it to stay around and offer tactical support or quickly return for another deployment.

SLAUGHTER IN THE SQUARE

Follow these fresh troops down the street, but watch out for explosions to the left and right. Adding to the chaos and mayhem, a flaming U/AV-17 Hawk careens through the sky and crashes into the roof of a nearby building. When Hale reaches the roundabout at the end of the street, find cover and get ready for a nasty firefight.

ENVIRONMENTAL INTERACTION

You can interact with many of the roadside objects and debris in some way. The dilapidated cars littering the streets serve as a prime example. Simply shoot out a vehicle's tires and it will list to one side, doors ajar.

However, be careful of what you stand behind. Some objects will break apart as they take repeated fire, while others, including the car in this example, will eventually catch fire and explode. The resulting explosion will cause harm to anyone within the blast radius.

Use various explosive objects (like cars, barrels, etc.) as offensive weapons. When Chimera are near these objects, detonate the objects to damage the enemies.

There are multiple Hybrids stationed in the square. Two of them are on the balcony of the house to the north (note, however, that one of them jumps down to engage Hale on the street). Another two emerge from the house and take up position behind the barriers to the northwest. Pick off as many of the foes as possible from the relative safety of cover.

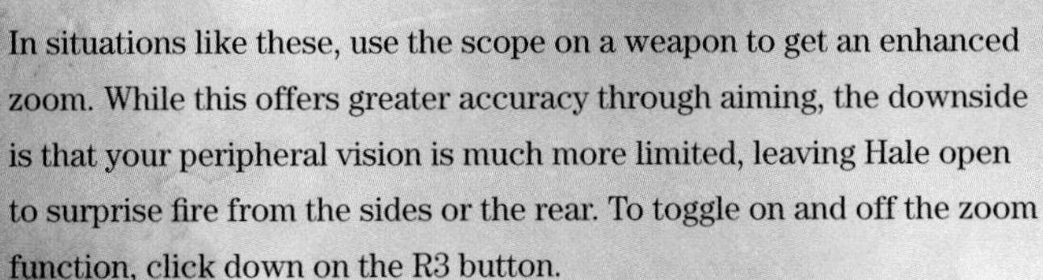

In situations like these, use the scope on a weapon to get an enhanced zoom. While this offers greater accuracy through aiming, the downside is that your peripheral vision is much more limited, leaving Hale open to surprise fire from the sides or the rear. To toggle on and off the zoom function, click down on the R3 button.

If the battle gets too intense and Hale starts taking too much damage, try using the Carbine's Grenade Launcher (press the L1 button), or simply lob a Frag Grenade onto the balcony or behind an enemy barricade by pressing the Circle button.

The Frag Grenade

WEAPON INTELLIGENCE

The No 22 Fragmentation Grenade is a standard issue, anti-personnel munition used throughout the British armed forces. The grenade has an exposed fuse that releases lots of smoke prior to detonation. While not hazardous in the quantities produced, the smoke does discourage a target from picking it up and throwing it back. The Fragmentation Grenade is ideal for assaulting entrenched enemy positions or attacking around corners.

When all of the Hybrids in the square are history, take a few minutes to recon the area and collect any leftover ammo. Although there are multiple rounds of ammo inside the shell of the burned out building to the west, there are no health or medical supplies to acquire. Hale must survive and go the rest of this mission without such items.

CLEANING HOUSE

Move forward into the house from where the Chimera originally appeared when Hale approached the square. Inside, a lone Hybrid dashes up the staircase. Don't hesitate and shoot the creature in the back. If you don't kill it, your allies at the top of the stairs will finish the task.

GRAB AND GO

`Before heading upstairs, take a few moments to scour the downstairs area, picking up extra ammo and Frag Grenades in the process.`

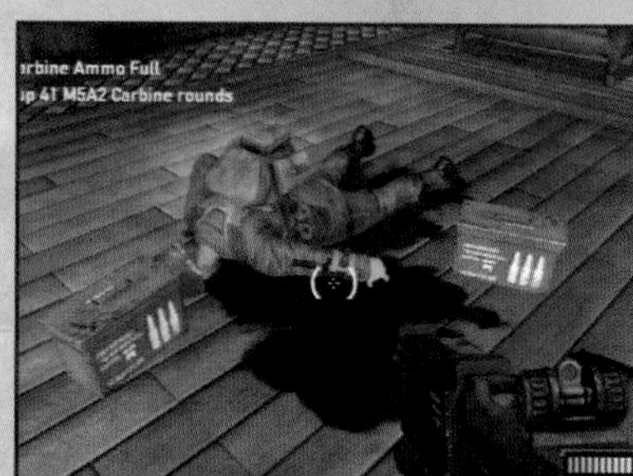

Upstairs, let the soldiers head into the doorway to the left first and have them fight the Hybrids inside the room beyond. After they start firing, follow them in and pick off any remaining foes. You may find two Hybrids hiding behind a set of stacked crates in the adjoining room. If Hale has a Frag Grenade in his inventory, use one to flush them out.

Continue to move from one room to the next, passing through the balcony area where you engaged the Chimera from the square below. Head back into the interior of the house to find two more Hybrids inside. The first one is near the doorway directly to the right, so dispose of it in a hurry.

The second one is hiding behind the doorway directly in front of Hale. To avoid a potential ambush, avoid passing through the doorway; instead, take the opposite doorway where you just killed the Chimera and turn the tables on the enemy by coming around and shooting it from behind.

THE HOLE IN THE FLOOR

There is a large hole in the floor of this second story room. Use it to drop down to the first floor, then search the area until you find the open room with windows facing the street outside. A lone, fallen soldier lies dead on the floor, but there is an envelope sitting in a pool of blood by his head. Approach the envelope and press △ to pick it up.

INTEL DOCUMENTS

You will find various Intel Items right in plain sight or tucked away in hard to find places. Use these top-secret documents to learn more about Hale's mission. To view any collected Intel Items, press the SELECT button to access Hale's Diary and then select "Intelligence." You can also pause the game (press the START button) and choose "Documents" from the Pause Menu.

When you're ready, return upstairs (either via the staircase or the makeshift ramp through the hole in the ceiling/floor) and then drop off of the balcony down onto the small street below.

Guidelines

This document is from the U.S. Army and details the guidelines of conduct for U.S. soldiers while on foreign soil.

Bullseye

WEAPON INTELLIGENCE

The Bullseye is the Chimeran's main battle rifle. It has a rapid cyclic rate and a high damage capability. Pressing the L1 button fires a Homing Tag. Once a foe is marked, the tag will draw the Bullseye's primary fire. Skillful placement of the tag allows for entire magazines of ammunition to be placed on a target from the safety of cover. It is also very effective against fast-moving targets.

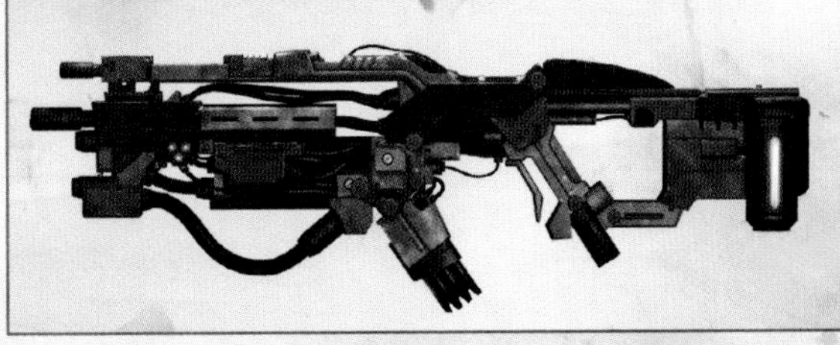

★ GET TO THE BUS DEPOT

Once back on the ground, continue along the street until you discover a new weapon lying on the ground. This weapon is referred to as the Bullseye! You get the chance to check out this new weapon at the makeshift set of barricades near the end of the street. To use the Bullseye's Homing Tag function, aim at one of the Hybrids and press the L1 button to shoot a sticky tag on your target. If successful, quickly switch to firing (press the R1 button) to send a stream of bullets homing in on your target.

THE QUICK SELECT SYSTEM

★ WEAPON INTELLIGENCE ★

When holding more than eight weapons, you can toggle between a second Quick Select Menu by holding R2 and pressing ●. In addition to the Weapon Quick Select System, you can cycle through your available weapons at any time by pressing R2. You can change weapon order on the wheel by highlighting a weapon, pressing ⊗ to select it, then highlighting a second weapon and pressing ⊗ to swap the weapons. Also, the "tap" select order is determined by the order of the Quick Select wheel.

The Weapon Quick Select System enables you to pull up your current weapon inventory and quickly choose a weapon. When open, the information in the center of the Quick Select Menu displays the name of your currently highlighted weapon, the amount of ammunition currently loaded, the total amount of ammo available for that weapon, and the amount of ammo available for the weapon's alternate fire.

To use the Weapon Quick Select, press and hold the R2 button to pause the game and pull up the Quick Select Menu. Next, use the left analog stick to select a weapon and then release R2 to equip the weapon and close the Quick Select Menu.

INTO THE OPEN

There is some ammo located around the area up the small stairs to the right (Bullseye, Carbine, and Frag Grenades). Pick the area clean, then return to the street and locate the small opening between two buildings along the left side of the street (its location is before the courtyard and the burning bus). A second Intel Item rests inside this alcove.

DOCUMENT INTELLIGENCE #2

Infections

This document, dated July 7th, 1951, details some firsthand observations from a Line Medic regarding bizarre creatures that enter and infect humans via their airways.

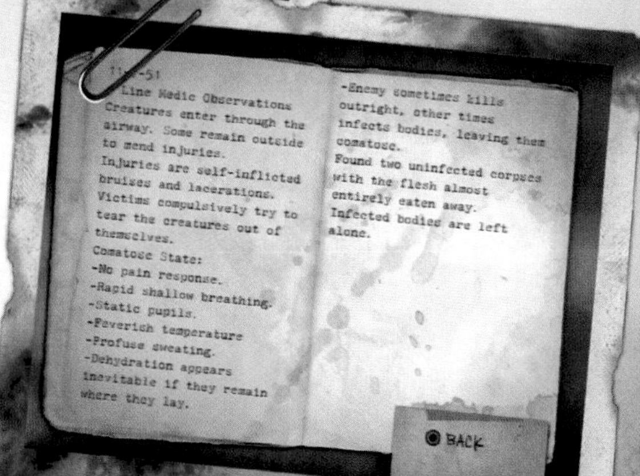

Return to the street and follow it out to a courtyard where another set of Hybrids is waiting to ambush Hale and his men. Quickly find cover and start picking them off one-by-one. Continue to use the Bullseye's Homing Tag function and resort to the Carbine when you've exhausted your supply of Bullseye ammo.

Exit the courtyard through the opening in the back and follow the path overlooking the creek bed around to the left. There are more Hybrids waiting for Hale here, but a group of soldiers down in the creek below should help even the odds. Drop down and follow the men along the misty creek bed until they reach the end of the area.

A LONE SURVIVOR

NORTHERN COMMAND
CLASSIFIED

York, England
11 July 1951—07:47 GMT

MISSION OVERVIEW

No one knows exactly how the Chimeran virus infected Hale. The only clue is a journal entry recovered from the body of a U.S. medic. It says that he encountered a number of comatose soldiers in a dry creek bed. One of the soldiers, a sergeant, suddenly woke up. Unlike the other soldiers, his body had no wounds at all. The sergeant refused any kind of medical treatment, insisting on catching up to the rest of the company. If that sergeant was in fact Nathan Hale, then he remains the only known person to wake up after being infected. Whether the Chimeran virus mutated within him, or whether his body had an innate resistance to it, remains a mystery.

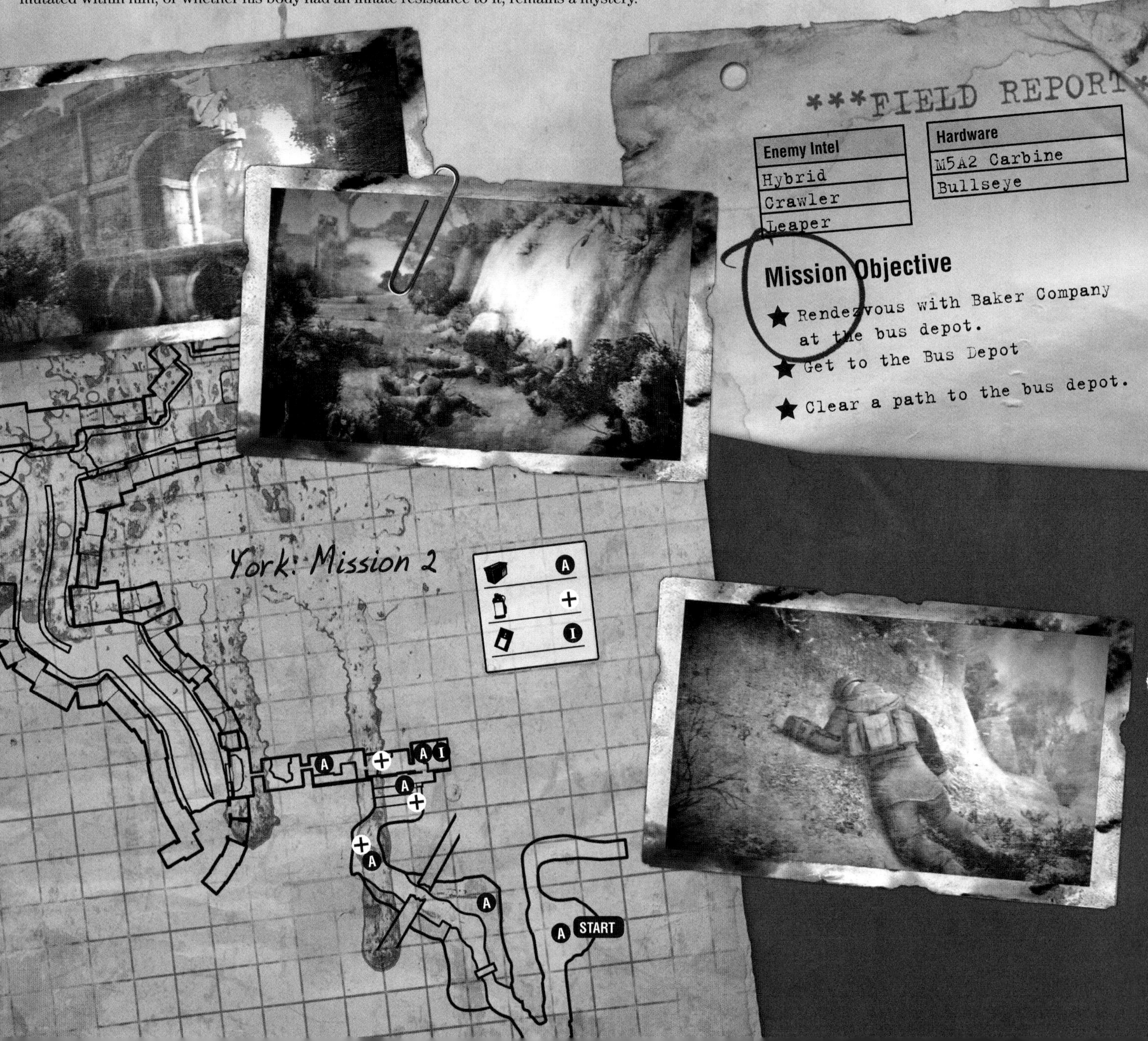

THE SWARM

★ Rendezvous with Baker Company at the Bus Depot

The creek bed turns out to be the final resting place of many of Hale's fellow men. He should have met his own death there, too, but for reasons unknown, the massive Crawler attack has left him alive and unharmed, but it has also altered him in some inexplicable way.

The Crawler

Crawlers are small, beetle-like creatures used to spread the Chimeran infection. Although capable of limited flight, they are most often delivered by Spire missiles. Upon finding victims, Crawlers penetrate their bodies, usually through the mouth and nose, and inject the Chimeran virus and quickly expire. The infected host falls into a coma as the virus begins the inexorable conversion of the host into a Chimeran creature.

When Hale comes to, he is met by an American medic who is on his way to rendezvous with the other soldiers at a nearby bus depot. Follow him along the creek bed, collecting ammo from your fallen comrades in the process.

Just down the path a couple of small, grotesque creatures skitter across the creek bed. Although they don't attack Hale and his fellow U.S. officer, their appearance can only mean the harbinger of bad things to come…

The Chimera Leaper

Crawlers that fail to infect a host will eventually evolve into Leapers. They first seek out sustenance, such as human or animal corpses. After gorging themselves, they develop protective pupae, a Leaper pod. They spawn from their pods upon maturation. The voracious young Leapers attack opponents with teeth and claws. It's best to fight these foes from a distance, if at all possible. Taking out a single foe isn't too difficult, but Leapers are lethal when they attack in large numbers.

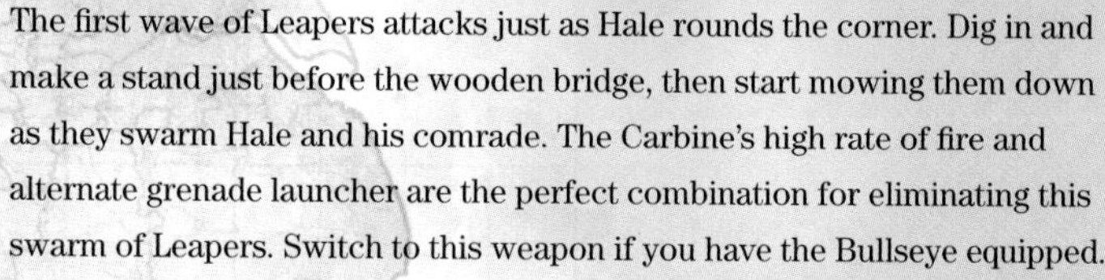

The first wave of Leapers attacks just as Hale rounds the corner. Dig in and make a stand just before the wooden bridge, then start mowing them down as they swarm Hale and his comrade. The Carbine's high rate of fire and alternate grenade launcher are the perfect combination for eliminating this swarm of Leapers. Switch to this weapon if you have the Bullseye equipped.

Continue down the creek bed until the next wave attacks. Once again, stay your ground and do your best to pick them off from afar. The Leapers come at Hale from the concrete barrier at the end of the path. Thankfully, a second officer joins in the fray from the stairs to Hale's left.

HERO MOMENT!

Keep an eye on the medic, as it's easy for him to become overwhelmed and killed by the Leaper horde—especially the second pack that attacks from the fence behind him. If an attack occurs, you will have a few moments to save him as he attempts to fight off the Leaper foes. Quickly come to his aid before he perishes!

THE ROOFTOPS

When it's safe to move on, take the stairs out of the creek bed and follow the path around to the bridge toward the concrete barrier beyond. It's very possible that Leaper reinforcements will attack Hale at this juncture. Hale's men will need to help dispose of these foes.

Continue across the bridge and along the path on the other side until you arrive at a set of boulders. Make this location your next stand against the approaching wave of Leapers. If you've been ensuring the safety of Hale's fellow men, they will be there to help even the odds.

Climb up the concrete barrier and drop down on the opposite side—the sight of another Chimeran massacre. Just around the bend, the creek bed abruptly ends at the base of a large building. Have your weapon at the ready and find some cover, as a trio of Hybrids appear on the walkway above.

TAG, YOU'RE DEAD!

Don't forget that the Bullseye has the capability of tagging an enemy and then homing in on it with its fire. Use the zoom function for pinpoint aiming and quickly tag a Hybrid from below, then fire a steady homing stream of ammunition at it until it is obliterated.

There are a few strange, glowing canisters lying next to the dead Hybrid carcasses and another one is on the landing of the stairs. Collecting them seems to have a positive effect on Hale's health.

Possibly due to Hale's mysterious survival from the Crawler attack, he can now automatically regenerate a quarter of his health if he doesn't take damage for a short period of time. In addition, he can use the Chimera Sym-Bac serum to heal himself. One canister of this bacteria-filled fluid also regenerates a quarter of his health!

DOCUMENT INTELLIGENCE #3

Regeneration

An excerpt from a Medical Journal dated March 23rd, 1950 written by Dr. Ian Coxen:

Further research into Chimeran physiology suggests their rapid regeneration ability may be the result of more than their metabolic rate alone. We have known for some time that sufficient damage will kill a Chimera outright and leave it with lasting wounds that the creature cannot heal. But recent research suggests that the Chimera have developed a symbiotic bacterium that complements and amplifies their healing abilities. The bacteria are suspended in a viscous yellowish fluid our researchers have dubbed the "Sym-Bac" serum. We believe the bacteria is likely destroyed during the healing process, which means that the Chimera would be dependent on further injections of the serum as they sustain damage.

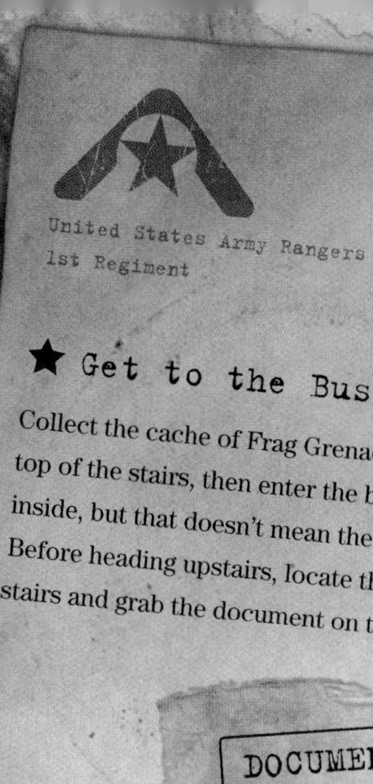

★ Get to the Bus Depot

Collect the cache of Frag Grenades and ammo at the top of the stairs, then enter the building. It's eerily quiet inside, but that doesn't mean the building is abandoned. Before heading upstairs, locate the closet at the base of the stairs and grab the document on the floor.

DOCUMENT INTELLIGENCE #4

Isolationism

This document from the US Isolationist League is a call for the United States to stay out of foreign wars.

The first and second floors of the building are devoid of life—either human or otherwise. The third floor, however, is teeming with Chimeran Hybrids. Take cover behind the metallic crate at the top of the stairs and start picking them off.

The Bullseye's tag function works especially well in situations such as this. Simply emerge from cover and tag an enemy, then duck back and shoot the foe from around a corner without the threat of taking damage. You will know when you have an enemy tagged by an audio cue and a red light emitting from the barrel of the gun.

DUCK AND COVER

In addition to hiding behind objects, you can duck down to ensure Hale is completely protected. To duck, press and hold the L2 button.

More Hybrids are positioned just beyond the third floor room. Eliminate the one up on the rooftop first, then turn your attention to the two hiding behind the wooden crates in the next room. Use any means necessary to eliminate them.

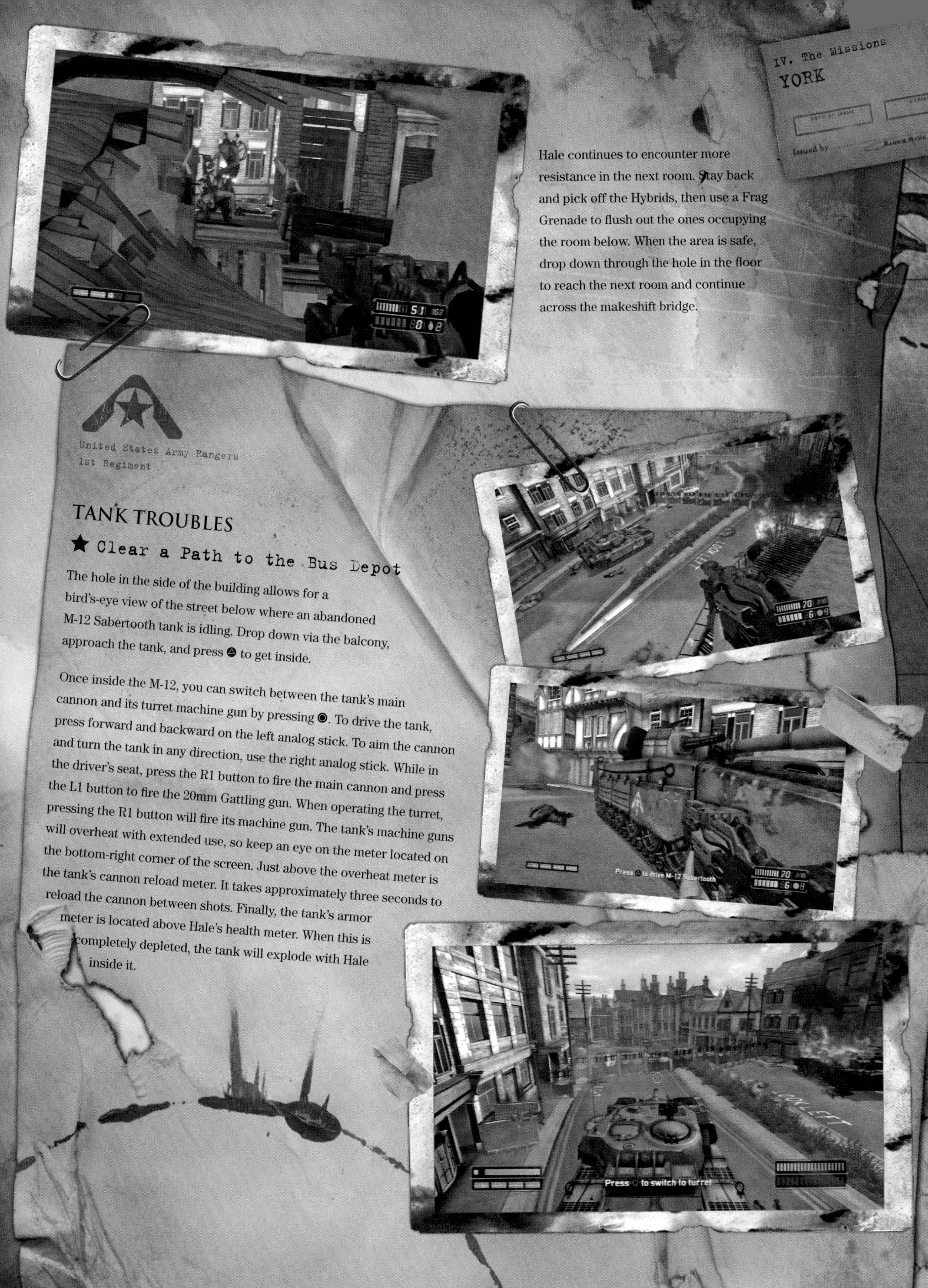

Hale continues to encounter more resistance in the next room. Stay back and pick off the Hybrids, then use a Frag Grenade to flush out the ones occupying the room below. When the area is safe, drop down through the hole in the floor to reach the next room and continue across the makeshift bridge.

TANK TROUBLES

★ Clear a Path to the Bus Depot

The hole in the side of the building allows for a bird's-eye view of the street below where an abandoned M-12 Sabertooth tank is idling. Drop down via the balcony, approach the tank, and press △ to get inside.

Once inside the M-12, you can switch between the tank's main cannon and its turret machine gun by pressing ◉. To drive the tank, press forward and backward on the left analog stick. To aim the cannon and turn the tank in any direction, use the right analog stick. While in the driver's seat, press the R1 button to fire the main cannon and press the L1 button to fire the 20mm Gattling gun. When operating the turret, pressing the R1 button will fire its machine gun. The tank's machine guns will overheat with extended use, so keep an eye on the meter located on the bottom-right corner of the screen. Just above the overheat meter is the tank's cannon reload meter. It takes approximately three seconds to reload the cannon between shots. Finally, the tank's armor meter is located above Hale's health meter. When this is completely depleted, the tank will explode with Hale inside it.

CLASSIFIED

NORTHERN COMMAND

Containment Facility

The M-12 Sabertooth Tank

The M-12 Sabertooth is the US light battle tank. The main turret supports an 80mm rifled tank cannon and a 20mm Gattling gun. A .50 caliber anti-personnel machine gun is mounted on a coaxial turret. A notable element of the tank's design is its ability to be carried for short distances by VTOL transport. Sabertooth brigades are commonly flown in for the final leg of an attack, known as "the pounce."

Getting to the bus depot to rendezvous with the rest of the troops is Hale's ultimate goal, and the M-12 is the safest and quickest way to reach it. Break through the flimsy barrier and start driving down the street.

Hale encounters Chimera resistance almost immediately. Use the cannon to dispose of multiple Hybrids with one strike. Watch for movement or enemy fire, then aim and shoot. It's just that easy!

THE EXPLODING

What self-respecting shooter wouldn't be complete without exploding barrels? Any time you see enemies in the vicinity of these containers filled with volatile fluids, detonate them to catch the enemy in the barrel's deadly blast radius.

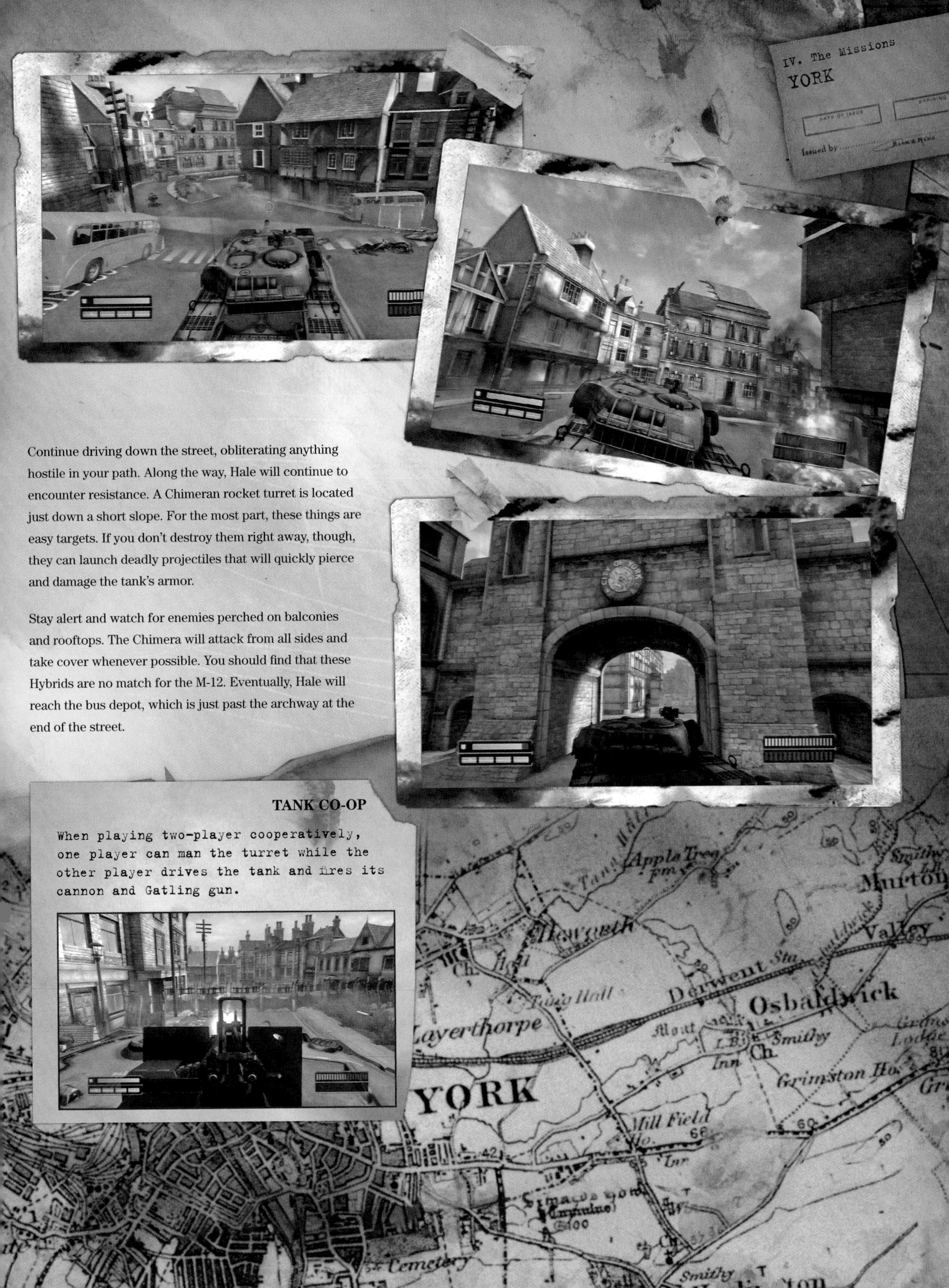

Continue driving down the street, obliterating anything hostile in your path. Along the way, Hale will continue to encounter resistance. A Chimeran rocket turret is located just down a short slope. For the most part, these things are easy targets. If you don't destroy them right away, though, they can launch deadly projectiles that will quickly pierce and damage the tank's armor.

Stay alert and watch for enemies perched on balconies and rooftops. The Chimera will attack from all sides and take cover whenever possible. You should find that these Hybrids are no match for the M-12. Eventually, Hale will reach the bus depot, which is just past the archway at the end of the street.

TANK CO-OP

When playing two-player cooperatively, one player can man the turret while the other player drives the tank and fires its cannon and Gatling gun.

SPIRES

Operation: Deliverance

York, England
11 July 1951—09:16 GMT

MISSION OVERVIEW

The Americans regrouped at an abandoned bus depot in southeast York. Under the command of a Captain Winters, they staged a daring tactical offensive. The Chimera had begun to close in on their position. If the Americans could secure the site, they would have a perfect landing zone, and the scales would tip in their favor.

FIELD REPORT

Enemy Intel
Hybrid

Hardware
M5A2 Carbine
Bullseye

Mission Objective

★ Destroy all enemy gun positions.

★ Find Captain Winters.

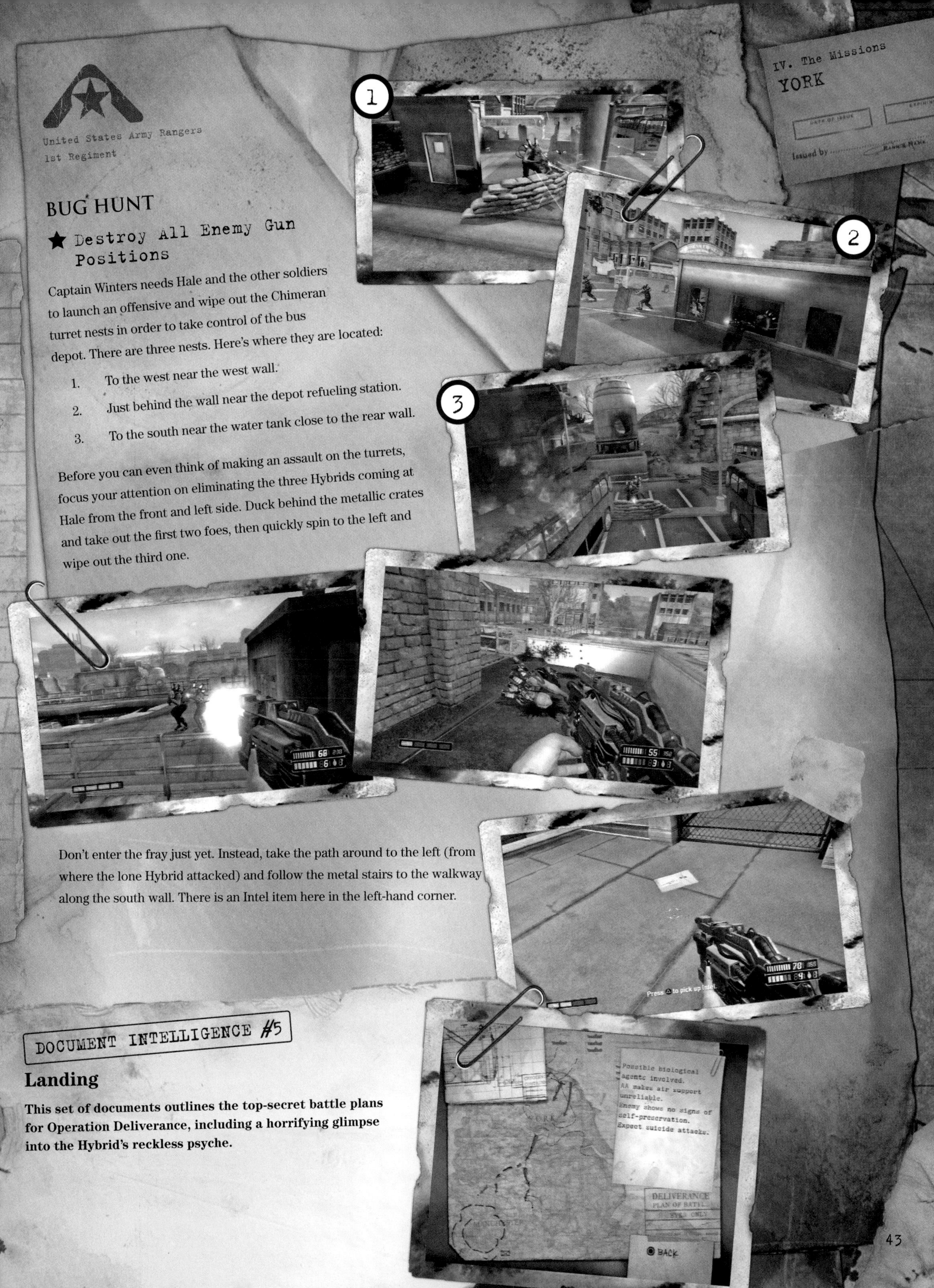

BUG HUNT

★ Destroy All Enemy Gun Positions

Captain Winters needs Hale and the other soldiers to launch an offensive and wipe out the Chimeran turret nests in order to take control of the bus depot. There are three nests. Here's where they are located:

1. To the west near the west wall.
2. Just behind the wall near the depot refueling station.
3. To the south near the water tank close to the rear wall.

Before you can even think of making an assault on the turrets, focus your attention on eliminating the three Hybrids coming at Hale from the front and left side. Duck behind the metallic crates and take out the first two foes, then quickly spin to the left and wipe out the third one.

Don't enter the fray just yet. Instead, take the path around to the left (from where the lone Hybrid attacked) and follow the metal stairs to the walkway along the south wall. There is an Intel item here in the left-hand corner.

DOCUMENT INTELLIGENCE #5

Landing

This set of documents outlines the top-secret battle plans for Operation Deliverance, including a horrifying glimpse into the Hybrid's reckless psyche.

ASSAULT ON TURRET NEST #1

Stay along the outer perimeter of the bus depot and follow the back wall toward the large tree to the west. From this location, charge down the hill and quickly take cover using the sand bag bunker on the right side.

MAN ON FIRE

If you use the sand bag bunker on the left for cover, stay as far away from the nearby bus as possible. If it catches fire, standing next to it will result in a quick—and painful—death.

Using the sand bag bunker for cover, stay low and wait out the barrage of rockets from the first turret. As soon as there is a momentary pause, pop out and tag the Hybrid at the controls. Next, duck back down, aim the Bullseye so that the barrel is pointing up in the air, and start shooting at the sky. The rifle's ammunition will home in and find its mark.

As soon as the coast is clear, make a beeline for the turret, but stay crouched to the side of it near the left wall. From this position, you can easily mow down any lingering Hybrids that are attempting to regain control over the turret. When they stop appearing, it's safe to move on.

MANNING TURRETS

Although it may be tempting to take over a turret and use it to mow down the Chimera, it's not necessarily a good idea in this instance. This is especially true because so many of the enemies are still mobile and moving about the area. Once Hale starts using a turret, your view and turning radius are limited and Hale is susceptible to unseen enemy attacks from the sides and rear. If you decide to jump on a turret, approach it and press △ to take control. To fire, press and hold R1. To exit, press △ a second time.

ASSAULT ON TURRET NEST #2

The second turret nest is just behind the first one, inside the small building near the refueling station. Scoot around the edge of the buildings along the west wall, then pick off any Hybrids nearby before making an assault.

If you can eliminate most of the Hybrids outside the building while only the ones inside the building remain, creep up along the side and then pop up and shoot them through a window or toss in a grenade. Once this area is completely devoid of enemies, move on to the third and final turret.

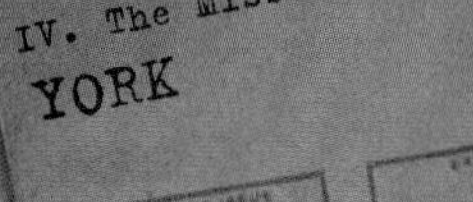

RUNNING ON EMPTY

Don't shoot the gas pumps at the refueling station. You can put their explosive effects to good use in just a little bit. Leave them along for now!

ASSAULT ON TURRET NEST #3

The third turret is located along the back wall in front of the water tank. Use the environment for cover and find a good vantage point from which to shoot. The garage near the entrance to the depot provides plenty of cover opportunities.

BREACH AT THE NORTH WALL

★ Find Captain Winters

Upon eliminating the final Chimera, the U.S. regains control of the turrets. However, don't go celebrating just yet! Captain Winters barks out orders that the north wall behind the water tank has been breached and an onslaught of Chimeras are about to come pouring in. Quickly take cover and start picking them off one-by-one.

BREACH AT THE WEST WALL

A second wave of Chimera foes attempt to recapture the bus depot from the west wall near the refueling station. Quickly head over to the sand bag bunkers and hunker down for another intense battle. Let them have it, but try to conserve your ammo.

For the last pack of foes, switch back to the tag and terminate tactic using the Bullseye. Remember that once you tag an enemy, you can stay under the protection of cover and kill them by using the Bullseye's homing shots. Defeat these remaining foes and the bus depot will be secure.

FILL 'ER UP!

The Hybrids conveniently position themselves in front of the gas pumps, thus providing the perfect opportunity to take them out in a blaze of glory. Use the Carbine and target each pump individually to get the most "bang" for your buck.

FATE WORSE THAN DEATH

Chimeran Conversion Center

NORTHERN COMMAND
CLASSIFIED

Grimsby, England
12 July 1951—03:15 GMT

MISSION OVERVIEW

We know from the craters that the Chimera ended the battle at the bus depot by launching Spires. There is no defense against a Spire attack. By the time you see them in the air, it's already too late. After impact, the Spires release swarms of Crawlers; literally thousands of them can come from a single Spire. Entire cities have been infected in minutes. After the Crawlers finish their work, the Chimera send in Carriers to collect the dormant victims.

The Carriers took Hale to a Conversion Center just west of Leeds. My convoy team and I were imprisoned at the same location. We had been captured uninfected, so we were put in makeshift pens until they could infect us.

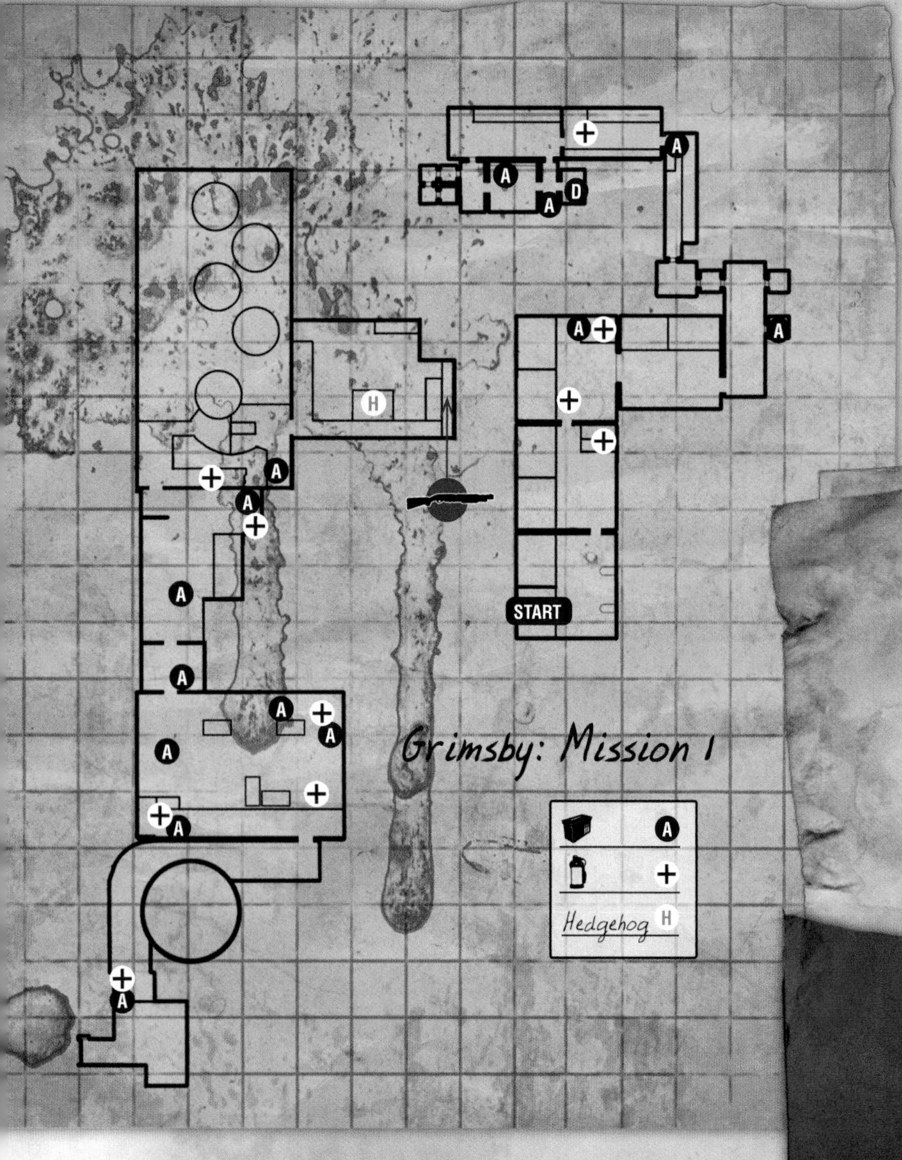

FIELD REPORT

Enemy Intel
Menial
Hybrid

Hardware
M5A2 Carbine
Bullseye
Rossmore 236 Combat Shotgun
Frag Grenades
Hedgehog

Mission Objective

★ Escape the Chimeran conversion cente

OUT OF THE FRYING PAN

★ Escape the Chimeran Conversion Center

The Spire assault on the bus depot resulted in another massacre of human life. Hale once again survived the attack, only to wake up a prisoner inside the Chimeran conversion facility where heinous and unspeakable things were being done to his fellow homosapiens.

Thankfully, Hale still has access to his weaponry. When he comes to, wait for the Chimera to turn its back and then shoot it dead.

The Chimera Menial

Unlike other Chimera intended for combat, the Menial strain is bred to be a tool for basic labor. Menials generally ignore other Chimera as they mindlessly handle their duties. Seldom encountered in combat, they are unarmed and appear sluggish and non-aggressive. However, like all Chimera, Menials are unpredictable. They should be considered dangerous, especially when cornered.

Although the Menials are easy targets, they are still extremely dangerous and deadly. If given the chance to get up close and personal, they can grapple Hale and start gnawing and gnashing at him with their sharp teeth. To break free from a grapple, just shake the controller back and forth.

Flashlight

WEAPON INTELLIGENCE

Hale has a flashlight that he can use to help him see in dark areas and spaces. To turn the flashlight on and off, press the right directional button. The flashlight does not drain any battery energy and can be used for as long or as little as needed.

Be prepared for a second Menial to appear from outside the holding pen. As long as you keep these disfigured creatures at bay, they are easily dispatched. Save your Bullseye ammo for the more deadly Hybrids and instead use the Carbine when fighting these worker drones.

Exit the holding pen and move through the makeshift operating room into the next area. Expect plenty more Menials as Hale moves through the conversion center. They may emerge from dark corners, lunging and grabbing with extreme quickness. Take your time and slowly maneuver through the facility and always have the Carbine at the ready.

The Power Cell

You'll often find glowing globes, called Power Cells, which are a source of energy for the Chimera. These objects are also highly volatile and explosive, meaning they can be used against the Chimera. To do so, shoot the cells to make them detonate.

MEET LIEUTENANT PARKER

Cautiously move through the conversion center, room-by-room, until Hale comes to the door with the switch next to it. Approach the switch and press ▲ to activate it.

Inside the next room, Hale encounters two British soldiers trapped in a conversion pen. Before he can figure out a way to free them, a swarm of Crawlers descend on the area. However, it's not too late for the woman in the nearby cell, Captain Rachel Parker of British Intelligence. Although Hale saves her from infection, she must figure her own way out.

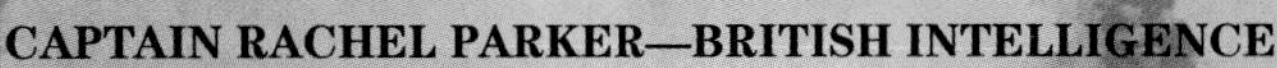

CAPTAIN RACHEL PARKER—BRITISH INTELLIGENCE

Depending on how you look at it, Rachel Parker is one of the lucky ones who was captured and taken alive to the Chimeran conversion center for later infection. Parker is resourceful, strong-willed, and has a wry sense of humor that helped her quickly move through the ranks. She is also the narrator of these unfolding events, and suspects there is something strange and unmistakably Chimeran behind Hale's eyes.

Take the only exit and move deeper into the conversion facility. The Menial's provide little in the way of serious threat or resistance as long as you proceed cautiously and shoot accurately when one appears. There are two of them in this next area, including one hiding in the room to the right.

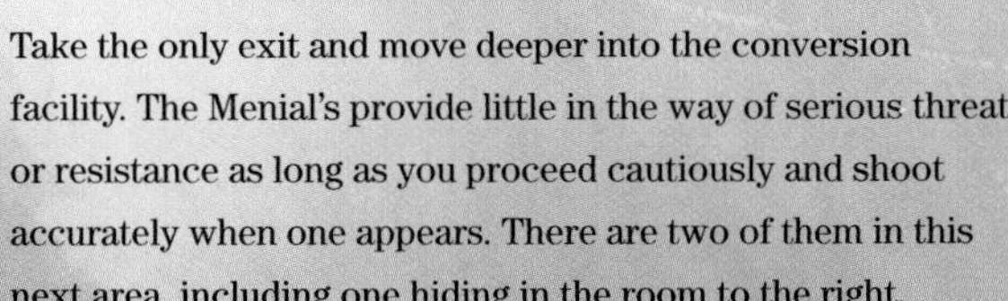

MENIAL MELTDOWN

When you spot a Menial carrying around a power cell, quickly target and shoot the explosive power source to blow it—and the Menial— sky high. Be careful though, as the Menial can turn the tables and toss the Power Cell at Hale, using it as a very large and deadly grenade.

INTO THE FIRE

Break through the boarded doorway using a melee attack and continue to wind your way through the facility. Eventually, Hale reaches an open room where he encounters a few Hybrids in addition to the drone-like Menials. Either stay back and use the Bullseye to target and kill them from afar, or get in close and shoot the container of Power Cells along the left wall to wipe out all of the Chimera foes inside the room in one fell swoop.

Take a quick detour by heading down the left corridor inside the next room. In addition to a cache of Frag Grenades at the end of the hallway, there is an Intel Item resting against the wall in the bathroom to the left.

DOCUMENT INTELLIGENCE #1

GUIDELINES

This document is a diary page from a hapless British soldier who is obviously trapped in a holding pen awaiting infection. In it, he describes the plight of the "Cloven," unfortunate Russian souls who chose a grisly suicide over being turned into Chimera.

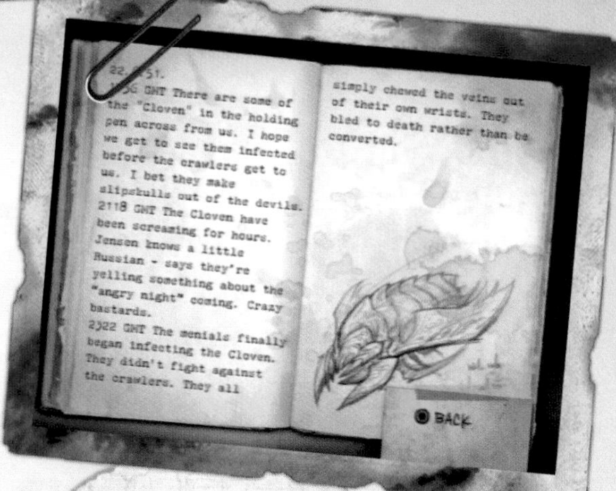

22. 51.
GMT There are some of the "Cloven" in the holding pen across from us. I hope we get to see them infected before the crawlers get to us. I bet they make slipskulls out of the devils.
2118 GMT The Cloven have been screaming for hours. Jensen knows a little Russian - says they're yelling something about the "angry night" coming. Crazy bastards.
2322 GMT The menials finally began infecting the Cloven. They didn't fight against the crawlers. They all simply chewed the veins out of their own wrists. They bled to death rather than be converted.

Return to the main room and continue to follow the path through the conversion center. If you need it, there is some Sym-Bac serum and ammo inside the kitchen area. There is a lift just down the opposite corridor from the kitchen. Hop into it and throw the switch to ride it up to the next level.

Now up on top, Hale finds that he is one step closer to freedom. Through the windows, the Menials work tirelessly to move the power cells and place them in strange receptacles.

There is yet another Hybrid just down the path and up on a walkway. There is very little in this area, so quickly target and eliminate it with either the Carbine or the Bullseye. Don't forget that you also can lob a Frag Grenade or use the Carbine's Grenade Launcher by pressing the L1 button.

Unfortunately, there is no way to get outside from here. The only way to progress is to drop down into the chamber via the twisted, broken metal walkway. Dispose of any visible enemies that are located below before dropping down.

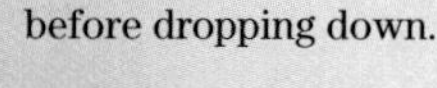

INTO THE NIGHT

The path temporarily leads outside to a quiet courtyard, but don't let the silence fool you. This area is protected by hovering mines that detect movement and emerge from small portals in the ground. If you don't quickly eliminate them, they emit a laser strike with deadly accuracy. The best defense against these mines is to tread slowly and keep one eye on the ground where Hale is walking. The portals are fairly visible, but some are covered by foliage or brush. Therefore if you're deliberate, you will see them and be prepared to counteract them before it's too late. You can also tell when a mine is about to be launched, as the lights around the portal will temporarily flash. If you do stumble upon one, take evasive action and strafe to the left or right while shooting.

Before exiting the courtyard via the staircase in the back corner, grab the Hedgehog Grenades on the platform in the center and the Rossmore 236 Shotgun from underneath the stairs.

Hedgehog Grenade

WEAPON INTELLIGENCE

The Hedgehog Grenade is a Chimeran anti-personnel munition that is thrown like an ordinary hand grenade. Upon landing, it springs up and expands into a spiny cluster. At its "kill height," the Hedgehog fires spines in all directions with enough force to pin targets against nearby walls. The effect is especially deadly in tight quarters.

Take the stairs up to the second floor, then head back inside the conversion center. Be ready for a few more mines just inside the doorway.

Rossmore 236 Combat Shotgun

WEAPON INTELLIGENCE

The Rossmore 236 Combat Shotgun is employed by the British Army for base defense and urban warfare. It is noted for its potent stopping power, especially in close-quarters engagements. Since the Chimeran invasion, soldiers have found the shotgun very adept at dispatching Howlers. Simply press the L1 button to discharge both barrels. This method is less efficient than firing the barrels one at a time, but using it effectively can sometimes mean the difference between life and death.

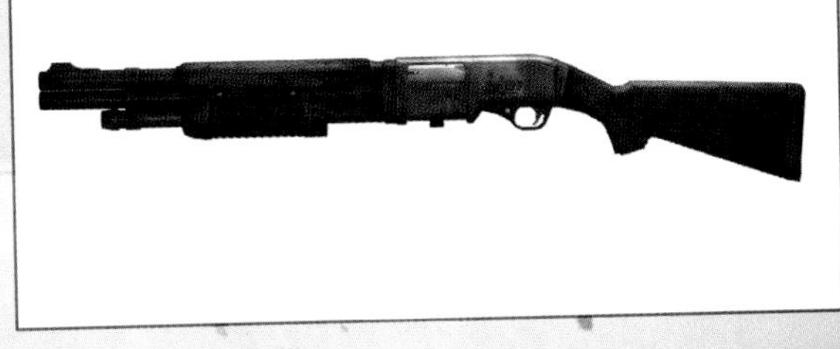

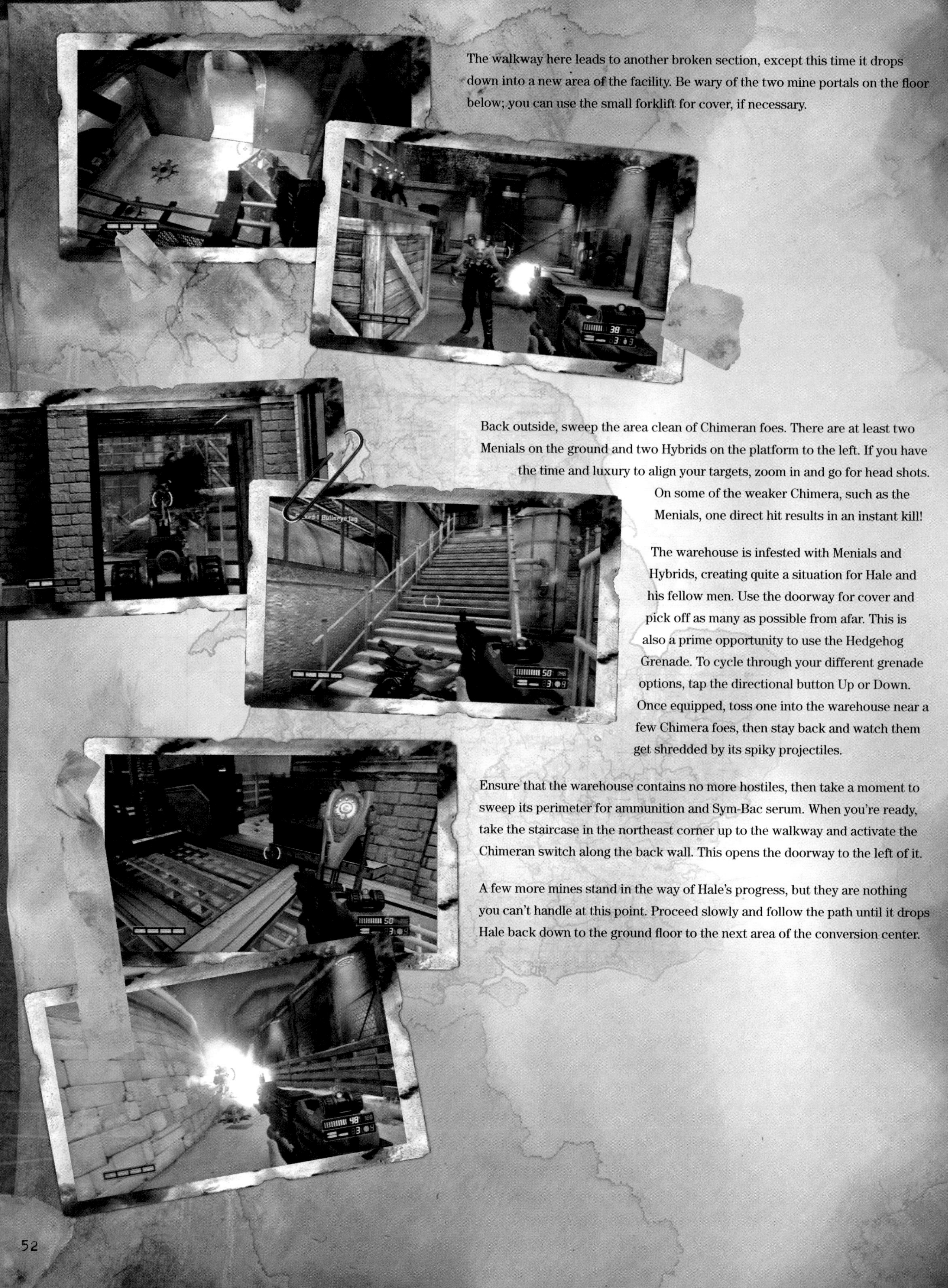

The walkway here leads to another broken section, except this time it drops down into a new area of the facility. Be wary of the two mine portals on the floor below; you can use the small forklift for cover, if necessary.

Back outside, sweep the area clean of Chimeran foes. There are at least two Menials on the ground and two Hybrids on the platform to the left. If you have the time and luxury to align your targets, zoom in and go for head shots. On some of the weaker Chimera, such as the Menials, one direct hit results in an instant kill!

The warehouse is infested with Menials and Hybrids, creating quite a situation for Hale and his fellow men. Use the doorway for cover and pick off as many as possible from afar. This is also a prime opportunity to use the Hedgehog Grenade. To cycle through your different grenade options, tap the directional button Up or Down. Once equipped, toss one into the warehouse near a few Chimera foes, then stay back and watch them get shredded by its spiky projectiles.

Ensure that the warehouse contains no more hostiles, then take a moment to sweep its perimeter for ammunition and Sym-Bac serum. When you're ready, take the staircase in the northeast corner up to the walkway and activate the Chimeran switch along the back wall. This opens the doorway to the left of it.

A few more mines stand in the way of Hale's progress, but they are nothing you can't handle at this point. Proceed slowly and follow the path until it drops Hale back down to the ground floor to the next area of the conversion center.

CONVERSION

Chimeran Conversion Center

Grimsby, England
12 July 1951—05:15 GMT

MISSION OVERVIEW

The conversion center was built atop an old fish cannery. Networks of tubes transported the bodies from one stage of the conversion to another.

Once the Chimeran virus infects humans, they fall into a coma. The virus begins changing their bodies from the inside out, eventually turning them into one of the Chimeran creatures. The conversion centers simply speed up the process. During the second phase of the process, the humans are wrapped in cocoons. This accelerates the final stages of the conversion. The strain of the virus determines what emerges from the cocoon. Also, a separate strain creates each Chimeran creature. What we call "Hybrids," the ones that most closely resemble humans, have the shortest gestation period. The more beastly creatures, which take months to create, are comprised of multiple human bodies.

FIELD REPORT

Enemy Intel
Menial
Hybrid

Hardware
M5A2 Carbine
Bullseye
Rossmore 236 Combat Shotgun
Frag Grenades

Mission Objective

★ Escape the Chimeran conversion center.

United States Army Rangers
1st Regiment

THE LABYRINTH

★ Escape the Chimeran Conversion Center

Getting closer to escaping this hellish factory of nightmares, Hale finds himself in a makeshift courtyard. It seems as if this area serves as some sort of transport system for Chimeran cocoons. Cross the courtyard and move into the next area through the open doorway. Follow the path to the base of the stairs and look out for an onslaught of Leapers.

The Chimera Cocoon

Once delivered to conversion centers, cocoons envelop the Chimera infection victims. Within each cocoon, a human body is broken down and recombined into a strain of Chimera. It is theorized that multiple human bodies are required for the larger strains. External measures are taken to keep the cocoons from overheating. This outside intervention suggests that the conversion process is not being performed in ideal circumstances. It is unknown if there is a more natural way for the Chimera to reproduce.

If you run through the Carbine's munitions during this onslaught, you can return to the alcove to the right of the doorway to replenish your stores. There is a second cache of ammo at the top of the stairs in the alcove to the left.

Another Leaper onslaught occurs at the top of the stars. Move into the alcove to the left (where the Carbine ammo is located), position Hale so that his back is against the wall, then start mowing them down.

When the last Leaper is history, throw the switch next to the back door and move into the chamber beyond. This eerie chamber contains multiple racks of pupae hanging from the ceiling. Their shells are rock solid; nothing from Hale's arsenal of weapons can penetrate it, so don't waste any ammo.

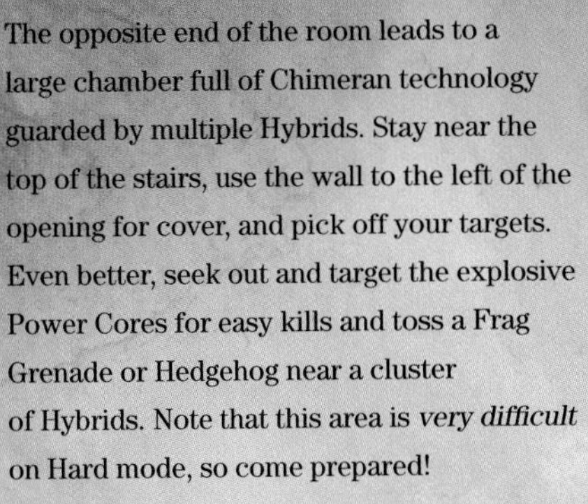

The opposite end of the room leads to a large chamber full of Chimeran technology guarded by multiple Hybrids. Stay near the top of the stairs, use the wall to the left of the opening for cover, and pick off your targets. Even better, seek out and target the explosive Power Cores for easy kills and toss a Frag Grenade or Hedgehog near a cluster of Hybrids. Note that this area is *very difficult* on Hard mode, so come prepared!

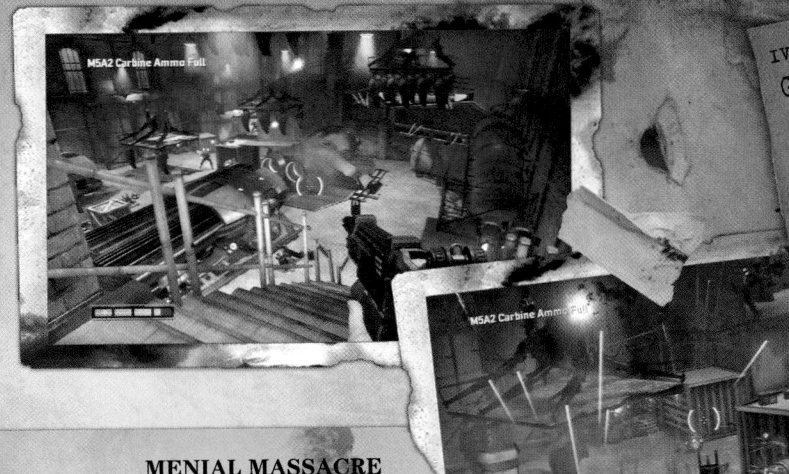

MENIAL MASSACRE

Although it may seem like no enemies remain, it's not the case. As soon as Hale steps foot into the open chamber, a bunch of Menials attack from the front and left sides. Have the Carbine locked and loaded to deal with this hostile situation.

There are even more Hybrids on the platform in the next portion of this chamber. Don't forget that the Bullseye's alternate fire can create a hovering arsenal of bullets that you can direct at your intended target. To do so, press and hold the L1 button, then unload a few rounds of rifle ammo. After doing so, use the barrel of the Bullseye to aim the bullets and press the L1 button a second time to send them on their way.

Collect all of the ammo and health in this area, then move into the next portion of the chamber where even more Hybrids await. Don't let your guard down until every last Chimeran foe has been eliminated. When the coast is clear, locate the doorway in the back-left corner and throw the nearby switch to unlock it.

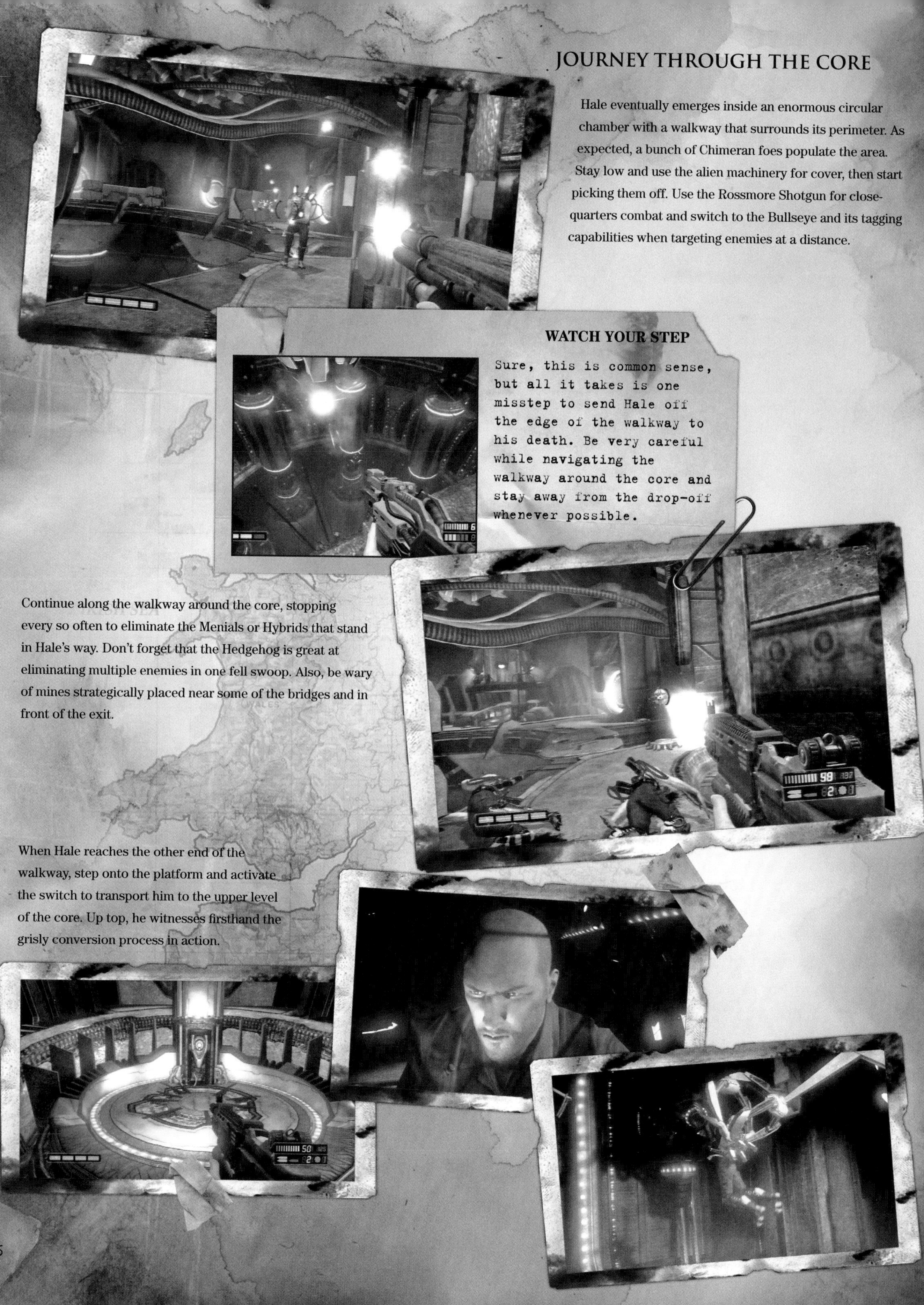

JOURNEY THROUGH THE CORE

Hale eventually emerges inside an enormous circular chamber with a walkway that surrounds its perimeter. As expected, a bunch of Chimeran foes populate the area. Stay low and use the alien machinery for cover, then start picking them off. Use the Rossmore Shotgun for close-quarters combat and switch to the Bullseye and its tagging capabilities when targeting enemies at a distance.

WATCH YOUR STEP

Sure, this is common sense, but all it takes is one misstep to send Hale off the edge of the walkway to his death. Be very careful while navigating the walkway around the core and stay away from the drop-off whenever possible.

Continue along the walkway around the core, stopping every so often to eliminate the Menials or Hybrids that stand in Hale's way. Don't forget that the Hedgehog is great at eliminating multiple enemies in one fell swoop. Also, be wary of mines strategically placed near some of the bridges and in front of the exit.

When Hale reaches the other end of the walkway, step onto the platform and activate the switch to transport him to the upper level of the core. Up top, he witnesses firsthand the grisly conversion process in action.

HUNTED DOWN

Chimeran Conversion Center

Grimsby, England
12 July 1951 — 07:38 GMT

MISSION OVERVIEW

The final stage of the Chimeran conversion process is known as the "birthing chamber." When the cocoons open, new Chimera are born. In the case of Hybrids, a cooling apparatus is fused into their bodies. The Chimeran metabolism is roughly twelve times that of humans. This results in remarkable healing abilities, but also raises their body temperatures significantly. Without the cooling apparatus, the hybrids would overheat and die.

Hale and I were in contact via radio, although I couldn't keep tabs on him while attempting my escape. I know firsthand his path through the conversion center must have been filled with peril.

FIELD REPORT

Enemy Intel
Menial
Hybrid

Hardware
M5A2 Carbine
Bullseye
Rossmore 236 Combat Shotgun
Frag Grenades

Mission Objective

★ Escape the Chimeran conversion center.

United States Army Rangers
1st Regiment

DOCKSIDE TERROR

★ Escape the Chimeran Conversion Center

Starting on the second level of the conversion center, follow the walkway around the core to find the exit at the opposite end. Although Hale is out of the facility, he still needs to free himself from the surrounding docks and outlying area. Cautiously follow the path between the structures, stopping near the doorway of the Café-Bar on the right.

Mines litter the dockside, so proceed cautiously. Listen for audio cues while walking, as the mines make a charging sound before firing off a laser strike. The first mine is inside the Café-Bar, near the doorway, while a second one is cleverly hidden behind the first pool table.

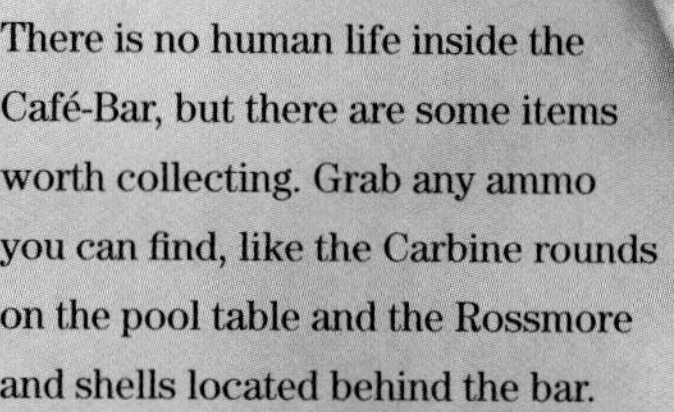

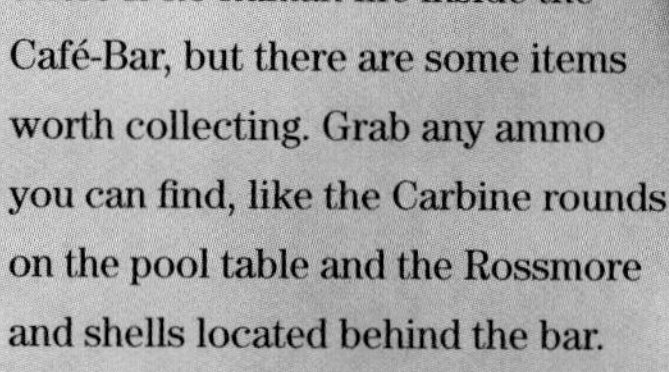

There is no human life inside the Café-Bar, but there are some items worth collecting. Grab any ammo you can find, like the Carbine rounds on the pool table and the Rossmore and shells located behind the bar.

SOLIDS OR STRIPES?

Although this has no bearing on Hale's attempt at escape, check out the cool physics in *Resistance: Fall of Man* by shooting/using the melee attack to move the balls around the pool table. If you're skilled enough, you can knock one off the table and send it rolling across the floor.

Exit the Café-Bar through the second doorway and be on the lookout for three more mines just up the path. As always, the best strategy is to take cover and pick them off in between charges if you can't shoot them all.

This path leads to the docks, but before heading this way, take a moment to enter the structure through the doorway to the right. There are more mines here just inside each of its doorways. Search the counter along the back of the room on the left-hand side to locate an Intel Item. Grab it before moving onward.

DOCUMENT INTELLIGENCE #7

CAPTURED

This document is a page from a diary of one Lt Cpl. Canning, who was captured during a patrol north of Liverpool and taken via Carrier to the conversion center. It chronicles Canning's capture and his attempt at escape.

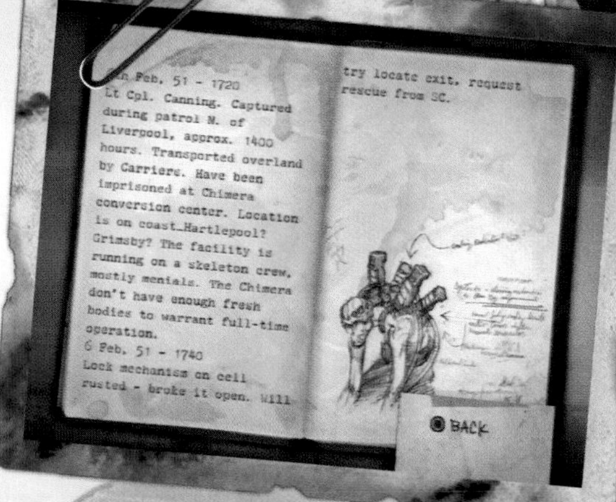
Feb. 51 - 1720
Lt Cpl. Canning. Captured during patrol N. of Liverpool, approx. 1400 hours. Transported overland by Carriers. Have been imprisoned at Chimera conversion center. Location is on coast_Hartlepool? Grimsby? The facility is running on a skeleton crew, mostly mentals. The Chimera don't have enough fresh bodies to warrant full-time operation.
6 Feb. 51 - 1740
Lock mechanism on cell rusted - broke it open. Will try locate exit, request rescue from SC.

BACK

Return to the path and follow it to the docks. Watch out for more mines down here; there is one in the middle of the first dock, three down the path to the right, and one at the end of the second dock. There are also two Hybrids hiding behind the corner at the end of the path. To dispose of them, target the nearby container of Power Cores to set off a chain reaction.

A SECOND SHOTGUN

You may have already picked up the Rossmore and plenty of shotgun ammo. If you passed it by in the previous areas, there is another one down the dead end path to the right, which is located between the walkway and the docks.

STANDOFF

Enter the building at the end of the path and get ready to dig in for a massive firefight! Equip the Bullseye and use the large sections of machinery for cover, then start acquiring your targets and taking them down.

The majority of the Hybrids in this area are located near the back of the room on the elevated platform. However, there are a few who are also patrolling the room and using the environment for cover. You can flush out these foes by tossing a few grenades their way.

To dispose of the Hybrids on the platform in the back, use the tag function on the Bullseye to target them from at a distance, then eliminate them from behind cover.

Make sure you completely clear the area of enemies before moving out. Once accomplished, take a moment to sweep the room for ammo and Sym-Bac serum, then follow the elevated platform around the corner to the right and into the next area.

Instead of stepping down into the room, use stealth and duck down behind the crates, then tag and take out the Hybrids patrolling the staircase and landing across the way. There are a few more Hybrids inside the room behind the conveyor belts. If you have any Frag Grenades, toss one of them, or use a Hedgehog, to wipe them out.

DON'T FORGET TO MELEE

Hale's melee attack is an effective defense against most close-range attacks. Always try to use it when things get a little too close for comfort. If an enemy attacks up close, quickly press △ to knock back the foe.

Before exiting the building, take a quick detour upstairs to the attic and collect an Intel Item. Look for it amongst the carnage and dead bodies that litter the floor.

DOCUMENT INTELLIGENCE #8

YORK SET UP

This document chronicles the observance of the "Cloven" and their interaction with the Chimera. The author begs the question of why they would lure the Chimera to York.

GRAB THE GRENADES

There is a cache of Frag Grenades next to a few canisters of Sym-Bac serum on top of the cargo next to the forklift. Before moving out, jump from the adjacent platform to the forklift and hop onto the cargo to grab them.

Return to the ground floor and exit the building through the doorway leading back outside. Luckily, this area is devoid of Chimeras, although this reprieve is only temporary.

This path leads up a small hill. At the top, a screeching sound foreshadows an attack by some Leapers. Back up to create plenty of distance, face the doorway from which they are coming, then start mowing them down as they pour out. The best strategy to take when combating these nasty creatures is to minimize Hale's exposure to them and keep them from spreading out.

More of these foes attack just as Hale reaches the stairwell inside. Quickly backtrack through the doorway to force them to bunch together and keep firing until they stop coming.

THE FINAL PUSH

Take the lift up to the vast warehouse, which is strangely devoid of Chimera. According to Parker, she has determined that they have set up a trap for Hale and are waiting to ambush him when he steps outside.

Locate the exit, use the doorway for cover, and start the final push toward freedom by eliminating any foes within view. Containers, crates, and other various items fill this area, so use them for cover from the enemies' fire. Cautiously move from one object to the next, peeking out to locate the Chimera and pick them off using the Bullseye. If you have any grenades, toss them into areas occupied by two or more enemies.

If you want to mix things up a bit, switch to the Rossmore. Remember, though, that this is more of a close-range weapon, meaning that it is most effective when an enemy is in the immediate vicinity.

The real trouble begins as Hale approaches the exit. Some Chimera, sitting behind a set of bunkers, are manning two turrets. If you peek out from cover, Hale will get caught in the crossfire. The most effective strategy is to either toss a grenade into the turret nests or use the Bullseye to tag and target the foes operating them.

PLAN B

There is another alternative to taking over the turret nests. Instead of fighting the Chimera head on, jump onto the trailer beds and go to the top of the crate that overlooks the turrets. From this vantage point, the foe can't use the turrets to target Hale. Instead, they will resort to their standard weaponry. This area also makes them much easier targets to hit.

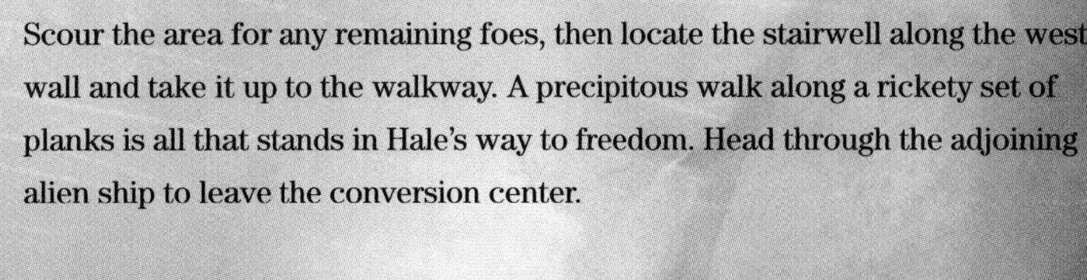

Scour the area for any remaining foes, then locate the stairwell along the west wall and take it up to the walkway. A precipitous walk along a rickety set of planks is all that stands in Hale's way to freedom. Head through the adjoining alien ship to leave the conversion center.

PATH OF LEAST RESISTANCE

Convoy Recovery

NORTHERN COMMAND

CLASSIFIED

Manchester, England
12 July 1951 — 09:38 GMT

MISSION OVERVIEW

Hale made it out of the conversion center shortly after. I looked for any further signs of conversion. Fever, nervous movement, paranoia. There was nothing. Just the gold-colored eyes. We flew directly to Manchester. Soldiers had been trying to recover the convoy ever since my squad was ambushed. They knew what was in it. They knew it was our last hope for defeating the Chimera. I wanted to take Hale back to Northern Command for debriefing. Maybe he could sense I was suspicious of him. He joined the Manchester squad before I could say a word…

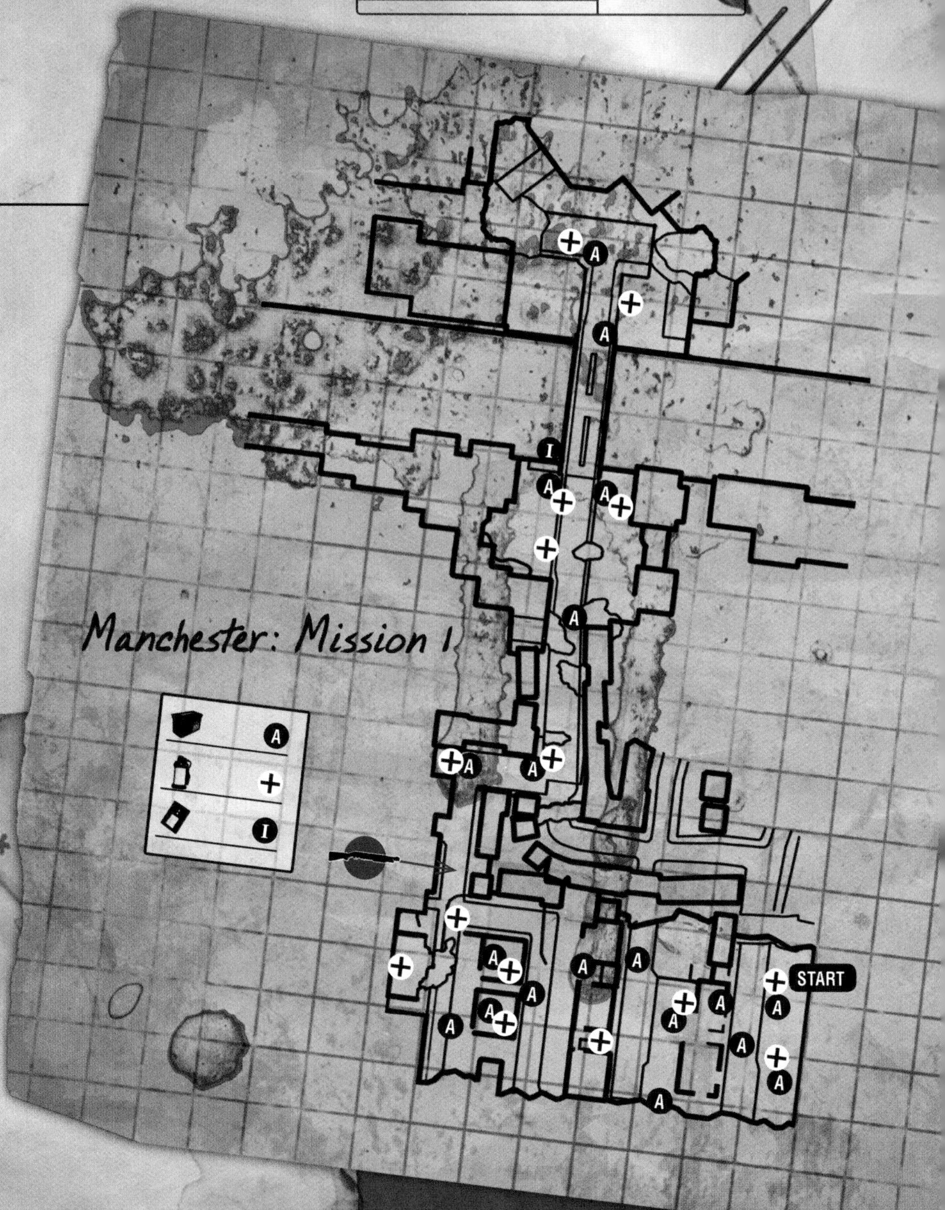

FIELD REPORT

Enemy Intel
Menial
Hybrid
Howler

Hardware
M5A2 Carbine
Bullseye
Rossmore 236
Combat Shotgun
Frag Grenades

Mission Objective

★ Get to the Convoy.

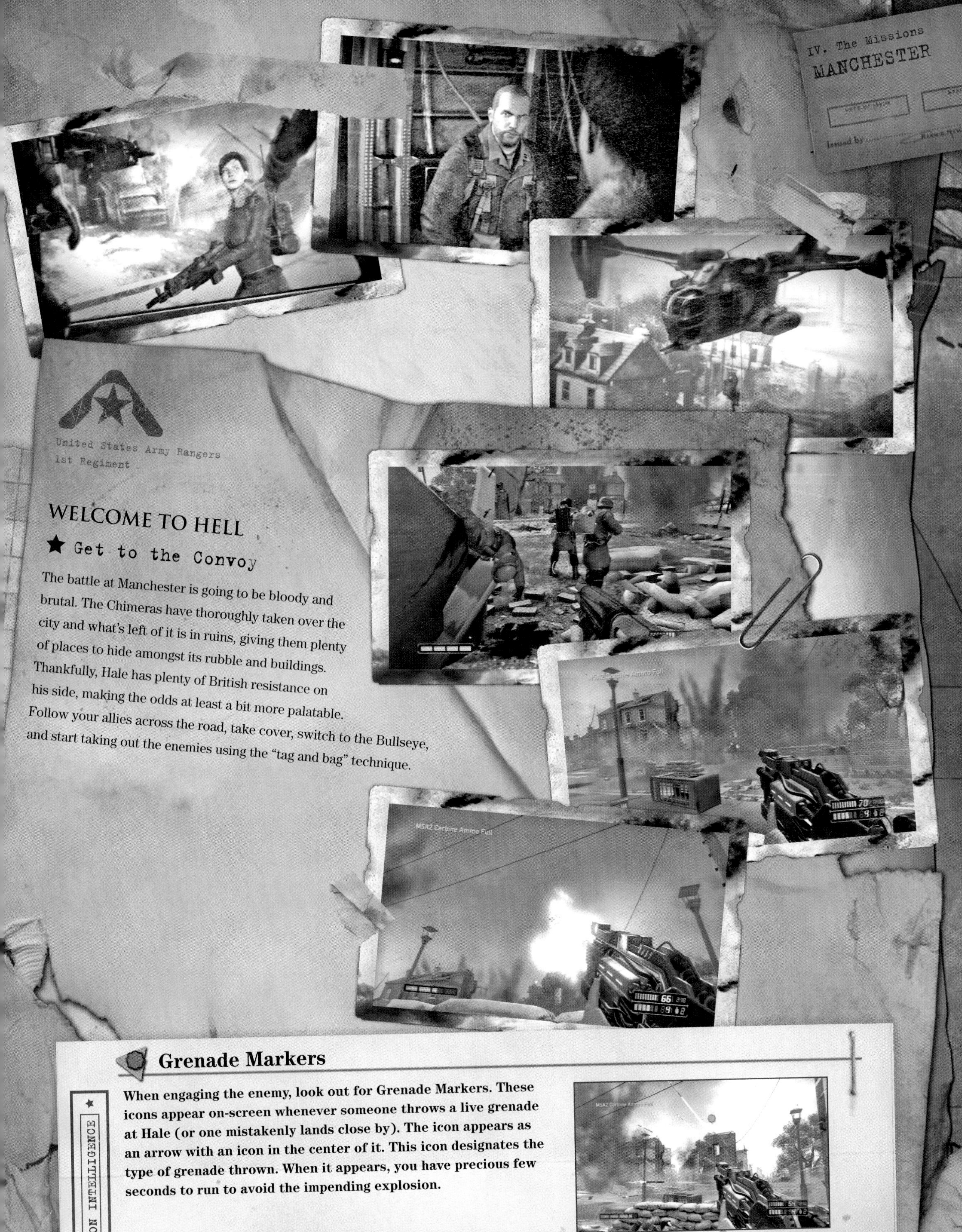

United States Army Rangers
1st Regiment

WELCOME TO HELL

★ Get to the Convoy

The battle at Manchester is going to be bloody and brutal. The Chimeras have thoroughly taken over the city and what's left of it is in ruins, giving them plenty of places to hide amongst its rubble and buildings. Thankfully, Hale has plenty of British resistance on his side, making the odds at least a bit more palatable. Follow your allies across the road, take cover, switch to the Bullseye, and start taking out the enemies using the "tag and bag" technique.

WEAPON INTELLIGENCE

Grenade Markers

When engaging the enemy, look out for Grenade Markers. These icons appear on-screen whenever someone throws a live grenade at Hale (or one mistakenly lands close by). The icon appears as an arrow with an icon in the center of it. This icon designates the type of grenade thrown. When it appears, you have precious few seconds to run to avoid the impending explosion.

Taking damage is inevitable, as there is an overwhelming number of foes to fight. Use the environment for cover and stay low if at all possible. Peek out from behind cover and fire at your targets to whittle them down.

Don't hold back and use plenty of Frag Grenades during this intense battle, especially against clusters of Chimera. One well-placed Frag Grenade can wipe out multiple foes in a hearbeat.

POWER IN NUMBERS

During this intense mission, Hale will have constant backup from his fellow allied soldiers. Do your best to stay close to at least one or two of them at all times, as they can provide cover fire and help keep the enemies busy by drawing their fire.

After the first wave of the assault, take a few moments to scour the surrounding area for Sym-Bac serum and ammo supplies. Now move out and continue down the hillside through the rubble.

It doesn't take long for the next wave of foes to attack. Once again, duck for cover and then pick them off with a Frag Grenade or Bullseye fire. Continue to advance by creeping a bit forward, taking cover, picking off the encroaching Chimera, then repeating.

SNIPERS IN THE WINDOWS

The Chimera are extremely crafty foes and will take advantage of the dilapidated buildings by sniping through their windows. Watch out for these sniper situations and quickly eliminate the shooter.

You can position Hale atop these crumbling buildings and fire at the enemies, too. Climb up to the second story of any open building, then use the elevated position to snipe any foes below.

The battle wages on as Hale and his allies slowly make their way down the remainder of the hill. Navigate through the rubble while engaging any foes in close-quarters combat until you reach the main thoroughfare of what used to be Manchester.

While making your way through the rubble, a Leaper onslaught occurs. Use the same drill here as discussed previously: Put some distance between Hale and the enemies, then rip ‘em to shreds with the Carbine.

HERO MOMENT!

Watch your nearby allies when the Leapers attack. More than likely, the onslaught will overwhelm one of them. If this occurs, offer your services and help him out!

A second Leaper attack occurs out on the street. This time, however, a horde of Bullseye-wielding Hybrids joins the fray. Don't forget that the Carbine also has a Grenade Launcher attachment; you can deal massive damage by pressing the L1 button.

THE ROAD TO THE CATHEDRAL

Continue the slow and bloody descent through the streets of Manchester, dealing with wave after wave of Chimera Hybrids. When Hale finally reaches the bottom of the hill, follow the main road due north, toward the cathedral off in the distance.

A last stand takes place near the entrance to the cathedral. Take cover and flush out the attacking foes blocking your progress. Before crossing the bridge, take a moment to locate this area's Intel Item. Look for it on the wharf side, down underneath the bridge. Locate the staircase to the left and take it down to the platform to grab it. Don't forget to pick up the 40mm grenade for your Carbine!

DOCUMENT INTELLIGENCE #8

OF HOWLERS

This is a page from a journal that documents the plight of a regiment barricaded inside the cathedral. In it, the author writes about a Chimeran beast called a Howler "as big as a horse and bulletproof." They were able to fell one using an old shotgun.

Return to the bridge and cautiously cross the river toward the cathedral. Expect heavy resistance as Hale and the allies approach the other end. Included in the resistance is a manned turret nest. Use quick weapons, such as the Carbine's Grenade Launcher, to take care of business.

THE HOWLER AT THE BRIDGE

The cathedral is Hale's ultimate destination. Locate the entrance and head straight over there. As Hale and his crew approach the cathedral's entrance, they are met by a new Chimeran creature—the Howler. Quickly equip the Rossmore shotgun and chip away at its tough hide while constantly retreating to keep a comfortable distance between it and Hale.

Here's a tactic for the really skilled player: Wait until the Howler gets close, then fire both shotgun barrels in the creature's face to drop him in two shots. Although this takes some skill, it does conserve ammo.

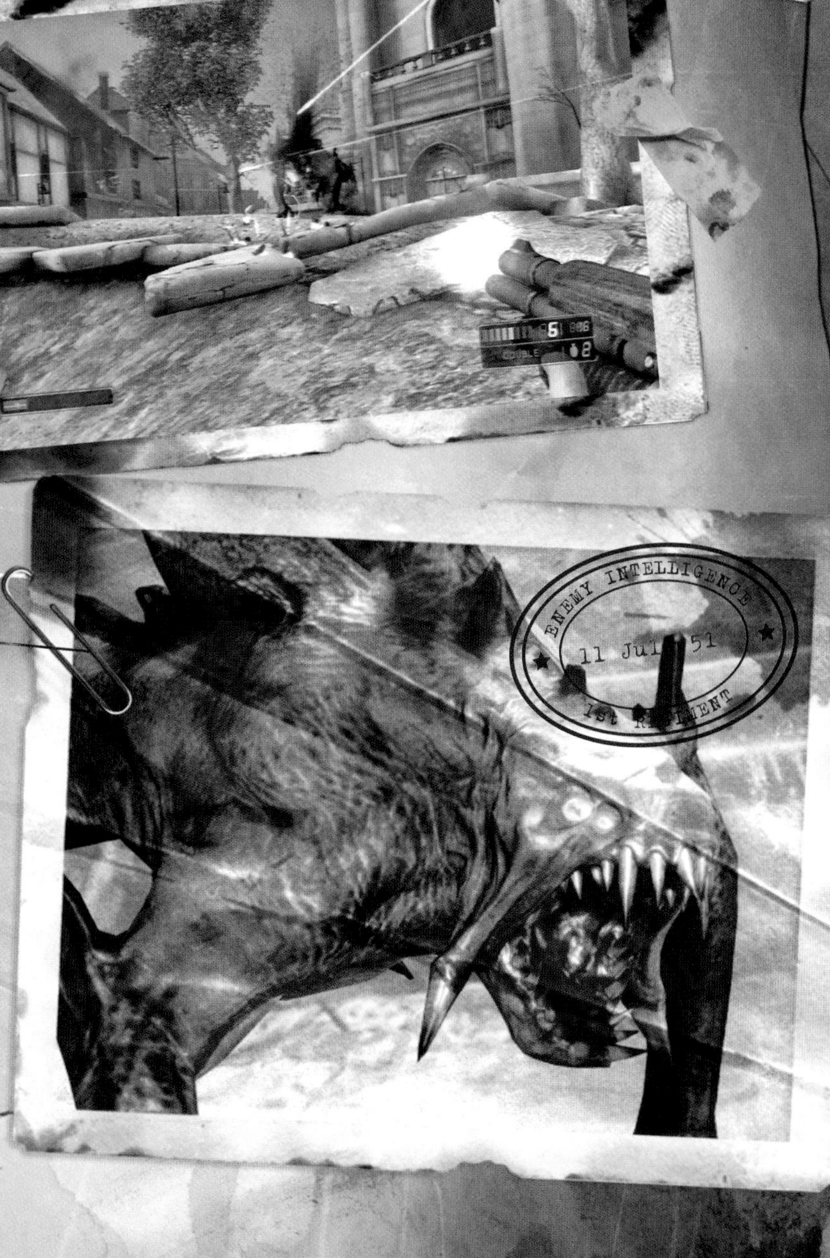

The Chimera Howler

A Howler is a large quadruple strain of Chimera. Their rudimentary vocalizations are rumored to provide the beasts with some level of communication. People can hear their calls for miles and the noise has a chilling effect on those familiar with the source. Howlers have a leathery hide that shrugs off most light-arms fire. Combat shotguns at close range have proven highly effective.

CATHEDRAL

Convoy Recovery

NORTHERN COMMAND

CLASSIFIED

Manchester, England
12 July 1951—11:14 GMT

MISSION OVERVIEW

The convoy was stranded on the west side of Manchester. The Chimera wanted it just as much as we did. Unfortunately, Stalkers guarded the site, so the only route in was on foot. The main path led Hale and the others through the Manchester Cathedral. The Cathedral was a field hospital during the war. It was abandoned in a hurry and still had some supplies and ammunition. Unfortunately, it was also a breeding ground for some of the lower forms of Chimera...

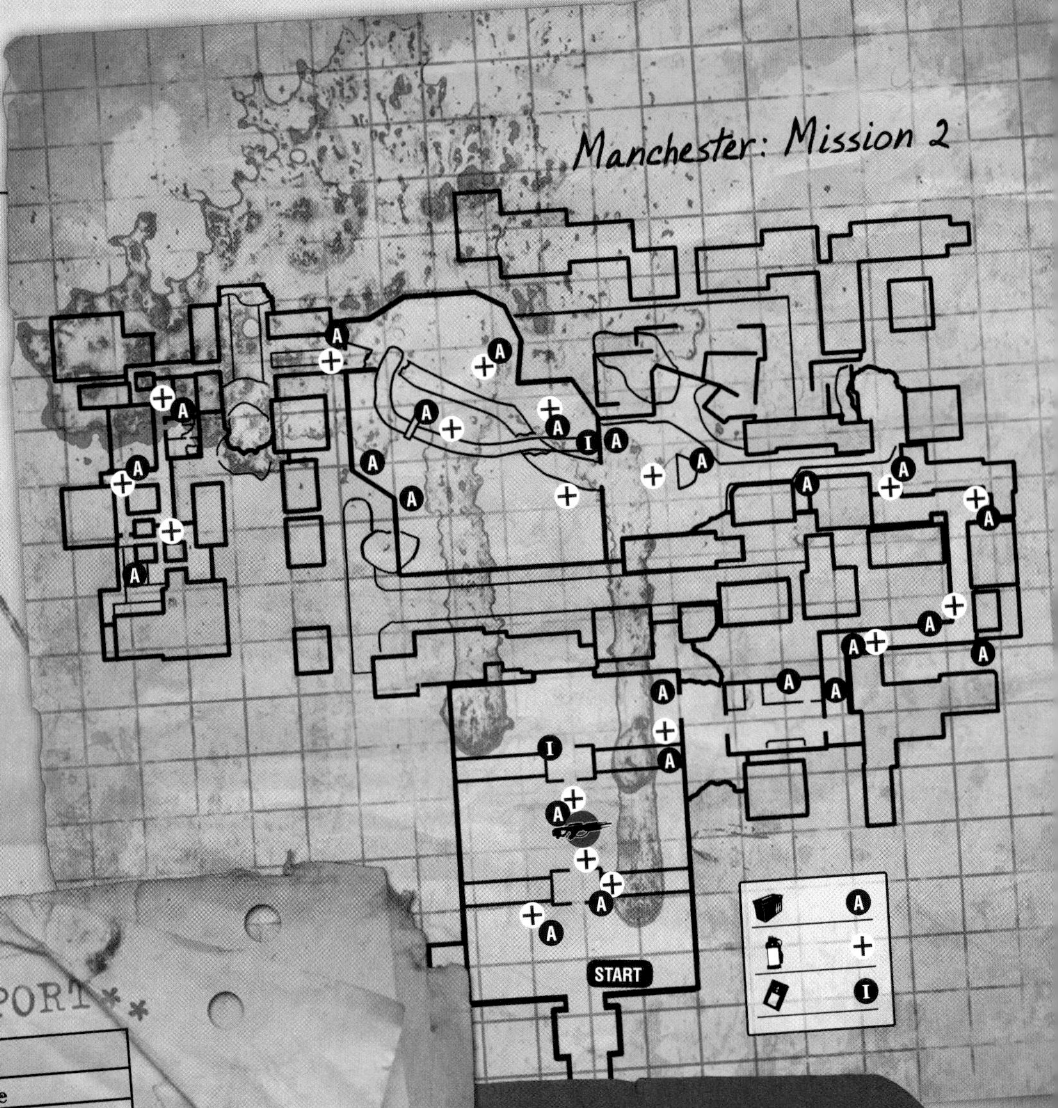

Manchester: Mission 2

START

FIELD REPORT

Enemy Intel
Hybrid
Howler
Steelhead

Hardware
M5A2 Carbine
Bullseye
Rossmore 236 Combat Shotgun
Auger
Frag Grenades
Hedgehog

Mission Objective

★ Get to the Convoy.

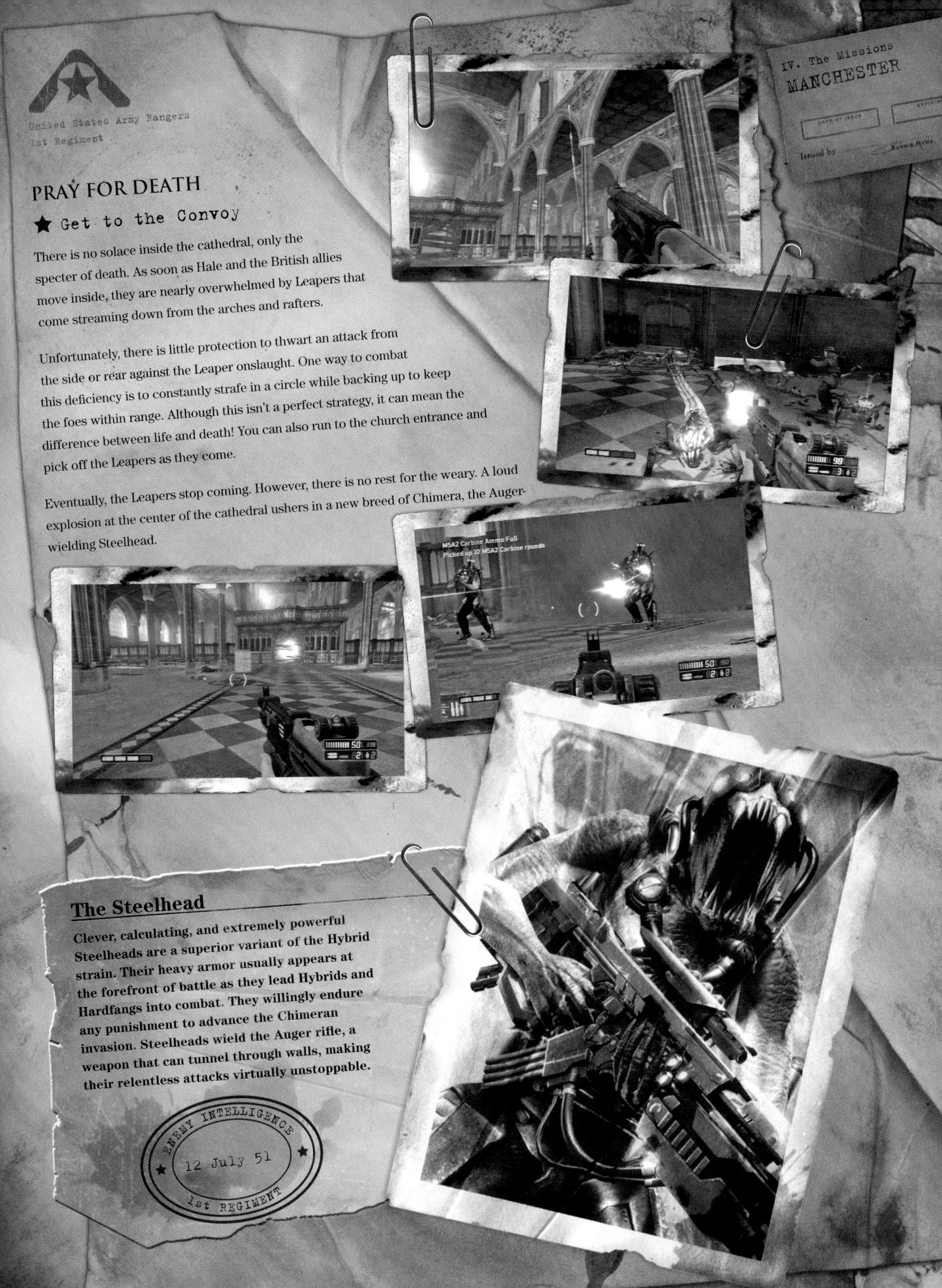

PRAY FOR DEATH

★ Get to the Convoy

There is no solace inside the cathedral, only the specter of death. As soon as Hale and the British allies move inside, they are nearly overwhelmed by Leapers that come streaming down from the arches and rafters.

Unfortunately, there is little protection to thwart an attack from the side or rear against the Leaper onslaught. One way to combat this deficiency is to constantly strafe in a circle while backing up to keep the foes within range. Although this isn't a perfect strategy, it can mean the difference between life and death! You can also run to the church entrance and pick off the Leapers as they come.

Eventually, the Leapers stop coming. However, there is no rest for the weary. A loud explosion at the center of the cathedral ushers in a new breed of Chimera, the Auger-wielding Steelhead.

The Steelhead

Clever, calculating, and extremely powerful Steelheads are a superior variant of the Hybrid strain. Their heavy armor usually appears at the forefront of battle as they lead Hybrids and Hardfangs into combat. They willingly endure any punishment to advance the Chimeran invasion. Steelheads wield the Auger rifle, a weapon that can tunnel through walls, making their relentless attacks virtually unstoppable.

There is no place to hide when dealing with these beasts, as their weapons have the power to shoot through solid objects—including walls. Keep moving and don't let them get a bead on Hale. Also, throw a Hedgehog Grenade to help soften them up a bit.

The Bullseye is effective against their armored hides, but it's much quicker and safer to use a grenade or the Carbine's Grenade Launcher to take them down. After defeating one of these foes, make sure to grab the Auger from their twisted claws.

Auger

WEAPON INTELLIGENCE

This rifle emits blasts of transient radiation that will tunnel through solid matter. The blasts increase in power with each object they pass through. Pressing the L1 button deploys a Force Barrier. This alters the Auger's energy blast to create a barrier that is impervious to all types of firepower except that from the Auger. Enemies will suffer injuries if they move through this barrier.

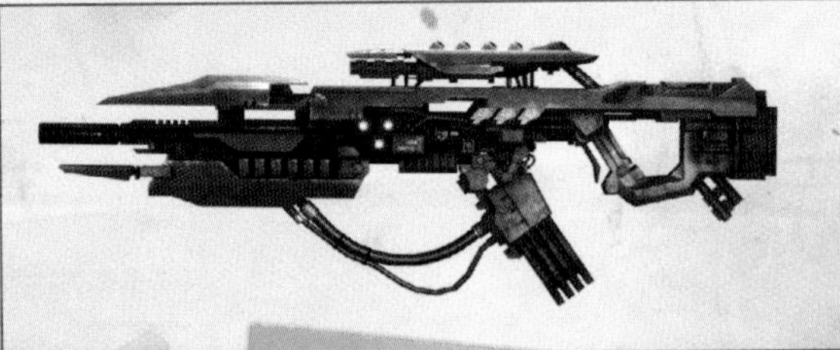

AUGER 101

The Auger is a powerful weapon that can literally shoot through any solid object. Use the targeting reticule for confirmation that there is an enemy on the other side of an object—it will turn red when an enemy is within its sights—and then start shooting. The Auger's radiation bolts travel slowly at first, so don't leave a protected position until you fire at least three of four blasts or receive confirmation that the target has been eliminated. By using the shield secondary fire, Hale can set up cover from which he can deploy Auger rounds. You need to watch out for any Steelheads in the area, though.

After defeating the Steelheads, take a moment to collect the Sym-Bac serum and ammo littered around this section of the cathedral. When the time is right, move toward the opening in the center of the room and engage the Hybrids in the second portion of the hall.

Don't let your guard down, even if you've eliminated the Hybrid on the other side of the cathedral. That growling sound indicates that there is a Howler nearby, and it's most likely already on its way to attack Hale. Switch to the Rossmore and return the favor.

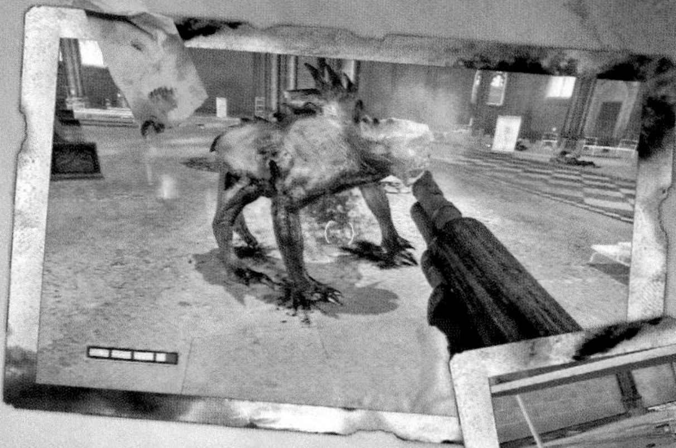

When it's safe to do so, sweep the second half of the cathedral for ammo and Sym-Bac serum. In addition to these pick-ups, there is also an Intel Item on one of the shelves along the left side of the hall.

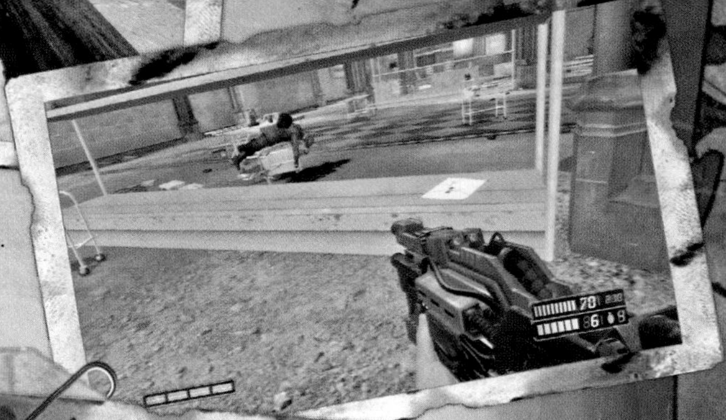

DOCUMENT INTELLIGENCE #9

Crawlers

A torn page from a medical journal by the Royal Army Medical Corps, this document details the horrific plight of the survivors at the cathedral and what happens when Crawlers get into an uninfected body.

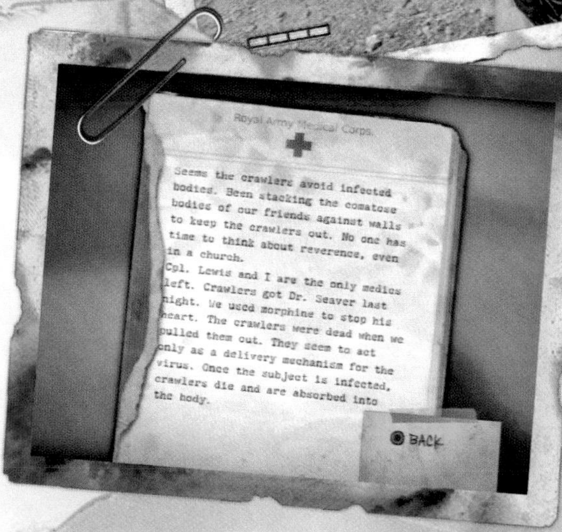

Royal Army Medical Corps.

Seems the crawlers avoid infected bodies. Been stacking the comatose bodies of our friends against walls to keep the crawlers out. No one has time to think about reverence, even in a church.

Cpl. Lewis and I are the only medics left. Crawlers got Dr. Seaver last night. We used morphine to stop his heart. The crawlers were dead when we pulled them out. They seem to act only as a delivery mechanism for the virus. Once the subject is infected, crawlers die and are absorbed into the body.

BACK

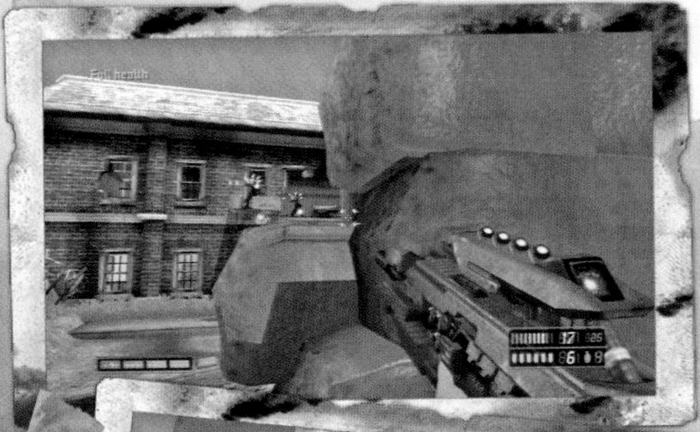

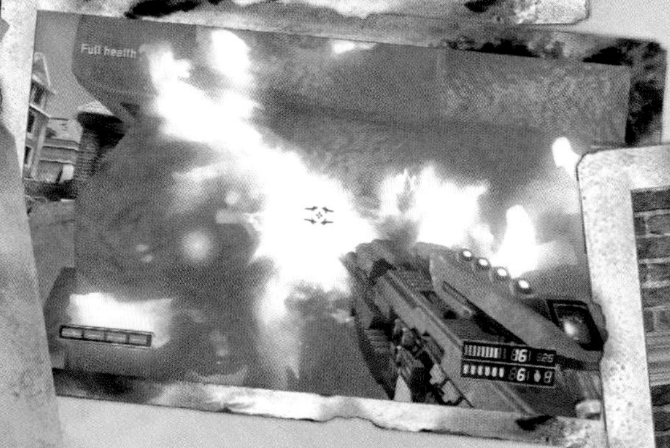

Prepare to exit the cathedral through the large hole in the wall along the back right side. Before doing so, though, take out the two Hybrids on the second floor of the building across the way. You can use the Auger to eliminate them by shooting through the cathedral's thick limestone walls.

You can also send the Chimera on the balcony plunging to its death by targeting the balcony's supports. Look for these instant-kill opportunities while making your way through the streets of Manchester.

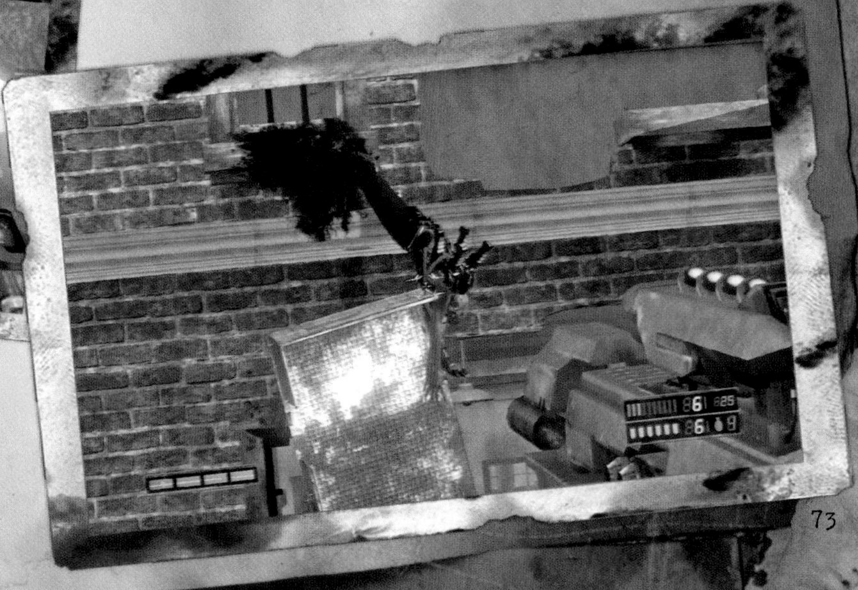

AMBUSHED

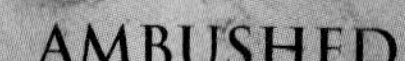

Move through the building across the street and head into the alleyway beyond. This is where Hale encounters a few surviving British soldiers. Gather your wits and head down the pathway between the buildings.

Around the corner, more Hybrids have hunkered down behind a sand bag bunker. Use the Auger to weed them out, then switch to the Carbine and obliterate the charging horde of Leapers in their wake.

Around the corner, more creatures ambush Hale and the surviving British troops. Take out the Steelhead first, then find cover and use grenades to flush out the Hybrids inside the storefronts on the right and at the end of the path. When the carnage ends, continue along the path and up the stairs, then through the archway to reach LLyod Street.

AUGER SHIELDING

Don't forget that the Auger has a secondary functionality. By pressing the L1 button, you can trigger a protective shield that blocks all weapon fire, with the exception of the Auger.

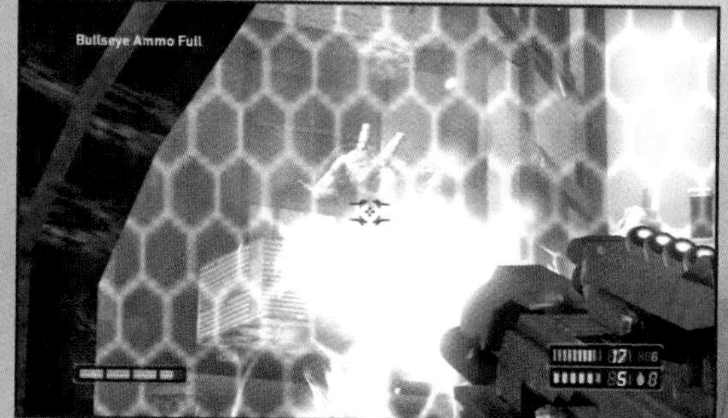

A WALK IN THE PARK

Head out due north toward the large tree in the square. The park in the distance is Hale's next destination. To reach it, though, you must get past two Howlers; switch to the Rossmore and keep them at bay. Although it's a risky proposition, it's possible to line them up, use the Rossmore's alternate fire (press the L1 button) to fire off a double round into their hides.

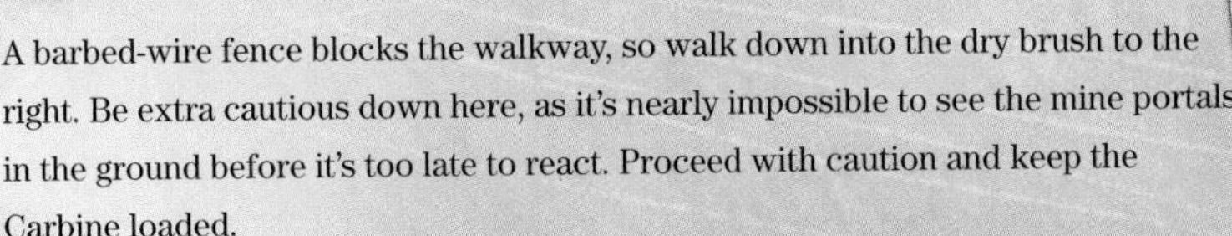

MINE TROUBLE #1—THE HEDGEHOG MINE

There are more mines just inside the park. These portals release exploding Hedgehog grenades into the air. One blast from a Hedgehog can be crippling and lethal. The best way to deal with these mines is to quickly shoot and destroy them before they can detonate. If this approach isn't possible, take evasive action before they detonate.

A barbed-wire fence blocks the walkway, so walk down into the dry brush to the right. Be extra cautious down here, as it's nearly impossible to see the mine portals in the ground before it's too late to react. Proceed with caution and keep the Carbine loaded.

MINE TROUBLE #2—THE RADIAL MINE

Hale encounters yet another new type of mine down here. Radial Mines emit a lethal, rippling shockwave of energy when they explode. The only way to survive a blast is to either jump over the shockwave or duck underneath it.

Look for the opening in the barbed-wire fence and drop off the makeshift bridge into the trench below. Before moving onward, search for the Intel Item at the end of the trench off to the right.

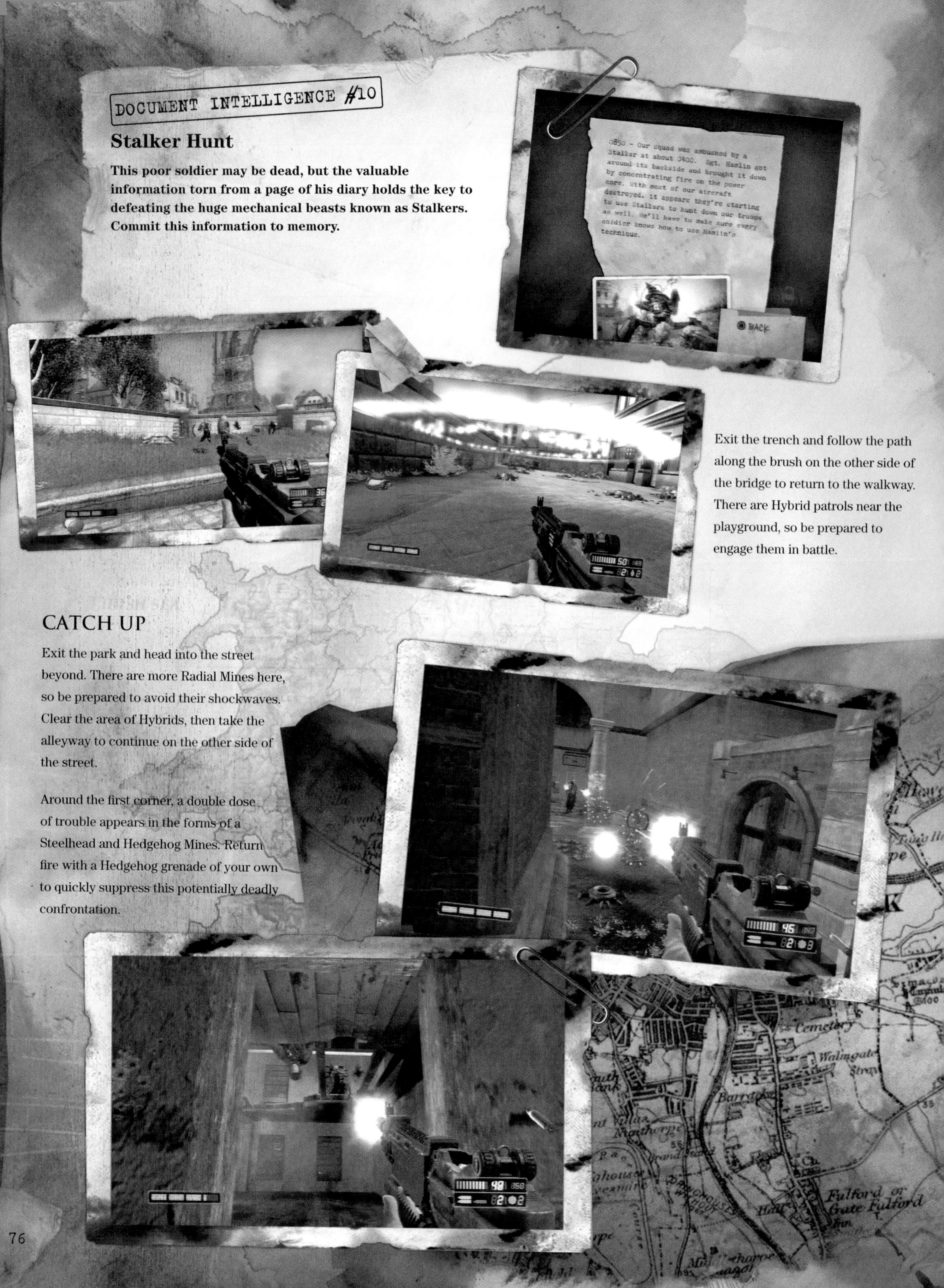

DOCUMENT INTELLIGENCE #10

Stalker Hunt

This poor soldier may be dead, but the valuable information torn from a page of his diary holds the key to defeating the huge mechanical beasts known as Stalkers. Commit this information to memory.

Exit the trench and follow the path along the brush on the other side of the bridge to return to the walkway. There are Hybrid patrols near the playground, so be prepared to engage them in battle.

CATCH UP

Exit the park and head into the street beyond. There are more Radial Mines here, so be prepared to avoid their shockwaves. Clear the area of Hybrids, then take the alleyway to continue on the other side of the street.

Around the first corner, a double dose of trouble appears in the forms of a Steelhead and Hedgehog Mines. Return fire with a Hedgehog grenade of your own to quickly suppress this potentially deadly confrontation.

There are lots of Hybrids in the courtyard and the next building. Move slowly and pick off the enemies as they appear. Enter the building and sweep it clean, then drop down through the hole in the upper floor to continue. Back outside, the path leads Hale to a Leaper ambush. As usual, stay back and switch to the Carbine to obliterate the enemies.

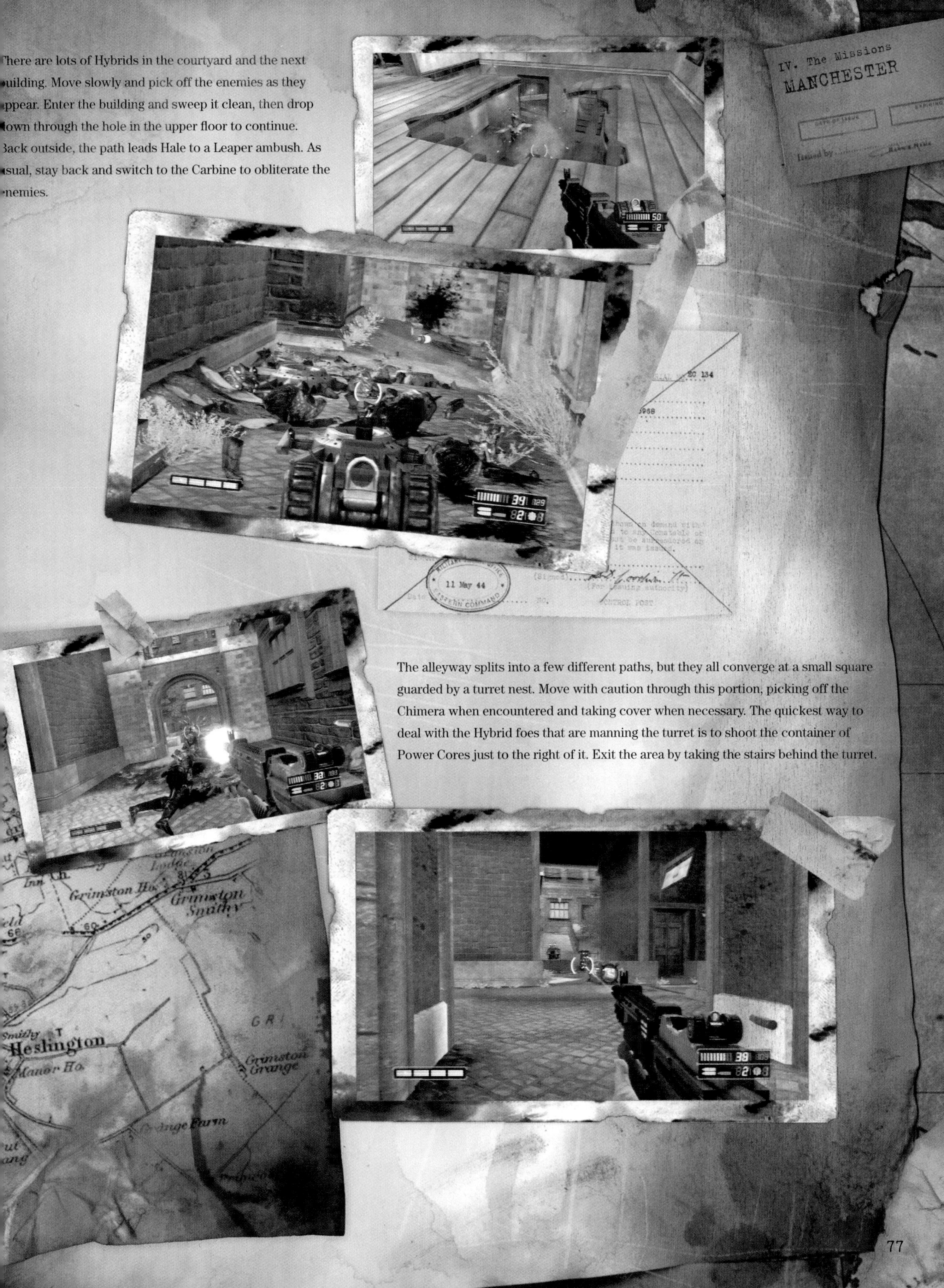

The alleyway splits into a few different paths, but they all converge at a small square guarded by a turret nest. Move with caution through this portion, picking off the Chimera when encountered and taking cover when necessary. The quickest way to deal with the Hybrid foes that are manning the turret is to shoot the container of Power Cores just to the right of it. Exit the area by taking the stairs behind the turret.

OUTGUNNED

Convoy Recovery

NORTHERN COMMAND
CLASSIFIED

Manchester, England
12 July 1951—13:35 GMT

MISSION OVERVIEW

Captain Mitchell's squad had located the convoy. Unfortunately, Stalker sightings in the area made immediate recovery impossible. The Stalker is one of the Chimera's most feared foes. They move quickly and fire anti-aircraft missiles with deadly accuracy. The technology used in the Stalker remains one of the most intriguing and frustrating mysteries of the Chimera.

FIELD REPORT

Enemy Intel
Hybrid
Steelhead
Stalker

Hardware
M5A2 Carbine
Bullseye
Rossmore 236
Combat Shotgun
Auger
Frag Grenades
Hedgehog

Mission Objective

- ★ Eliminate the Chimera and Recover the Convoy.
- ★ Defend the Convoy.
- ★ Destroy the Stalker.

THE CONVOY OFFENSIVE—DISPATCH

★ Eliminate the Chimera and Recover the Convoy

The dangerous trek through Nottingham was nothing compared to the deadly battle about to take place. Hale and the British troops have located the convoy, which houses the mysterious piece of machinery that the Americans were hoping to get their hands on. To recover it, Hale and his fellow allies must take over the square and eliminate the Chimera foes.

Things are going to get very intense in a matter of moments. A quick glance at the square through the scope of Hale's weapon illustrates the impossibility of this upcoming firefight. First, try to pick off as many Chimera as possible from the safety of cover. Use the Bullseye to tag and bag, too. When this no longer works, move from cover to cover to get close enough to resume this killing spree.

Take this portion of the battle slowly and pick off packs of Chimera before moving to the next trouble spot. Start with the area to the left and work your way around the perimeter of the battlefield in a clockwise fashion. When an area contains no more enemies, take over the spot and find cover, then turn your attention to the next group of foes.

SHIELD STRATEGY

Use the Auger to your advantage on the battlefield by employing its shield function. Not only does the shield temporarily protect Hale while repelling the enemies' fire back at them, it also creates an opportunity to switch to another weapon and pick off a few of these nasty beasts in the process.

GRENADE TACTICS

Don't forget that Frag Grenade and Hedgehog Grenades (as well as the Carbine's Grenade Launcher) can eliminate multiple enemies with one direct hit. Make sure to use them whenever you encounter a cluster of enemies.

During this shootout, locate the truck along the perimeter and blow it up with continuous fire to take out the Chimera standing next to it. The truck is also significant in that the area surrounding it is littered with pick-ups, ranging from multiple vials of Sym-Bac serum to a variety of munitions and grenades. Come back here often to restock and replenish.

United States Army Rangers
1st Regiment

THE CONVOY OFFENSIVE—DEFEND

Defend the Convoy

Unfortunately, things are about to go from bad to worse. Once the first wave of Chimera is history, a second wave drops in from the north. Take cover in the overgrown fountain in the middle of the square, throw down a shield with the Auger, and start depleting the foes that come streaming out of the drop ship container. You can also throw a Hedgehog Grenade or two as the dropship container opens.

FLANK THE ENEMY

If you're feeling lucky, try to flank the enemy and come at them from the side. Let the allies keep the Chimera busy, equip the Rossmore, and come at them from the east or west.

In addition to Hybrids, there are a few Steelheads in the mix. Locate and target these beasts as quickly as possible. These foes can cause a great deal of damage, quickly sending Hale's health plummeting to dangerously low levels.

United States Army Rangers
1st Regiment

THE CONVOY OFFENSIVE—DESTROY

★ Destroy the Stalker

After clearing the area of Chimera for a second time, the guest of honor arrives—a huge mechanical behemoth affectionately referred as the "Stalker."

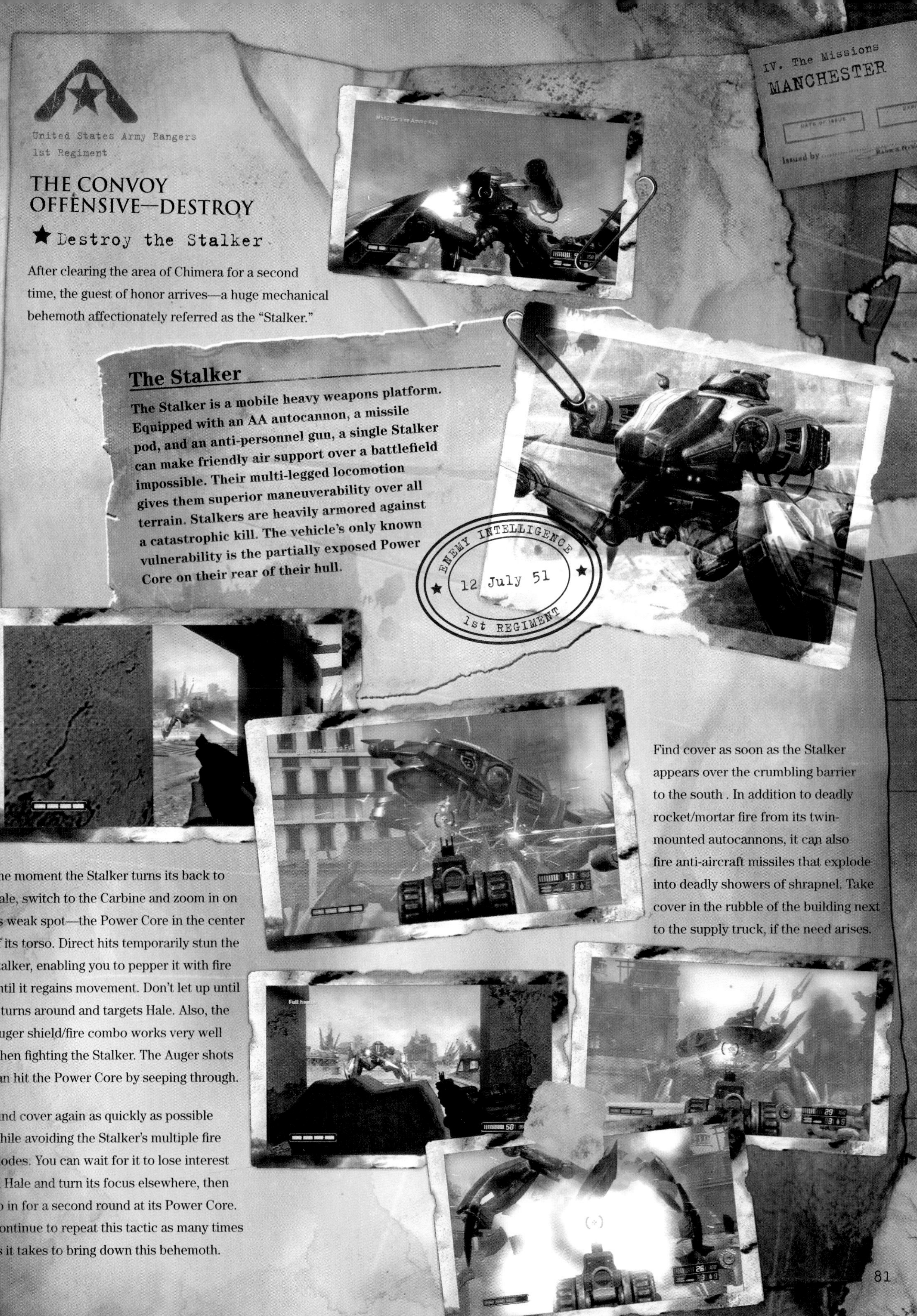

The Stalker

The Stalker is a mobile heavy weapons platform. Equipped with an AA autocannon, a missile pod, and an anti-personnel gun, a single Stalker can make friendly air support over a battlefield impossible. Their multi-legged locomotion gives them superior maneuverability over all terrain. Stalkers are heavily armored against a catastrophic kill. The vehicle's only known vulnerability is the partially exposed Power Core on their rear of their hull.

Find cover as soon as the Stalker appears over the crumbling barrier to the south . In addition to deadly rocket/mortar fire from its twin-mounted autocannons, it can also fire anti-aircraft missiles that explode into deadly showers of shrapnel. Take cover in the rubble of the building next to the supply truck, if the need arises.

The moment the Stalker turns its back to Hale, switch to the Carbine and zoom in on its weak spot—the Power Core in the center of its torso. Direct hits temporarily stun the Stalker, enabling you to pepper it with fire until it regains movement. Don't let up until it turns around and targets Hale. Also, the Auger shield/fire combo works very well when fighting the Stalker. The Auger shots can hit the Power Core by seeping through.

Find cover again as quickly as possible while avoiding the Stalker's multiple fire modes. You can wait for it to lose interest in Hale and turn its focus elsewhere, then go in for a second round at its Power Core. Continue to repeat this tactic as many times as it takes to bring down this behemoth.

INTO THE FIRE

Chimeran Tunnel Nexus

NORTHERN COMMAND
CLASSIFIED

Nottingham: Mission 1

Nottingham, England
12 July 1951—16:48 GMT

MISSION OVERVIEW

I picked up Hale after the mission. I saw him approach the containment cell on the convoy. The cell had 14-inch lead walls, but even so, given Hale's condition, I didn't want him anywhere near it. With the Stalkers gone, we were able to airlift the cell back to northern command. The exchange with the Americans would have to wait. We were about to execute a very risky offensive operation. The Chimera had been using a network of underground tunnels to attack undetected. The tunnels formed a nexus in Nottingham, and if we sealed them off we would at least briefly have the upper hand.

START

FIELD REPORT

Enemy Intel
Hybrid
Steelhead
Menial

Hardware
M5A2 Carbine
Bullseye
Rossmore 236
Combat Shotgun
Auger
Frag Grenades
Hedgehog

Mission Objective

★ Eliminate the Mortar Team.

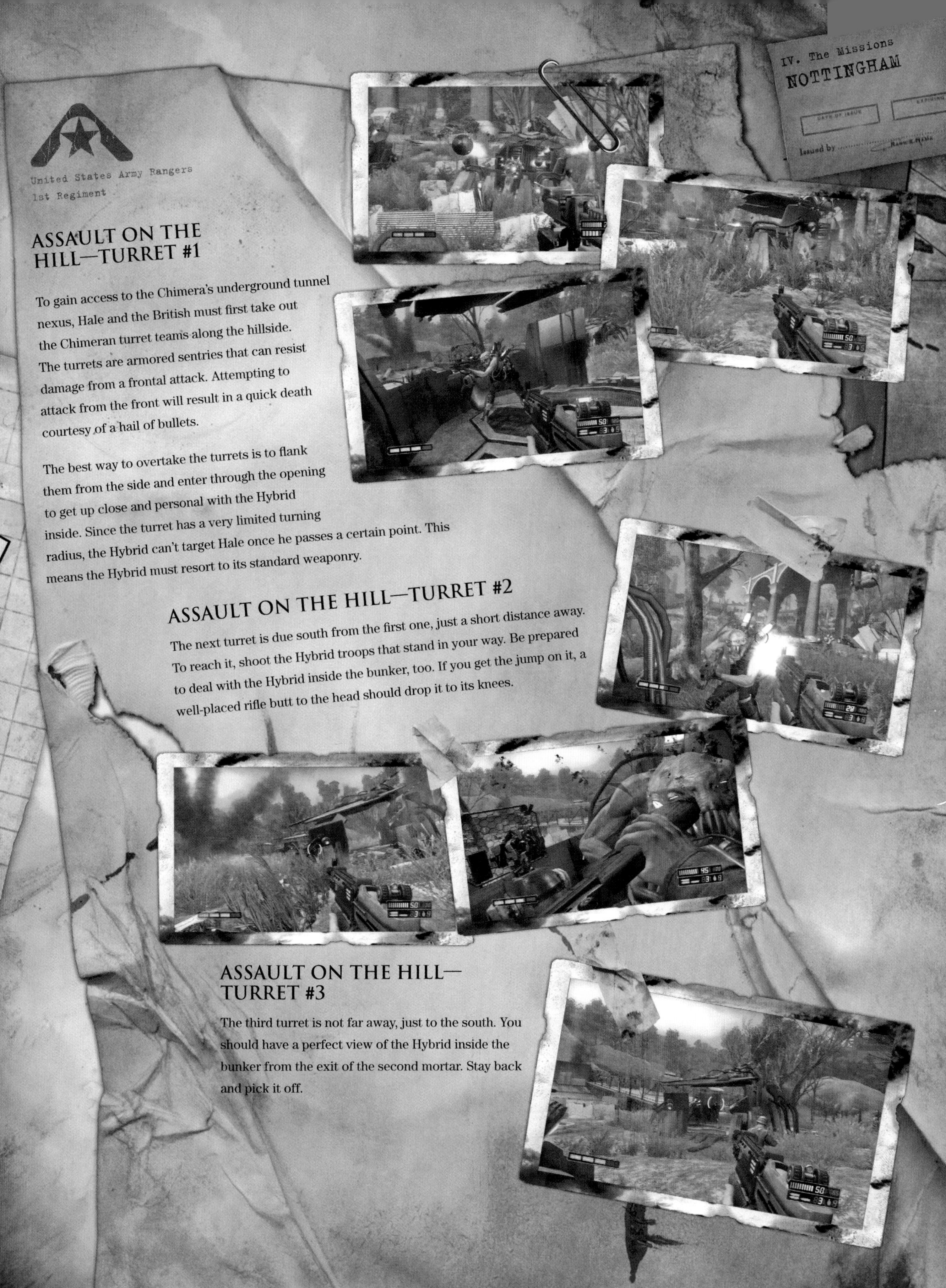

ASSAULT ON THE HILL—TURRET #1

To gain access to the Chimera's underground tunnel nexus, Hale and the British must first take out the Chimeran turret teams along the hillside. The turrets are armored sentries that can resist damage from a frontal attack. Attempting to attack from the front will result in a quick death courtesy of a hail of bullets.

The best way to overtake the turrets is to flank them from the side and enter through the opening to get up close and personal with the Hybrid inside. Since the turret has a very limited turning radius, the Hybrid can't target Hale once he passes a certain point. This means the Hybrid must resort to its standard weaponry.

ASSAULT ON THE HILL—TURRET #2

The next turret is due south from the first one, just a short distance away. To reach it, shoot the Hybrid troops that stand in your way. Be prepared to deal with the Hybrid inside the bunker, too. If you get the jump on it, a well-placed rifle butt to the head should drop it to its knees.

ASSAULT ON THE HILL—TURRET #3

The third turret is not far away, just to the south. You should have a perfect view of the Hybrid inside the bunker from the exit of the second mortar. Stay back and pick it off.

INTO THE TRENCHES

Turn around and locate the trenches behind the second bunker. The area down here is swarming with Chimera, so tread carefully. The trenches branch off in multiple directions, but they all end up at a dead end or converge into one. For the moment, simply concentrate on clearing the immediate area of enemies.

EXPLOSIVE RESULTS

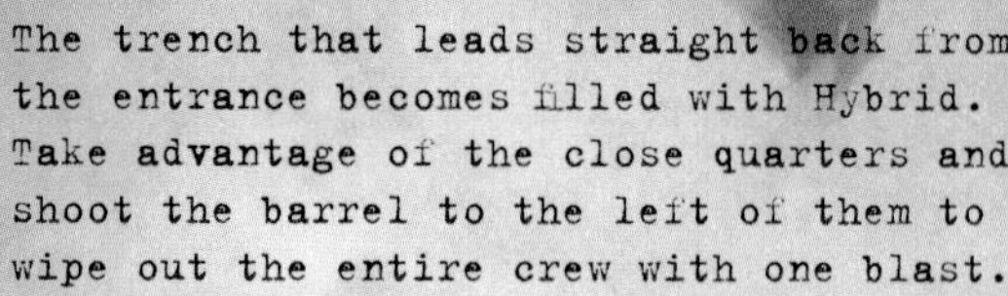

The trench that leads straight back from the entrance becomes filled with Hybrid. Take advantage of the close quarters and shoot the barrel to the left of them to wipe out the entire crew with one blast.

Follow the main path along the trenches, taking out any remaining Hybrid, until Hale reaches the stairs at the opposite end. Exit the trenches and continue to clear the area of enemy resistance. There is a fourth bunker here, but it's inoperable.

ASSAULT ON THE HILL—TURRET #4

Slowly move up the hill and stay in a crouched position. The next turret isn't far away and it is definitely operable and in use! Use the environment for cover and move through the brush to avoid the turret's fire.

DESTRUCTIBLE COVER

Be very careful when taking cover. Some of the items and objects in the environment may crumble apart after they take repeated fire. Look for cracks and other visual signs to help determine the stability of such objects.

Continue to stealthily make your way up and around to the mortar until you reach its side, then kill the Hybrid inside.

HOUSE ON THE HILL

After taking the turret, locate the next set of trenches and dispose of any enemies. Be aware of the manned turret nest around the corner to the right. Launch a grenade from the Carbine to cripple the machine.

Before moving any farther, locate the tunnel in the trench wall and head through it to reach a small room. In addition to plenty of munitions and Sym-Bac stores, there is an Intel Item on the desk.

DOCUMENT INTELLIGENCE #11

Harbinger

The page from the medical journal lists more grisly details regarding these strange "Cloven."

Royal Army Medical Corps

7.10.51
Dexter pulled me off my rounds this morning to join a commando patrol. He wouldn't go into specifics, or even tell me why they needed a med. officer.
Commandos had found more corpses left by the Cloven. Beneath their uniforms, the corpses were just bones. Only the hands remain -their fingers slashed in the way of the Cloven. The Cloven had eaten away the flesh, just like the Chimera do.

Follow the trench up to the house on the hill. Its interior is fiercely guarded by Chimera, but one or two well-placed Hedgehog Grenades can eliminate the infestation. As a bonus, the grenades may set off the explosive barrels that are inside. Finish off any surviving Chimera, then locate the Intel item on the desk at the base of the stairs.

DOCUMENT INTELLIGENCE #12

Tunnels

These documents detail the location of a system of Chimeran tunnels that appear to be a strategic junction for the enemy.

Tunnels converge in Nottingham. Appears to be strategic junction for Chimera.

If you have some grenades, toss one up to the floor above from the bottom of the stairs. Then head up and eliminate any remaining enemies. In addition to a Steelhead and Hybrid, there are a few Menials shuffling about. After disposing of the last Chimeran, the British Army regains control of the area.

CONDUITS

Chimeran Tunnel Nexus

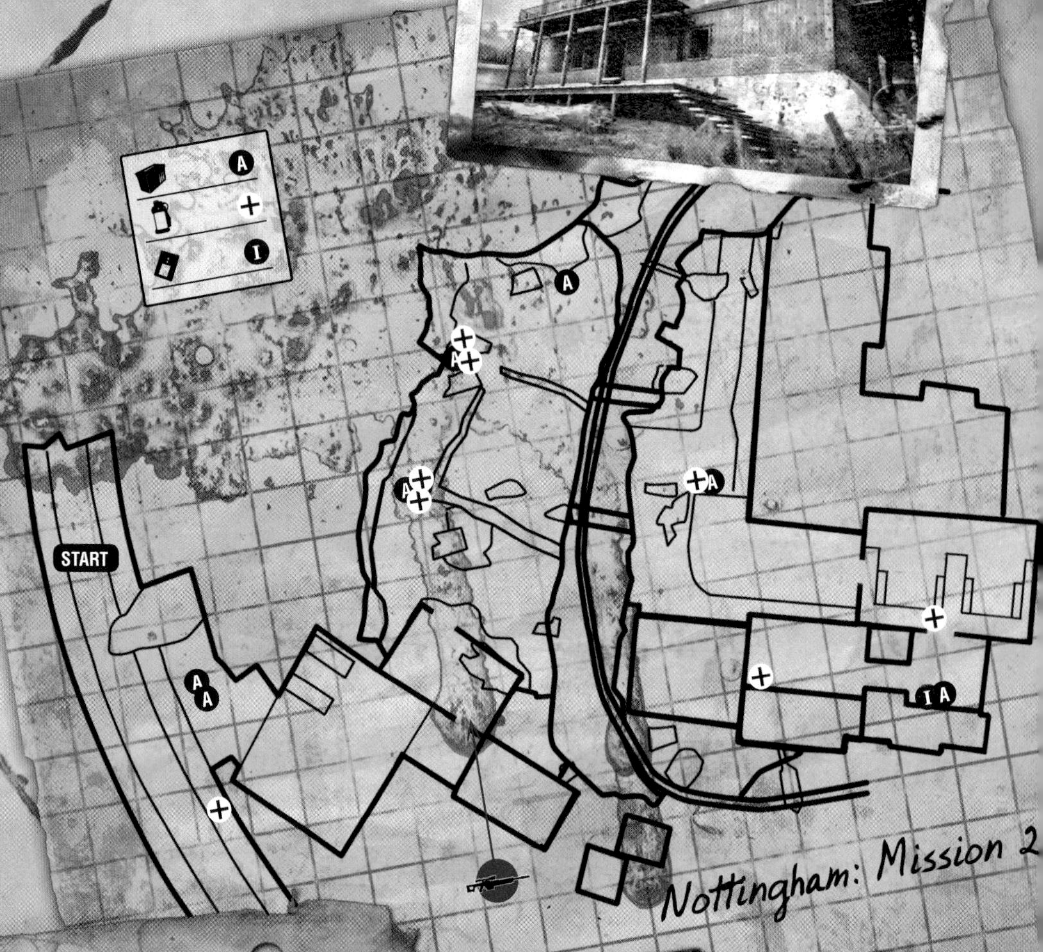

Nottingham, England
12 July 1951—20:23 GMT

MISSION OVERVIEW

A group of soldiers just stormed a Chimeran mortar position with Hale being the only one to make it out. I radioed him to look for a shortcut through an old train tunnel. The tunnel was mostly blocked by a Chimeran power conduit, but I knew if Hale could find a way through, it would turn the tide of the battle.

FIELD REPORT

Enemy Intel
Hybrid
Steelhead
Menial
Titan

Hardware
M5A2 Carbine
Bullseye
Rossmore 236
Combat Shotgun
Auger
L23 Fareye
Frag Grenades
Hedgehog

Mission Objective

- ★ Catch up with K Troop.
- ★ Find Lt. Cartwright.

United States Army Rangers
1st Regiment

HALE AND GOLIATH

★ Catch up with K Troop

Hale finds himself inside a dark train tunnel that's blocked by debris at both ends. His current objective is to catch up with an allied troop. However, to move forward, he needs to find a way into the generator facility to his left.

The sounds coming from beyond the fence are from K Troop; they're currently engaged in a fight for their lives against a new, never before seen Chimeran enemy—the Titan.

PRECIOUS CARGO

Hop inside the first train car and grab the Carbine Grenade ammo before heading up onto the platform to the left. Hale is going to need that ammo in just a moment.

The Titan

The Titan strain represents the limit of Chimeran evolution of the human form. They are massively strong and wield weapons more commonly found on vehicles, such as Stalker heavy siege pods. Titans aren't known to wear any form of body armor. Their calloused hides are sufficiently thick to protect them in the fiercest firefights.

The Titan doesn't waste any time mopping the floor with the allies, then turns its attention on Hale. The good news is that this behemoth has busted through the gate, giving Hale a way to continue on. The bad news is that it is now in the same room and bearing down on him. Equip the Rossmore and start shooting it as many times as possible.

The Titan is extremely strong and has a variety of attacks it can execute. If you're close enough, it raises its fist in the air and then brings it down, attempting to pummel you. It also fires bolts of flaming energy from its Stalker heavy siege pod; a single direct hit temporarily deafens Hale and causes a critical amount of damage.

The most effective strategy is to tag him with the Bullseye, then circle strafe. This tactic drops him in no time. Just stay patient and continue to pummel the beast with the Bullseye.

When the battle is finished, lick your wounds and head through the broken gate. The remains of the Troop K foes litter the floor, although there are still survivors. Locate the gate on the other side of the room and the soldier lets Hale through.

★ Find Lt. Cartwright

The soldier leads Hale into a large attic; a portion of its roof has been ripped off. A new weapon is leaning against the door frame—the L23 Fareye.

L23 Fareye

WEAPON INTELLIGENCE

The L23 Fareye is the weapon of choice for British Royal Marine Commando sniper teams. The rifle chambers a .303 Mk 10 round with a muzzle velocity of nearly 3400ft/s.

Press R3 to engage the scope. The directional button Down zooms out. The directional button Up zooms in. Press the directional buttons Left and Right to quickly swap between varying levels of magnification.

The Fareye also offers the ability to focus your concentration. This provides the sensation of slowing down time. All outside distractions are eliminated. Enemy movements become predictable, and fatal head-shots become inevitable.

To engage focus, press and hold L1. When engaged, a Focus Meter slowly fills along the button of your weapon HUD. When it's completely filled, you can no longer focus and time reverts to its normal pace.

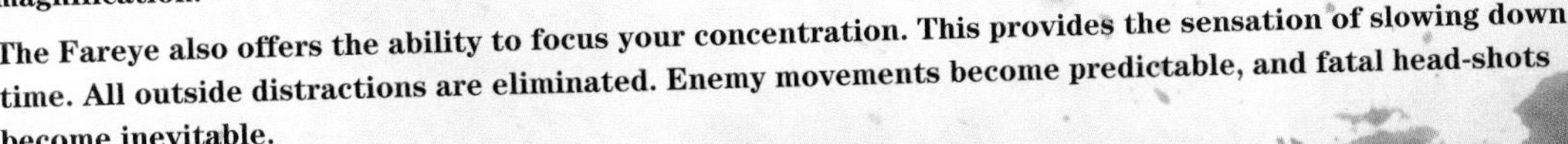

Hale gets the chance to try out the Fareye right away. Step up to one of the open windows, click down R3 to bring up the scope, acquire a target, and zoom in by holding the directional button Up. Line up a solid head shot, then pull the trigger for satisfying results.

USING FOCUS

Take a few moments to get comfortable with the Fareye's focus function. As long as you are holding down L1 and there is focus energy in the Focus Meter, time slows to a crawl. It's possible to use the extra seconds to get multiple precision kills while simultaneously dodging the Chimera's fire.

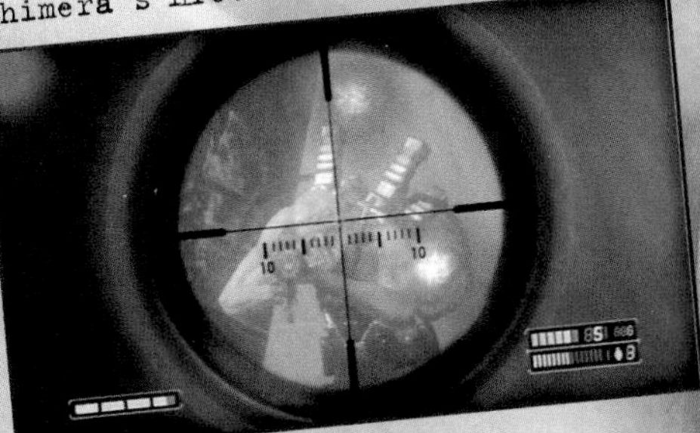

RAINY DAY

Spend some time picking off more of the Hybrid in the distance, but save a few rounds for later, as they might come in handy.

THE BATTLE OF THE BRIDGE

When you're ready to move on, drop to the bottom floor of the building through the hole and head outside. Out here, the combat is intense and it's an all-out war between the Chimera and the British Troops. Hop down into the large trench to the north and aid the allies in battle.

GRENADE OPPORTUNITY

This is a perfect opportunity to lob or launch a few grenades at the cluster of Hybrid down the trench. One or two direct hits send the whole pack flying into the air.

Stock up at these weapon caches along the trench. Not only do they offer the gamut in munitions, there are also a few canisters of Sym-Bac serum.

The large trench leads to an area with two bridges spanning a huge chasm. The closest bridge promptly gets destroyed when a huge hanging container drops its explosive cargo from above. Make a stand and do your best to stem the Hybrid onslaught at this location, noting that the concrete barriers are destructible and provide little in the way of cover.

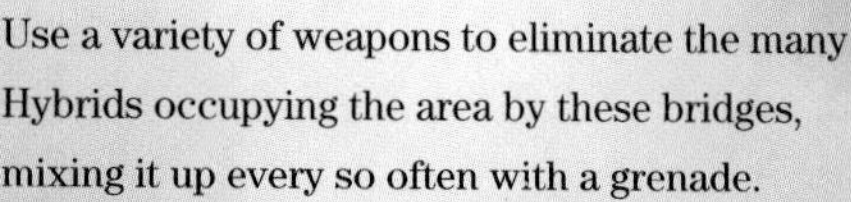

Use a variety of weapons to eliminate the many Hybrids occupying the area by these bridges, mixing it up every so often with a grenade.

It seems like an endless stream of Chimera is coming from the other side of the chasm. Continue to focus your attention on eliminating them until not a single one remains. When the dust settles, head across the still-intact second bridge.

On the other side, the influx of Chimera continues. However, since Hale is also accompanied by British allies, the Hybrid are scattered, allowing you to go in and knock them down/kill them before they have much opportunity to retaliate. One almost feels sorry for them… almost.

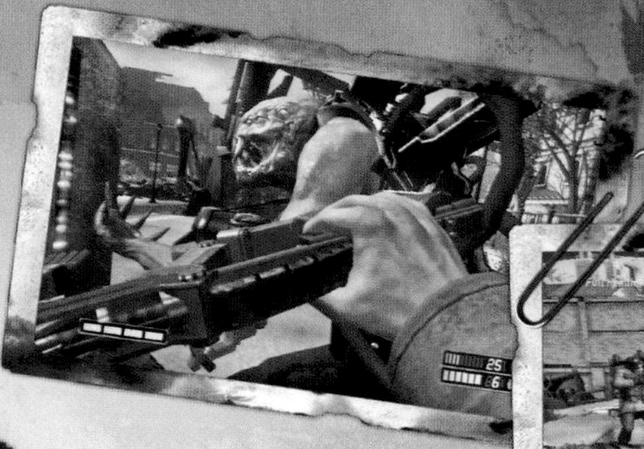

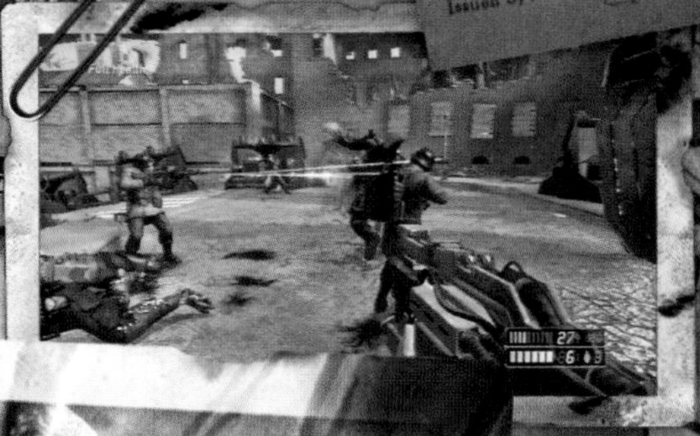

Before leaving, take a peek into the chasm. If you haven't noticed these floating creatures before, you'll get a glimpse of the Carriers now.

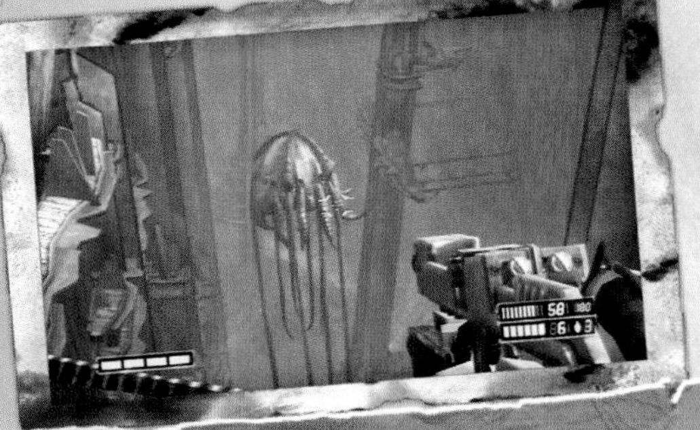

The Carrier

Carriers collect infected humans from the battlefield after a Crawler attack and ferry their catch to the nearest conversion center. As these infected bodies are also the Carrier's food source, not all of them survive to be converted. Early in the Chimeran invasion of Britain, Carriers formed caravans hundreds of miles long. It is unknown if the Carriers have found a new role now that fewer victims are available for conversion.

ENEMY INTELLIGENCE
12 July 51
1st REGIMENT

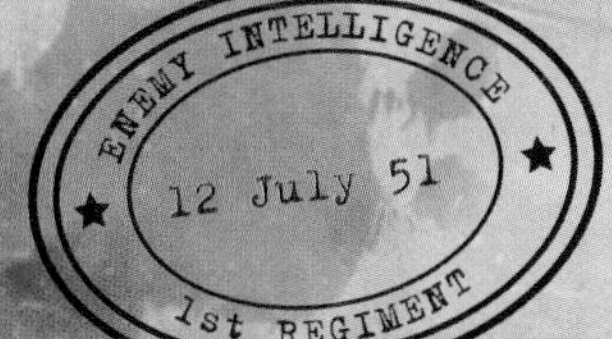

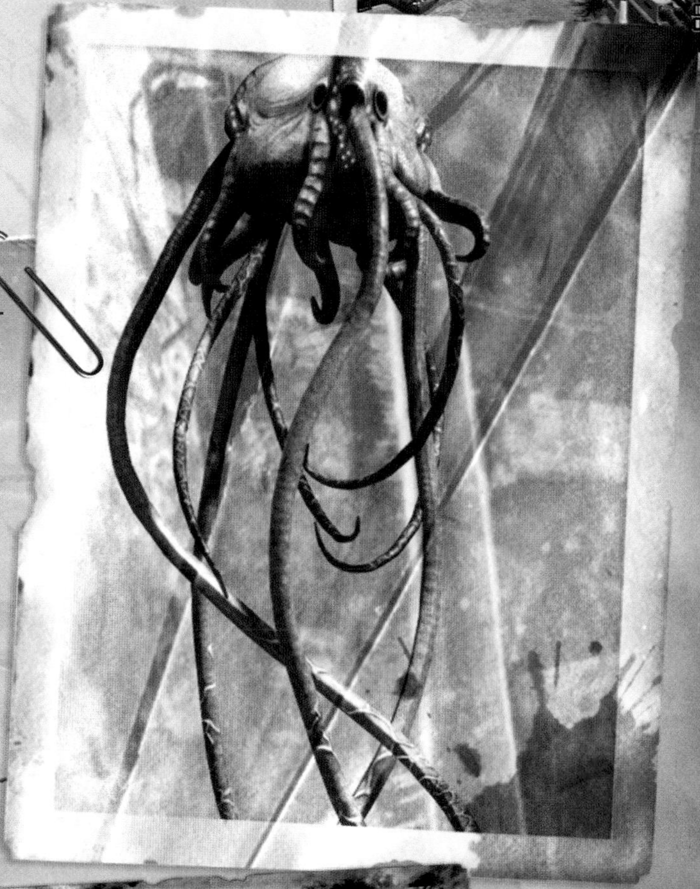

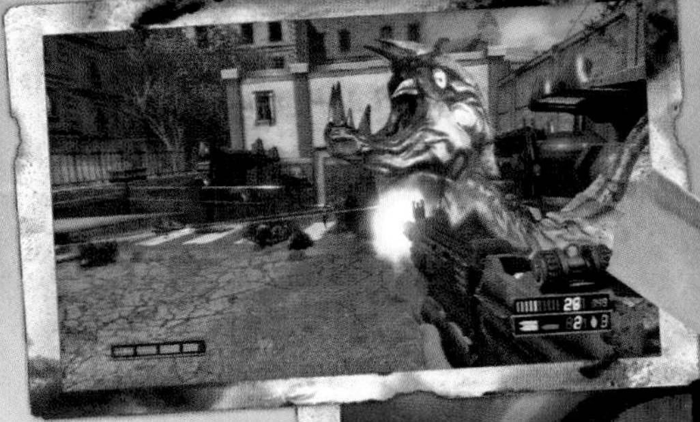

Leave those grotesque gas bags to their own devices and follow the road as it slopes down toward a large indoor loading dock. As Hale begins to move toward the building, the now familiar screech of the Leapers signals an onslaught. Equip the Carbine and start shooting them to bits.

The Leapers are backed up by a patrol of Hybrids inside the loading dock. If you saved some ammo from earlier, switch to the Fareye, focus, and pick them off from far away.

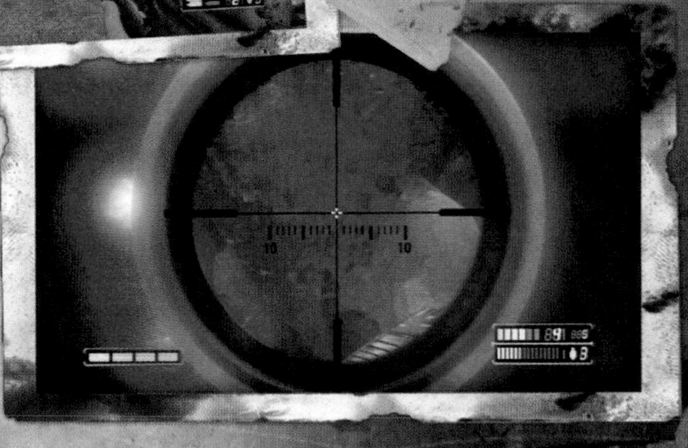

LOCATE THE LIEUTENANT

Enter the loading dock and head into the warehouse through the large opening to the right. You can opt to search the loading area below, but there's nothing of interest down there. However, there is something of interest in the warehouse. Locate the Intel Item on the shelves toward the back of the room and pick it up before moving on.

DOCUMENT INTELLIGENCE #13

REGARDING CLOVEN

This journal entry documents the strange behavior of the strange "Cloven." What are there motives? Who are they? Unfortunately, these questions remain unanswered for the time being.

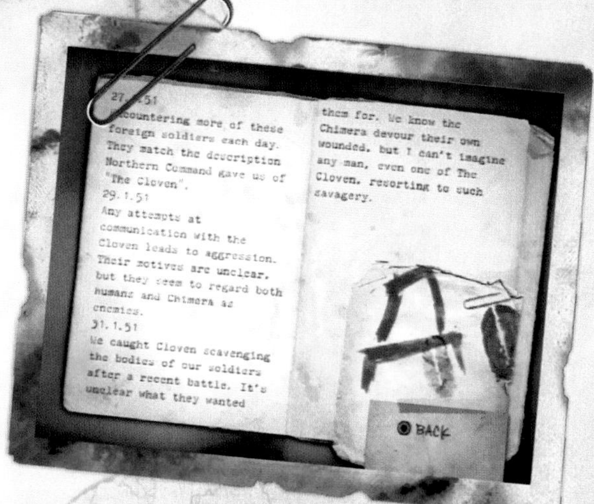

27.1.51
Encountering more of these foreign soldiers each day. They match the description Northern Command gave us of "The Cloven".
29.1.51
Any attempts at communication with the Cloven leads to aggression. Their motives are unclear, but they seem to regard both humans and Chimera as enemies.
31.1.51
We caught Cloven scavenging the bodies of our soldiers after a recent battle. It's unclear what they wanted them for. We know the Chimera devour their own wounded, but I can't imagine any man, even one of The Cloven, resorting to such savagery.

BACK

The ramp to the right leads to Lt. Cartwright, who is surveying the Chimeran activity outside. He welcomes Hale in his own way, marking the end of this area.

VIPER'S NEST

Chimeran Tunnel Nexus

Nottingham, England
12 July 1951—22:58 GMT

MISSION OVERVIEW

By the time Hale reached Lieutenant Cartwright, word had already spread about what Hale did in Manchester. However, Cartwright wasn't the type to be easily impressed—especially by an American. Cartwright's team had found something suspicious at the site. Instead of just making tunnels, the Chimera were digging something out of the ground. At the time, we passed it off as just another Chimeran mystery. Our priority was to seal off the tunnels.

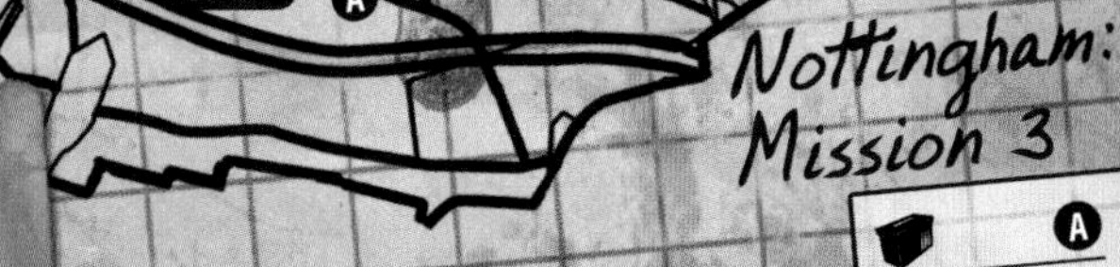

Enemy Intel
Hybrid
Menial
Titan

Hardware
M5A2 Carbine
Bullseye
Rossmore 236
Combat Shotgun
Auger
L23 Fareye
Frag Grenades
Hedgehog

Mission Objective

★ Destroy the sentry gun on the second pylon.

★ Clear out the final tunnel.

United States Army Rangers
1st Regiment

TEMPEST

★ Destroy the Sentry Gun on the Second Pylon

The excavations site is massive—whatever the Chimera are digging for must be enormous! To finish this mission and seal off the tunnels, Hale must put himself in the middle of another dangerous offensive. The British Royal Marines, led by Lt. Cartwright, are putting up a good fight.

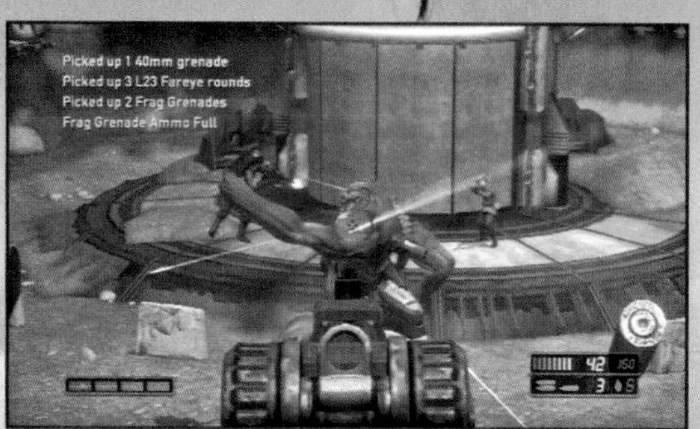

HERO MOMENT!

A battle against a Titan rages on down at the base of the site. The enormous creature grabbed a poor sap and the fellow is moments away from death. Stay at the top of the path and focus your weapon's fire at the beast until it drops.

It's not long before Hale is discovered by the Titan, causing the beast to turn its attention—and weapon—on Hale. To inflict major damage to the Titan, use the Bullseye or Auger shield/fire combo. The Auger is the safer route, as it's possible to hit the beast from behind cover.

TEMPORARY COVER

There is some cover down at the base of the site where the Titan battle takes place. You can use it for protection, but it's obvious it wasn't built to withstand the advances of a Titan. One solid blast will send the flimsy metal barrier flying.

To make matters worse, a group of Hybrids come pouring out of the pylon behind the Titan. You can let the troops deal with them for a little bit, or launch a grenade to wipe out a bunch of them immediately. If you choose the grenade approach, make sure your allies stay out of the blast radius.

Continue to focus your attention on the Titan, unleashing everything you have, including grenades. This creature is strong, but it is definitely not invincible. It will eventually fall in a spectacular blaze of blood and guts.

ASCENSION

Hale's main objective is to take out the sentry gunners on the pylons. To reach their location, head into the opening at the base and ride the lift to the walkway high above. Now up on top, follow the walkway around the pylon. Hale encounters some Hybrid resistance along the way.

When the coast is clear, locate the two gunners on the pylon across the way (there is one on each side) and use the Fareye to target and take each out. Use the network of small bridges to access the second pylon. There are some Hybrids here who are willing to take up the sentry guns if given the chance. Follow the walkway around the pylon while eliminating any resistance, then jump on the turret and use it to mow down any others on the tower across the way.

ACTIVATE THE BRIDGE

To reach the next pylon, you must activate the bridge. Turn back and follow the walkway to the right until you reach a second bridge.

On the other side, follow the walkway around to the right but watch out for the Menials blocking Hale's path, as well as the bullets coming from the tower to the right. When the threat is gone, locate and activate the switch at the end of the walkway. Activating the switch lowers the bridge back the way you came.

Return to the bridge and cross over to the pylon. To defeat the Hybrids in the distance, use a well placed Hedgehog Grenade or a few sniper shots. Don't forget that the Auger can provide a temporary shield, which can serve as the perfect solution when there is no available cover.

TITAN TERROR

★ Clear Out the Final Tunnel

The only way off the pylon is down. Don't be scared by the fact that there is no platform to whisk Hale to the ground—just walk off into the empty space inside the center and a jet of air will allow him to float harmlessly to the bottom.

Hale's final objective is to clear out the remaining tunnel at the excavation site. However, a Titan has been sent out to stop him. Unfortunately, you're own your own this time—there are no British troops nearby to help.

Start with the Rossmore and start shooting the Titan. Remember to stay mobile and not to let the beast get a bead on Hale with its massive weapon. As noted earlier, perhaps the best option against the Titan is the Bullseye or the Auger. Both weapons will drop this foe in no time at all. It's a nasty battle, but, with diligence, the Titan goes down and the tunnel is yours.

NO WAY OUT

Northern Command

Cheshire, England
13 July 1951—3:34 GMT

MISSION OVERVIEW

The Nottingham operation was a success. I sent the troops back to Southern Command for some well-earned rest. I was taking Hale to the intelligence division at Northern Command for debriefing. After Hale's heroics in Manchester and Nottingham, there were going to be a lot of questions. Hale was the one who really deserved the answers, but I didn't have any. I radioed Northern Command on our approach. No response. As we landed, I could already sense the worst. The whole place was deathly silent...

FIELD REPORT

Enemy Intel
Hybrid
Steelhead
Slipskull
Howler

Hardware
M5A2 Carbine
Bullseye
Rossmore 236
Combat Shotgun
Auger
L23 Fareye
Frag Grenades
Hedgehog
Fuel-Air Grenades

Mission Objective

★ Restore auxiliary power to Northern Command.

★ Escape Northern Command.

SEPARATION ANXIETY

★ Restore Auxiliary Power to Northern Command

Northern Command, once a bustling hub of resistance activity, is now a deserted mausoleum. It's clear the Chimera wiped out the entire military workforce and, from the sound of it, the enemy is still here. Before anyone has a chance to react, the underground bunker experiences a cave-in and Hale becomes separated from Parker and her men.

It's clear that Hale is on his own. Unfortunately, he doesn't have long to ponder the situation, as the Chimera launch an attack from beyond the thick dust and smoke choking the main tunnel. Quickly duck and take cover on either side of the tunnel entrance while shooting and lobbing grenades into the opening to hold back the assault.

After stifling these foes, move into the tunnel and use the pipes along the wall for cover or throw down a force shield with the Auger to keep the next set of Hybrid at bay. Exterminate the Chimeran resistance while slowly moving forward.

The hub of Northern command is connected via a complex system of tunnels, creating a maze-like labyrinth. However, most of the doors are shut and locked, forcing Hale down a specific path. Whenever you approach a junction or intersection, make sure to explore every nook and cranny for extra munitions and Sym-Bac serum.

REVITALIZE

If the need arises, retrace Hale's steps back to the tunnel entrance. There are two gated pathways that lead to dead ends, but one has a few canisters of Sym-Bac serum while the other path leads to some Carbine ammo.

KITCHEN CONUNDRUM

The tunnel leads Hale into the mess hall and it looks like he's the main course! When the sound of the Leapers pierces the air, back out into the tunnel and force the onslaught into a bottleneck for easier kills.

When the coast is clear, search through the mess hall and the kitchen behind it to find some ammo and Sym-Bac serum. After doing so, walk through the open doorway in the back-left corner and exit the mess hall.

CHILLS AND THRILLS

It's bad enough that the power is out and the claustrophobic tunnels are poorly lit, but when a Chimera bolts across the tunnel in front of Hale, it's enough to make your heart leap out of your throat! Brace yourself and continue down the corridor.

THE DARKNESS

Follow the Chimera by taking a right at the intersection, then take a left and prepare to fight it out with some Hybrids and Steelheads. While these tight spaces aren't really made for sniping, use the Fareye (and its focus ability) to quickly target the enemy.

Continue along the tunnel system. The next intersection leads to two paths, both of which have small sets of stairs that lead to another area. Take the left set first, defeat the Hybrid, then follow the tunnel to the left. Although this is basically a dead end, there is a nice stash of munitions here. Now return back to the other path.

Continue up the opposite set of stairs into what resembles a generator room. There is more Chimera resistance here, but it's nothing too difficult. Also, look for the Intel Item on the floor.

Unfortunately, there is no way to turn on the auxiliary power from this room, so continue onward. The next area is like a train depot of sorts and home to a Chimeran squad of Hybrids and a Steelhead. Focus on the Steelhead first (look behind one of the railcars), then go after the pack of Chimera near the back-left part of the room. Or, shoot the barrel behind the Hybrids to eliminate them in spectacular fashion!

DOCUMENT INTELLIGENCE #15

INVASION

This map shows the rapid Chimeran proliferation from Russia into Europe and beyond.

The depot is filled with makeshift bunk beds, stacked crates, and other debris. Follow the back wall to get by the obstacles and access the second half of the room. Next, cross back over the train tracks and move into the next set of tunnels on the other side.

There are more foes, including a Steelhead, in the room attached to the right side of the main tunnel. The enemies are emerging from a hole in the wall along the right side of the locker room. Take aim and lob/launch a few grenades, then duck for cover and pick off the rest of the foes as they pour out of the entrance.

Continue down the main tunnel until it reaches a dead end. As Hale approaches the gate, he feels a strange force. His vision blurs and turns yellow. Could this effect have something to do with the twisted, grotesque carcass of a new Chimeran enemy lying dead on the ground?

The Slipskull

Slipskulls are cunning opportunists who prefer to take pot shots rather than face their opponents. With their speed and stealth, they excel as scouts and ambushers. When a Slipskull makes an appearance, quickly dispose of it before it summons any reinforcements. Use explosives against them for the best results.

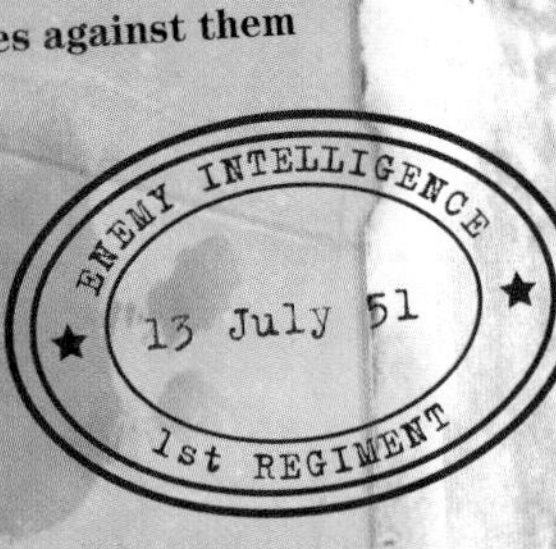

Return to the locker room and enter the hole in the wall. Now inside the chamber, follow the path to reach another series of tunnels. These tunnels lead to the Living Quarters, home to the first appearance of some live Slipskulls. The Auger is a good choice against these powerful foes.

The Living Quarters is basically a large underground tunnel with rooms built into its sides. Explore each room in search of ammo and supplies. Be methodical and start with the first set of rooms and clear each room before moving to the next one.

The last room on the right is only accessible via the tunnel in the room prior to it. Climb through the tunnel and locate the two objects on the desk in the corner: an Intel Item and a cache of Air-Fuel Grenades.

DOCUMENT INTELLIGENCE #16

Specimen Tank

These blueprints are for some kind of strange storage tank built to hold mysterious cargo.

WEAPON INTELLIGENCE

Air-Fuel Grenade

The No 42 Air-Fuel Grenade has been issued for combating Chimera in the tight spaces commonly found in urban conflicts. A thrown grenade adheres to most surfaces and immediately releases a cloud of flammable vapor. Once deployed, the cloud ignites and creates a massive explosion. The resulting heat and pressure wave will cause vast injuries to anything caught in the blast.

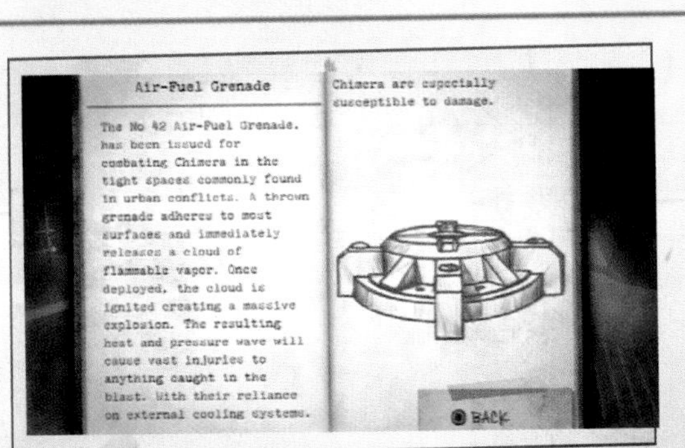

TUNNEL TERROR

Exit the Living Quarters by going through the gate at the opposite end of the tunnel. While moving down the tunnel, a huge creature burrows through the walls directly in front of Hale. The dust and debris are too thick to get a good look at it, but its size is massive!

Jump into the tunnel and follow it until you reach an opening that leads to a large boiler room. Of course, it's patrolled by Chimera—in this instance, a Steelhead and a Hybrid. Equip the Fareye and use focus to slow down time and pick them off without getting hit by their fire.

When it's safe to do so, drop down into the boiler room and climb the stairs to the top level. Throw the switch against the wall at the top of the stairs to activate the auxiliary power.

FIRST ENCOUNTERS

★ Restore auxiliary power to Northern Command

INTO THE CORE

This switch also opens the doorway on the second floor, so find a good vantage point and take aim. Use the open door to enter the massive core around the corner to the right. Follow the walkway around its perimeter, then take the stairs that lead down to the floor level.

AIR-FUEL SURPRISE

This is a good opportunity to use your newly acquired Air-Fuel Grenades. Toss one into the doorway (don't worry about accuracy, it sticks to just about any surface), then sit back and watch as the air fills with volatile gas that erupts into flames!

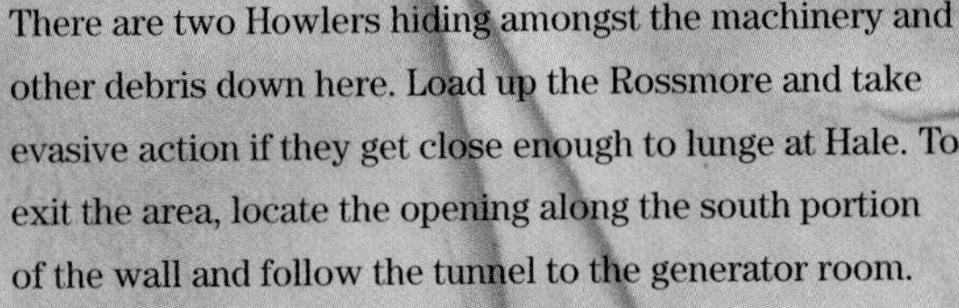

There are two Howlers hiding amongst the machinery and other debris down here. Load up the Rossmore and take evasive action if they get close enough to lunge at Hale. To exit the area, locate the opening along the south portion of the wall and follow the tunnel to the generator room.

NORTHERN COMMAND
CLASSIFIED

Cheshire, England
13 July 1951—6:12 GMT

MISSION OVERVIEW

I had been trying to radio Hale since the cave-in. I knew how the Chimera had found Northern Command. And more importantly, I knew why. They were after the containment cell from the convoy. If the Chimera opened the cell, the results would be devastating. But if Hale opened the cell, I had no idea what effect it might have. It could kill him. Or worse. It could control him…

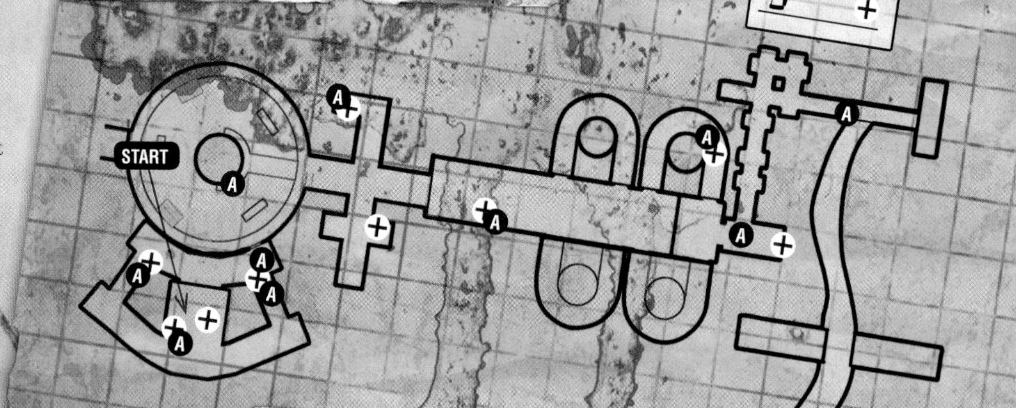

Cheshire: Mission 2

START

FIELD REPORT

Enemy Intel
Hybrid
Steelhead
Leaper

Hardware
M5A2 Carbine
Bullseye
Rossmore 236
Combat Shotgun
Auger
L23 Fareye
Frag Grenades
Hedgehog
Fuel-Air Grenades

Mission Objective

★ Escape Northern Command.

FEAR AND LOATHING

★ Escape Northern Command

The level picks up right where it left off, inside the generator room with the power fully restored to Northern Command. Unfortunately, this means that the Chimera can now see Hale. To escape Northern Command, you must backtrack the way you came. Return to the core just around the corner and begin picking off any visible enemies.

FEEL THE HEAT

Don't enter into the core until it's absolutely necessary, as it's infested with a variety of Chimera, including Steelheads. Target the trio of explosive barrels beyond the doorway, or use a few Air-Fuel grenades to help stack the odds in your favor

Locate the staircase inside the core and climb to the walkway. Defeat the Chimera up here and enter the tunnel leading to the Battery Bloc through the large blast door. Inside, Hale finds dead bodies everywhere—not a good sign.

The tunnel branches off into three directions, although the paths to the right and left eventually reach dead ends. Continue straight and enter the dark Battery Bloc, which is a large, open chamber with very few areas for cover. It only takes a second for the Chimera to sense Hale's presence and come at him in full force.

PROVIDE YOUR OWN COVER

When there is little cover, you can create your own by using the Auger. Lay down a shield to provide a quick breather and some temporary protection.

Utilize all of the weapons you've acquired thus far. Use some grenades against any nearby enemies, and use the Fareye to eliminate the ones on the walkway in the distance. In addition, there are some explosive barrels lining the chamber's left wall.

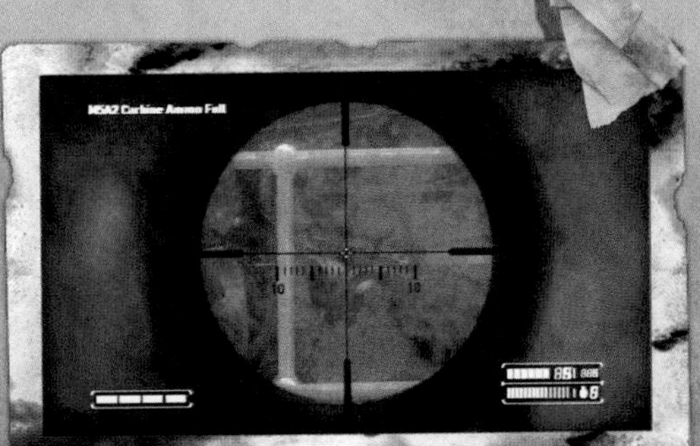

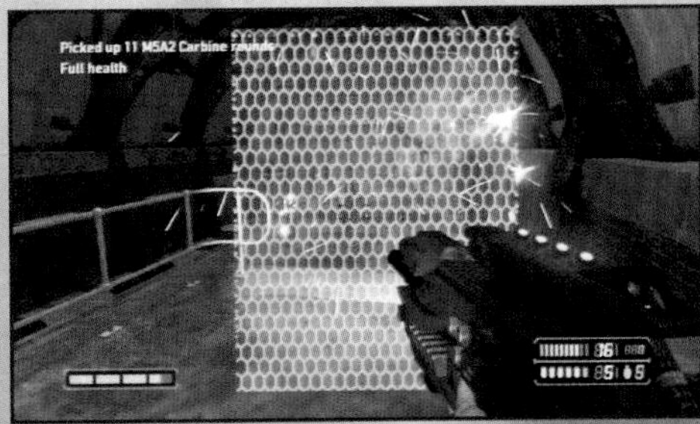

A WAY OUT

The open set of gates along the left wall lead to a tunnel system. Drop down into the small culvert and follow it into the opening. Have the Carbine at the ready, as the tunnels are crawling with Leapers.

Take the first left and then another left at the next junction to reach a second culvert. The tunnel system continues on the other side, but it leads to a dead end. The objective here is to exit this room, enter the large connecting room, then locate a switch on the left-hand wall.

Throw the switch to open the doorway to the right. Head inside, collect the munitions and Sym-Bac serum around the small set of stairs, then take the open door to the left. Some Auger-wielding Steelheads patrol the tunnel beyond the doorway. There is no cover here, so use grenades or the Bullseye to avoid any unnecessary damage. When it's safe to move on, take the dust-filled entrance straight ahead.

MEN IN BLACK

Just inside the doorway, Hale encounters the dead body of a soldier. This one is different than the others, though, as he is dressed in a black uniform with heavy body armor, including a gas mask. There is definitely something strange and mysterious about him...

LAIR OF THE LEAPER

The only way to continue is to go through the large tunnel burrowed into the wall. Take a right and slowly follow the path. A short distance into it, Hale encounters a seemingly never-ending onslaught of Leapers.

A little further down the tunnel, Hale comes across the source of the Leapers—strange pulsating pods attached to the sides and floor. An Air-Fuel grenade works quite nicely for clearing them out.

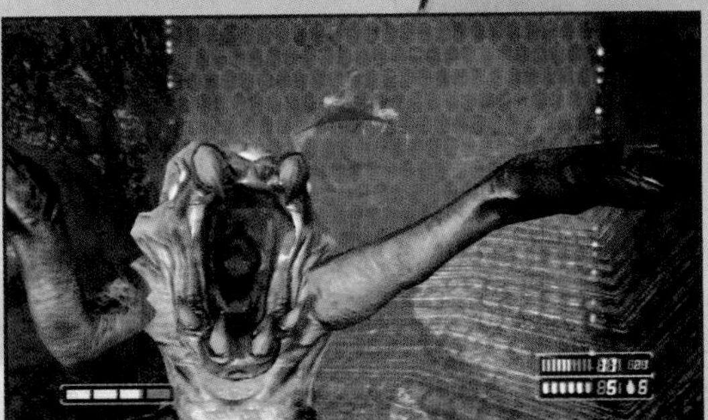

LATCHING LEAPERS

If a Leaper gets close enough to lunge at Hale, it can attach itself and start chomping away at his neck, face and chest. The quickest way to detach a Leaper is to shake the SIXAXIS controller if the Tilt function is set to ON, or quickly move the analog sticks back and forth.

The Leaper Pod

Leapers spawn from membranous sacs known as Leaper pods. It is believed these pods are deposited by other Chimeran strains, possibly Widowmakers. Spawning is triggered by local vibrations. The pods function as living mines. Caution should be observed in Chimeran-held territory, as early detection of Leaper pods has the potential to save lives. Explosives, such as grenades and rockets, can destroy the pods before they release the Leapers within.

REVELATIONS

When Hale reaches the other end of the tunnel, he reemerges back inside Northern Command. To the right is an open doorway leading into the Map Room/ Laboratory 2, the heart of Northern Command. Enter the area to complete this part of the mission.

ANGEL

Northern Command

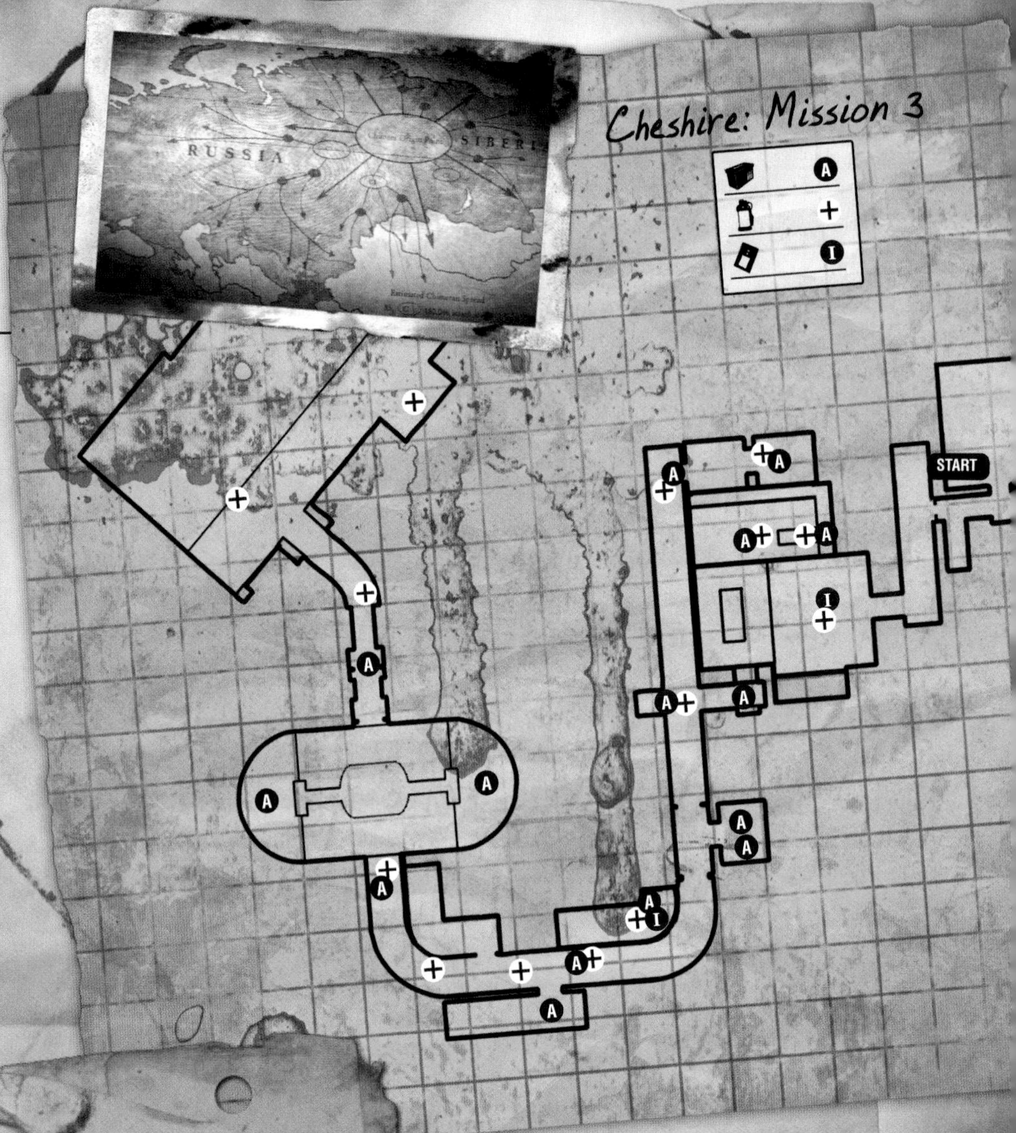

Cheshire: Mission 3

START

Cheshire, England
13 July 1951—8:03 GMT

MISSION OVERVIEW

I knew Hale would eventually find the Map Room. He would see all of British Command's most closely guarded secrets. Everything we had learned about the Chimera in the past two decades was in there. We had maps of the Chimeran invasion spreading through Russia, autopsy records of Chimeran creatures…even charts of the death tolls across Europe. These were numbers we didn't even disclose to our own soldiers. We had plotted the progression of the Chimeran virus in humans. In over six thousand cases, there was no record of any form of human resistance. There were also detailed schematics of the containment cell and what was in it. We call them Angels. They're the most powerful of the Chimera. We believe the Angels control other forms of Chimera via some form of telepathy. For all I knew, it was already controlling Hale.

FIELD REPORT

Enemy Intel
Hybrid
Steelhead
Menial
Gray Jack

Hardware
M5A2 Carbine
Bullseye
Rossmore 236
Combat Shotgun
Auger
L23 Fareye
Frag Grenades
Hedgehog
Fuel-Air Grenades

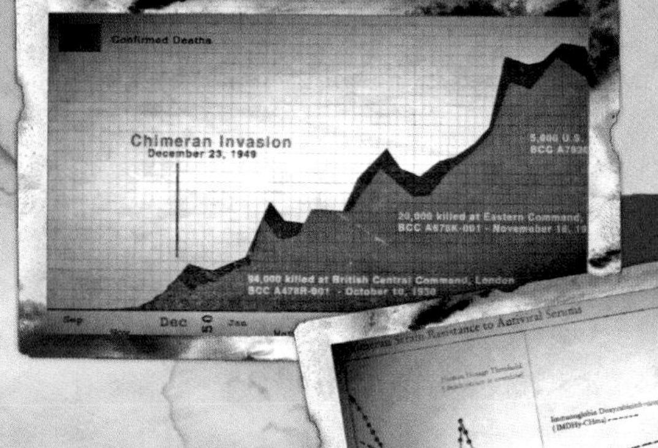

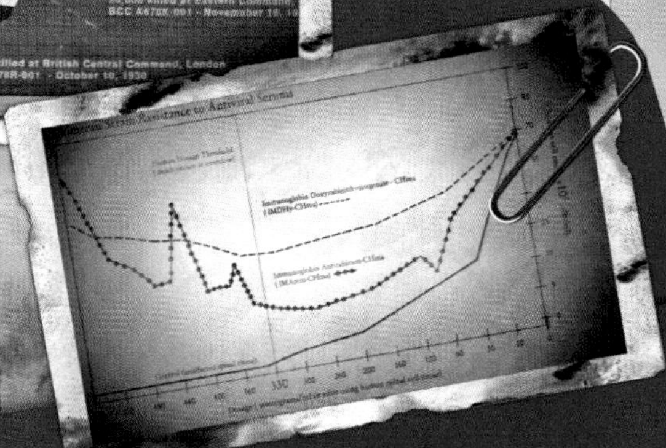

Mission Objective

★ Escape Northern Command. ★ Defend the specimen tank.

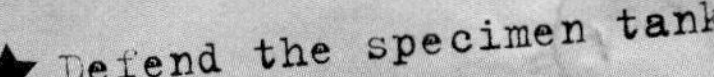

United States Army Rangers
1st Regiment

HARBINGER

★ Escape Northern Command

Inside the Map Room, Hale learns about the Angel. This is what was inside the container the convoy was escorting back in Manchester. When you're ready, exit through the Map Room's rear door and enter the corridor.

The tunnel to the right is a dead end. To continue, take the path straight ahead. A gate at the end of the tunnel blocks access; however, the doorway to the right automatically opens when Hale approaches.

THE MENIALS IN THE MORGUE

Stay back and don't enter the Morgue, as it's filled with Menials. Instead, use the Carbine from the doorway, wait for the Menials to get close to the barrels, and then detonate them! The blast radius doesn't dispose of all the foes, so hold your position and pick them off as they approach.

Enter the Morgue and search the area until you find the desk in the center of the room. Pick up the Intel Item and keep moving.

DOCUMENT INTELLIGENCE #17

Post Mortem

This medical autopsy report documents the details of the Chimera virus and the ability of its host to rapidly heal with little to no scarring.

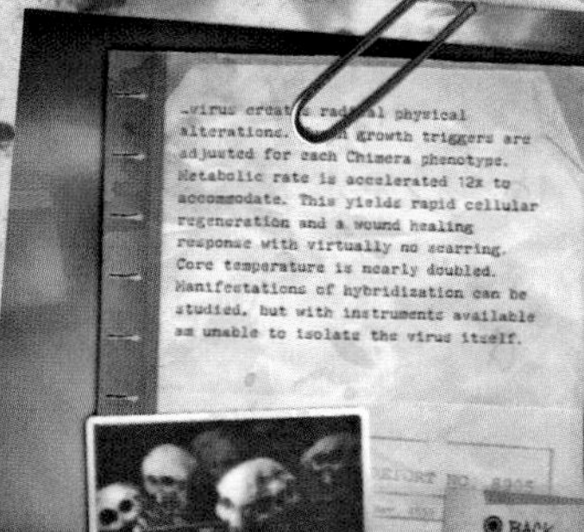

...virus creat... rad...al physical alterations. ...h growth triggers are adjusted for each Chimera phenotype. Metabolic rate is accelerated 12x to accommodate. This yields rapid cellular regeneration and a wound healing response with virtually no scarring. Core temperature is nearly doubled. Manifestations of hybridization can be studied, but with instruments available we are unable to isolate the virus itself.

The only way to exit the Morgue is to break the glass windows lining the wall, then hop through the hole. Perform a solid melee attack to shatter the glass.

At the top of the stairs, Hale encounters more resistance in the form Hybrids on the other side of the glass windows. Break the glass, toss an Air-Fuel grenade through the opening, and then watch the Chimera go up in flames.

Watch out for the Auger-wielding Steelhead in the next room. Dispose of this beast and enter the main corridor. Down at the bottom of the stairs, Hale encounters more Hybrids followed by some Leapers.

101 USES FOR A BARREL

Locate the stacked barrels on the cart at the top of the stairs. There is a block holding the cart. Shoot the block to make the barrels break loose and start rolling. Once this occurs, a stray spark will ignite them and take out the Leapers rushing up the stairs.

WHAT'S HAPPENING TO ME?

The blurry, orange-colored vision and sharp jolts of pain to Hale's head become more frequent as he moves deeper into Northern Command. Could this have something to do with the "Angel," which is contained inside a storage tank somewhere deep within the facility?

AMBUSHED!

Although the Infirmary windows along the right side of the corridor may be covered with blinds, they don't keep the Chimera on the other side at bay. As soon as you walk in front of the windows, the Hybrids unleash their arsenal of weaponry. Enter the Infirmary and locate the Intel Item on the table in the back before you move.

There are three Infirmaries along this main corridor. The second one contains no Chimera, but the last has a bunch of Hybrids inside. Use the Auger and target them from the safety of cover while you remain inside the second Infirmary or the main hall.

DOCUMENT INTELLIGENCE #18

Autopsy

This is a continuation of the last set of medical papers detailing the Chimera autopsy. According to the performing physician, the Chimera have two hearts and use a heat-exchanging device to lower their blood temperature and prevent necrosis (the death of cells in a tissue or organ caused by disease or injury). It also mentions a new type of Chimera called the "Gray Jack."

United States Army Rangers
1st Regiment

GRAY JACK

★ Defend the Specimen Tank

When you're ready, walk through the blast door at the end of the main corridor to reach the next area. Inside this room, Hale finds a British ally about to be eviscerated by a strange, new Chimera—the Gray Jack.

The Chimera Gray Jack

Gray Jacks are decrepit Hybrids that have nearly outgrown their bodies. As they approach death, their cooling units get over-taxed and their rampant metabolism steadily cooks them from the inside out. The resulting necrosis gives Gray Jacks an odor of decaying flesh. Although unarmed and seemingly frail, the long reach of their wicked claws can be deadly.

ENEMY INTELLIGENCE
13 July 51
1st REGIMENT

HERO MOMENT!

You can save the poor sap before he succumbs to the Gray Jack. Quickly target this beast's head or body and fill it full of ammo. If you're quick enough, the British solder will survive and fight by Hale's side.

Glass canisters holding live Gray Jack specimens rise from the floor, and the contents inside break free and attack. If you have some Fareye ammo, use the Sniper Rifle to pick them off from afar. If not, let them run in and hit them with both barrels from the Rossmore. As the fight rages on, more Gray Jacks rise from the ground.

USE YOUR ALLY

Keep an eye on your ally, if you saved him earlier. He provides extra firepower and support, and the direction of his weapon's fire pinpoints the location of the Gray Jacks, as they can sneak up and attack from behind.

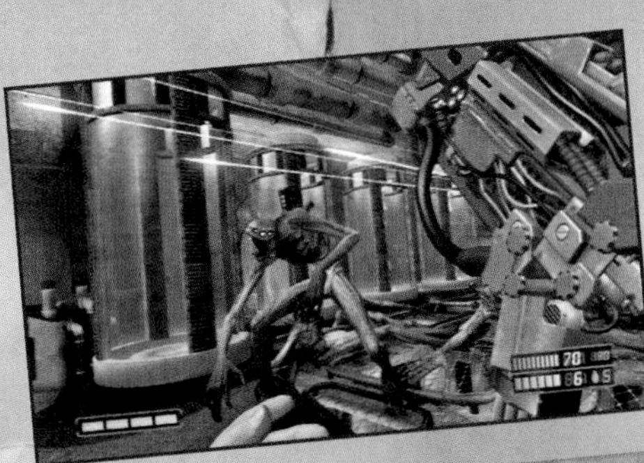

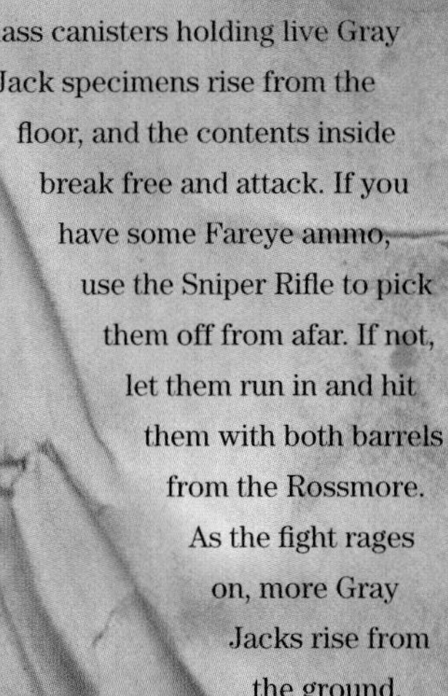

It's a bloody and brutal massacre. After disposing of the last Gray Jack, locate the open blast door to exit this chamber of death. Next, take the stairs up to another train depot. This one holds what Hale is looking for—the storage tank containing the Angel!

STAND OFF

Hale walks into the middle of a full-scale attack between the British troops and the Chimera. The allies are bravely defending the storage tank from the ferocious Hybrid assault. Join the fray and let loose a few grenades, then duck and take cover to pick off the ones that remain.

After the first wave is eliminated, a huge transport vehicle bursts through the train depot wall and drops off another wave of Chimera, which includes Steelheads. After the vehicle breaks through, look for the open door. Once it's open, throw a Hedgehog or Frag Grenade to clear out the Chimera before they can advance. Do your best to stay under the protection of cover, and use a combination of Hedgehogs, the Bullseye, and the Auger to take care of them.

Once the final Chimera falls, the battle for the Angel is over. However, Hale throws the switch to reveal the creature inside the tank, which has devastating effects on his mind.

SEARCH AND RESCUE

Cheddar Gorge

IV. The Missions
SOMERSET

NORTHERN COMMAND
CLASSIFIED

Somerset: Mission 1

START

Somerset, England
13 July 1951—9:52 GMT

MISSION OVERVIEW

We tracked Chimera leaving Northern Command heading toward a gorge in Somerset. Cartwright took some commandos and went after them. Three hours later, they still had not reported in. I was about to set out for Somerset when I saw Hale coming up the lift. I could tell from his face that he had found the Angel. There was no point asking questions. If he was alive then the Angel was dead.

Hale was starting to show more Chimeran traits. His movements had the unnatural quickness of the hybrids. There were also several bullet holes in his uniform, yet almost no blood. I could tell from his eyes that he knew what I was thinking, but I still had no answers. Hale volunteered to go after Cartwright. I sensed he knew his time was running out. Maybe he wanted some kind of vengeance against the Chimera for what they were slowly doing to him. I'll probably never know. I took Hale to the location we had last heard from Cartwright. Of course, if I had known what he would find in that gorge I would have sent in every soldier we had.

FIELD REPORT

Enemy Intel
Hybrid
Steelhead
Slipskull
Howler

Hardware
M5A2 Carbine
Bullseye
Rossmore 236
Combat Shotgun
Auger
L23 Fareye
XR-005 Hailstorm
Frag Grenades
Hedgehog
Fuel-Air Grenades

Mission Objective

★ Find Cartwright's Team.

★ Help Cartwright eliminate the Chimera.

United States Army Rangers
1st Regiment

THE CRUCIBLE

★ Find Cartwright's Team.

The VTOL drops Hale off in the sleepy town of Somerset; however, things are not as tranquil as they seem. Hale is charged with catching up with Lt. Cartwright and his men, who are somewhere in this village, most likely engaged in battle with the Chimera. Follow the cobblestone path to exit the yard. Another one of the mysterious black soldiers lies at the end of the path. There's also a humongous assault rifle in front of him, so add it to your arsenal.

WEAPON INTELLIGENCE

XR-005 Hailstorm

The XR-005 "Hailstorm" is believed to be of US origin. The weapon fires subsonic bolts that are designed to ricochet off hard surfaces and they will continue to travel until they find a soft target or are exhausted. Kills outside the line of sight are possible with banked shots. Pressing L1 launches the remainder of the Hailstorm's clip. This creates an Auto-turret as the clip fires its bolts at nearby targets. The recoil from the bolts will even allow the clip to hang in mid-air. Note that Hailstorm ammo is quite sparse until later levels in the game

Out on the street, the Chimera quickly take cover and disappear from sight. If you're diligent and stealthy, you can eliminate one or two of them without alerting the full force of the troops. Use the Bullseye and try to tag at least one or two before they disappear behind the buildings.

Use the environment for cover and slowly make your way down the street. Avoid any open spaces, and be prepared to return fire from random Chimera. Not far down the street, a Howler appears and charges at Hale. Do your best to avoid its strikes while pumping it full of lead from the Rossmore.

SNIPE TOWN

There are some Chimera down at the end of the street, up on a ledge to the east. You can use the Fareye to snipe them from afar.

Cartwright and his men are holed up inside a building to the east. Before you come to their aid, take a moment to locate the park at the end of the street to the northwest. Search the area near the body of a one of those mysterious black ops soldiers to find an Intel Item.

DOCUMENT INTELLIGENCE #17

Field Guide 1

This practical field guide was created to aid soldiers on the battlefield against the varying Chimera species. The logo in the top-right corner mysteriously matches the one on the black ops soldiers...

United States Army Rangers
1st Regiment

CLUSTER

★ Help Cartwright Eliminate the Chimera

Return to the street and take the small set of stairs up to the platform near the burning bus. The next set of stairs leads up to a higher platform with some Hybrids. These foes have their weapons targeted on the building where Lt. Cartwright and his men are pinned inside.

Use a strong weapon, such as the Hailstorm, to quickly eliminate the Hybrids on the platform. In addition to the two foes straight ahead, there are two more to the left around the corner. Locate the metal fence dividing the street. There is a small hole here that is perfectly sized for the Fareye. Use this area to clear out any remaining Chimera. You can find several Fareye ammo pick-ups in one of the buildings on the other side of the street. Don't forget to explore that empty house if your ammo runs low!

This is where things get very intense. Down below, roughly six or seven Chimera are focused on keeping Cartwright and his men pinned down. When they become aware of Hale's presence, they turn their full attention on him. The best way to make it through this battle alive is to quickly wipe out at least half of their forces with a grenade. Toss a Hedgehog or an Air-Fuel grenade at one of the two clusters, then quickly take cover.

After the grenade detonates, stay down behind cover until it's safe to pop up. Then toss another grenade, or start picking off any foes that remain.

There is more Chimeran resistance around the corner, near the base of the stairs. Look for more Hybrids to emerge from the building across the way. In addition, a few Slipskulls cling to the walls and roam the street. Use the Fareye in this situation to slow things down and pick them off with headshots.

Continue to take cover and pick off the remaining Chimera until the street is quiet. Once the final Hybrid has been eliminated, Hale is reunited with Cartwright.

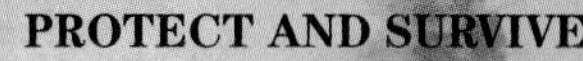

PROTECT AND SURVIVE

Cover is extremely important during this battle, as the Chimera are fierce and relentless. If Hale stays out in the open, they will cut him down in no time.

COMMON GROUND

Cheddar Gorge

Somerset, England
13 July 1951—11:37 GMT

MISSION OVERVIEW

Cartwright was the best soldier in my command. Nothing got past him. He must have known Hale was infected when they first met in Nottingham. Fortunately, Cartwright never cared too much about the small stuff. The Chimera were protecting something in the gorge, and the only way to reach it was with four wheels and a fifty-caliber turret.

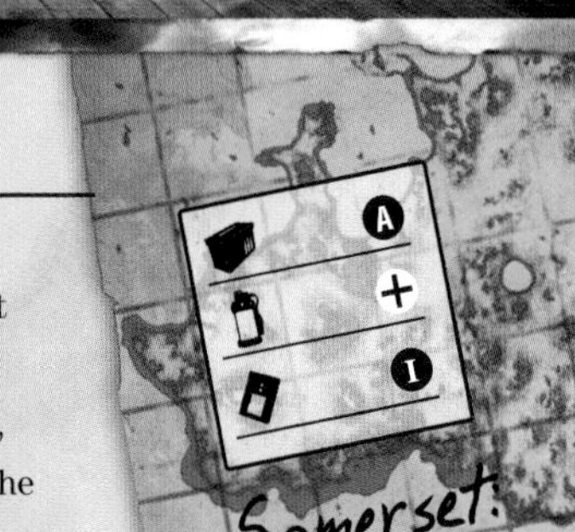

START

FIELD REPORT

Enemy Intel
Hybrid
Steelhead
Menial

Hardware
M5A2 Carbine
Bullseye
Rossmore 236
Combat Shotgun
Auger
L23 Fareye
XR-005 Hailstorm
Frag Grenades
Hedgehog
Fuel-Air Grenades

Mission Objective

★ Find the Source of the Chimera.

HELL ON WHEELS

★ Find the Source of the Chimera

According to Cartwright, the Chimera that gutted Northern Command came from this gorge. If the resistance is to gain the upper hand, Cartwright and Hale must find the source. They'll need a tough vehicle, and the LU-P Lynx is the one for the job.

The LU-P Lynx is a British Army, all-terrain, light-utility vehicle used for long range patrols. Although it lacks armor, the Lynx is extremely durable due to its reinforced chassis. It has four-wheel drive and a deceptively wide track, which keeps it from tipping over in tight turns. The Lynx is outfitted with a 360-degree, shock-dampened turret equipped with an L-650 12.7mm general purpose machine gun.

Vehicle Intelligence-LU-P Lynx

Most of this mission takes place inside the Lynx, however, Hale must go it on foot to get past a series of gates. Step on the gas and ram through the first barricade, then veer off-road to the left and head northwest.

There are two Chimera-filled bunkers dead ahead. These bunkers contain switches that open the gates blocking the path. To move onward, you must first clear out the Chimera and throw the switches.

SNIPE FROM AFAR

The Chimera have become much more fierce and aggressive, so much so that running in guns blazing is essentially a death sentence. Before you get too close, stop the Lynx, and hop out. Now use the Fareye and snipe any Hybrids wandering around or inside the bunker, paying special attention to the ones on the second level.

ASSAULT ON GATE BUNKERS #1 AND #2

When the Fareye runs out of ammunition, hop back into the Lynx and head into enemy territory. Next, run over any remaining Chimera for some easy kills

Drive the Lynx right up to the bunker's ramp (unfortunately, the vehicle is too big to fit through the opening) and hop out. Now let Cartwright provide cover and have Hale eliminate any Chimera with his machine gun. Don't worry about Cartwright's health; he's a sharpshooter and can take care of himself.

Now back on foot, quickly switch to a strong weapon (the Auger or Hailstorm are particularly handy in close-quarters combat) and head into the bunker, quickly eliminating any Chimera inside. Pay particular attention to the ramps leading to the second floor, as enemies can use them to shoot down from above.

TAKE COVER!

Once inside a bunker, make a mad dash for the back to find a large piece of machinery that provides good cover. There a few Sym-Bac serum canisters nearby, and this area enables you to take a brief respite from enemy fire and prepare for the next assault.

It's likely that a few Chimera still remain above, putting Hale in a precarious position. One or two well-tossed grenades can help even the odds. After doing so, go in and mop up the remaining foes.

When the coast is clear, locate the switch and throw it to raise one of the two gate bars blocking the path outside. Return to the Lynx and drive over to the second bunker, which is just to the left of the first bunker. As before, take a few moments to run down any Hybrids around the bunker's outer perimeter, then drive onto the ramp and exit the vehicle.

BLAST THROUGH THE BUNKER

To make things easier, use the Auger to pinpoint and eliminate the Chimera inside the bunker by shooting through its walls and ceiling. The Auger's shield force barrier also comes in handy during these bunker assaults.

Go for a repeat performance—head inside, use the machinery in back for cover, toss a grenade or two onto the second floor, then activate the switch. Doing so raises the second gate bar, thus allowing Hale and Cartwright to continue.

Once past the first set of gates, take a quick detour to the northeast. You need to find a small, deserted cabin at the base of a hill. Inside the cabin, you find some Hailstorm ammo and an Intel Item.

DOCUMENT INTELLIGENCE #20

Spires

This document, dated Nov. 23rd, 1950, is a diary excerpt detailing an encounter with a soldier named Buckler who mysteriously survived a Crawler attack.

23rd Nov.50
Found a soldier on pat[...]
outside Exeter. Looks li[...]
he's been on his own for
quite a while. Doesn't talk
much, but he ate a day's
rations in about five
minutes.
25th Nov '50
The soldier's finally coming
around. His name's Buckler.
He was there when the
Chimera took Salisbury. They
had prepared for a ground
war - fortified trenches,
tanks, the full Monty. But
the Chimera attacked with
spires. Crawlers infected
all of Salisbury in minutes.

[...]uckler won't say how he
survived. Everyone thinks he
just plain ran. Nobody would
blame him.

BACK

Return to the Lynx and head due north through a small gully. Be very alert, though, as a bunch of Leapers immediately attack the vehicle. Plow through as many foes as possible and let Cartwright take care of his fair share. Just on the other side of the gully, some more Hybrids attempt to stop the vehicle. Just run them down and keep going.

MAJOR AIR

Looking for some major air? Although there's no real reason to do this other than for fun (and the Lynx doesn't take damage), you can jump off this makeshift ramp and catch some serious air.

ASSAULT ON GATE BUNKERS #3 AND #4

There are more gate bunkers ahead. As before, you must throw the switches at the top of each one to raise a set of gates.

Engage in similar tactics as before: Drive straight up to the ramp and let Cartwright target the Chimera within the immediate vicinity. Hop out of the vehicle and eliminate the enemies inside and around the bunker's perimeter. Run in and take cover, grabbing the Sym-Bac serum on the ground. Finally, toss a few grenades onto the second floor to clear out the enemies, then flip the switch.

There is a fourth bunker to the east of the third one. As before, the same strategy applies. Just make sure you use all of your available weapon resources, including the Auger's force shield and some grenades. When the area is safe, throw the switch to raise the gates, then jump back into the Lynx.

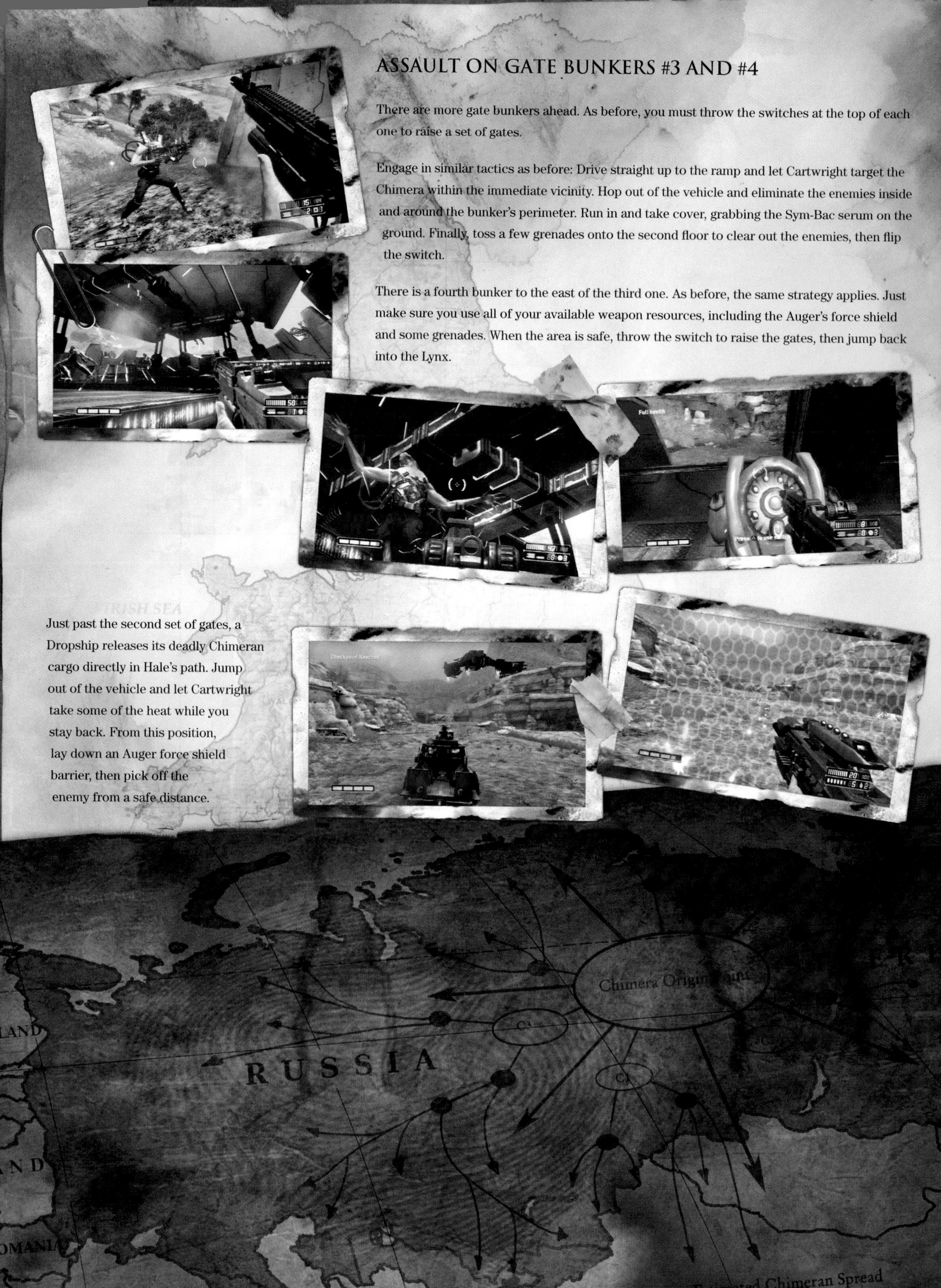

Just past the second set of gates, a Dropship releases its deadly Chimeran cargo directly in Hale's path. Jump out of the vehicle and let Cartwright take some of the heat while you stay back. From this position, lay down an Auger force shield barrier, then pick off the enemy from a safe distance.

When the skirmish ends, return to the Lynx and take the high or low path to find the paved road. Then once again head off-road but this time go to the east. This winding path leads to a small pocket of Chimeran resistance.

ASSAULT ON GATE BUNKERS #5 AND #6

Continue up the hill to the south and prepare for a third and final set of bunkers. These next foes are extremely fierce and are capable of overwhelming Hale in a matter of seconds if given the chance. Before you even think of going in, hop out of the Lynx and start lobbing some grenades.

When things calm down, head into the closest bunker and take care of the remaining Chimera inside. Don't forget that you can use the Auger to target the enemies through the ceiling. This approach also prevents Hale from taking unnecessary damage.

TURRET TAKEOVER

Usually, these turrets aren't very useful for retaliation purposes. However, you can turn this one on the nearby bunker. Use it to eliminate a few of the enemies on the top floor.

Clear both bunkers and throw the switches, then return to the Lynx. Now locate the road and head through the raised set of gates to the north. Continue driving north, then veer off-road one last time and crash through the barriers leading to a small canyon. The source of the Chimeran assault is dead ahead.

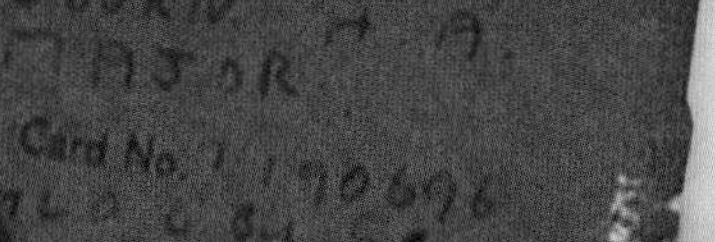

A DISTURBING DISCOVERY

Cheddar Gorge

Somerset, England
13 July 1951—12:20 GMT

MISSION OVERVIEW

The Chimeran forces were protecting something in the gorge. It wasn't like them to play defense. Whatever they were guarding had to be a potential weakness. The gorge contained factories that built Stalkers and Dropships, but we had seen them before. Deeper into the gorge, the Chimera were hiding something far more disturbing.

NORTHERN COMMAND

Somerset: Mission 3

START

FIELD REPORT

Enemy Intel
Hybrid
Steelhead
Menial
Slipskull
Leaper
Gray Jack

Hardware
M5A2 Carbine
Bullseye
Rossmore 236
Combat Shotgun
Auger
L23 Fareye
XR-005 Hailstorm
XR-003 Sapper
Hedgehog

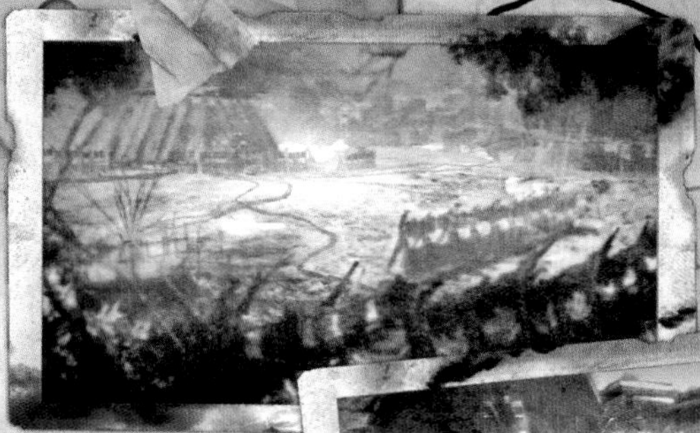

Mission Objective

- Find the source of the Chimera.
- Find the Chimeran base.
- Escape the gorge.

United States Army Rangers
1st Regiment

THE HIVE

★ Find the Source of the Chimera

Cartwright decides it would be best served to split up for the time being. He takes the left path, leaving Hale the right path. Press the switch to lower the gate and proceed.

A Hybrid and a Steelhead patrol near a path close to a large Chimeran structure. Use the surrounding environment for cover and pick them off, or equip the Fareye and snipe for some headshots. If you choose to take some headshots, save a few bullets for the enemies inside.

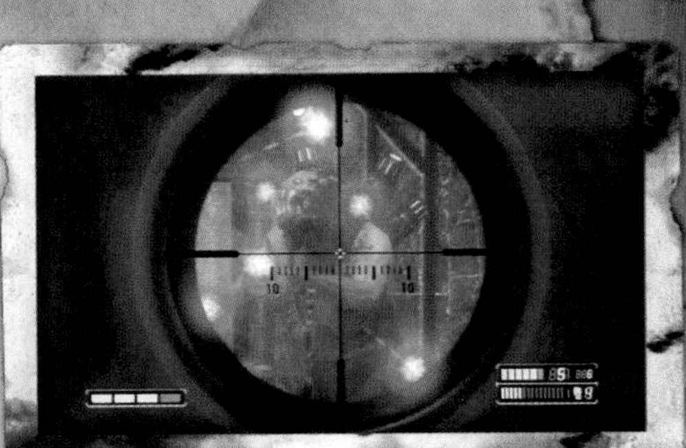

Once the shooting begins, the large door to the structure opens to reveal a pack of Menials. Switch to the Carbine and send a steady stream of bullets their way. Stay back and don't let them get too close.

Re-equip the Fareye and pinpoint the location of the Hybrids on the walkway inside the structure. Try to snipe them from this location using focus and dodge their Bullseye fire.

BEWARE THE MENIAL

Although the structure may initially look empty, some Menials emerge as soon as Hale enters. Stay near the entrance or back out a few paces, then mow them down with the Carbine.

Near the back of the structure, locate the two doorways with switches and use the door to the left first. Although this leads to a dead end, an Intel Item makes it worth the trip.

Back outside, some Chimera (including an Auger-wielding Steelhead) put up a very strong fight. Defeat the Steelhead first (try using the Bullseye), then take cover and pick off the remaining foes. At the end of the path, Hale finds his prize.

DOCUMENT INTELLIGENCE #21

Field Guide 2

This is a special black ops document that details more of the known Chimeran units. Some of the drawings show only portions of the Chimera, which include enemies Hale has not yet encountered.

Return to the structure and activate the switch for the main door that is located against the back wall. Also, pick up the new weapon—the XR-003 Sapper—that was dropped by one of these mysterious black ops soldiers.

XR-004 Sapper

The XR-003 "Sapper" mine launcher is believed to be a product of secret US weapons programs. This weapon fires a stream of organic cluster mines. Each mine is encased in a living cell similar to those used by the Widowmaker. The mines stick to most surfaces, including each other. In combat, you can use the Sapper to set large cluster mine traps against ambushing Chimera.

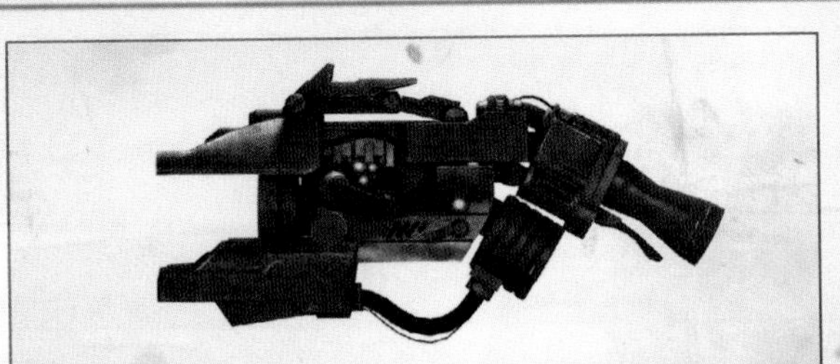

The open doorway leads back out to open spaces, where more Menials appear. Save your Sapper ammo for the moment and use the Carbine to get rid of these pesky foes. Outside, the field is littered with Chimeran debris, including the remnants of a few inoperable Stalkers. Ignore them for now and follow the path to the left.

As Hale rounds the corner, a vicious Steelhead and its Hybrid brethren launch an attack. A good way to combat this situation is to equip the Fareye and use focus to slow things down for a clean headshot, or use the Carbine.

MINE FIELD

Stealth saves the day inside this second structure. The floor contains multiple laser mines. Equip the Carbine and creep along, activating only one at a time so they are easy to target and shoot.

In addition to the mines, there are even more Menials shuffling around the interior of this structure. Eliminate all of them, then activate the switch next to the door to the left to venture outside.

The Chimeran assault continues out here. In addition to more Menials, two ultra-quick Gray Jacks will close the gap on Hale very quickly. Use the Bullseye or Carbine to quickly eliminate them before they can cause any damage.

REUNITED

Lt. Cartwright's location is just on the other side of the bridge. To reach him, you must first clear a path through the approaching Chimera. Stay back and use the Fareye to pick them off from the base.

On the other side, join Cartwright in a sniping battle with the Chimera on the ridge. Use the Fareye from a distance or the Carbine to dispense of them.

The Chimera continue to attack from the trench to the right. Follow Cartwright's lead, take cover, and eliminate them. The Auger is a good weapon to use here, as its fire effortlessly slices through the barriers the Hybrids are using for cover. When the coast is clear, climb the ridge to see what is really going on.

United States Army Rangers
1st Regiment

THE TOWER

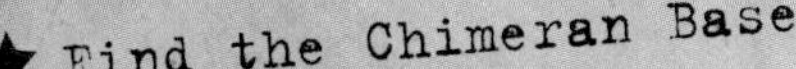

★ Find the Chimeran Base

At the top of the ridge, Hale and Cartwright observe a huge Chimeran tower. Something within triggers another jolt within Hale and a painful vision of the Angel appears in his mind.

Cartwright takes off down the ridge, calling on Hale to follow him. Stay on his heels and let him lead you to the next area. When he reaches the destination, Cartwright kindly lets Hale go in first.

There are multiple pieces of Chimeran equipment inside this open area that will provide lots of places to hide from enemy fire. But before you can even take cover, a Gray Jack comes barreling down the path.

Once it's out of the way, take on the arduous process of picking off the multiple Chimera in this area. Use the equipment for cover and eliminate them one-by-one. As usual, the Bullseye is a strong weapon for tight duck-and-cover situations.

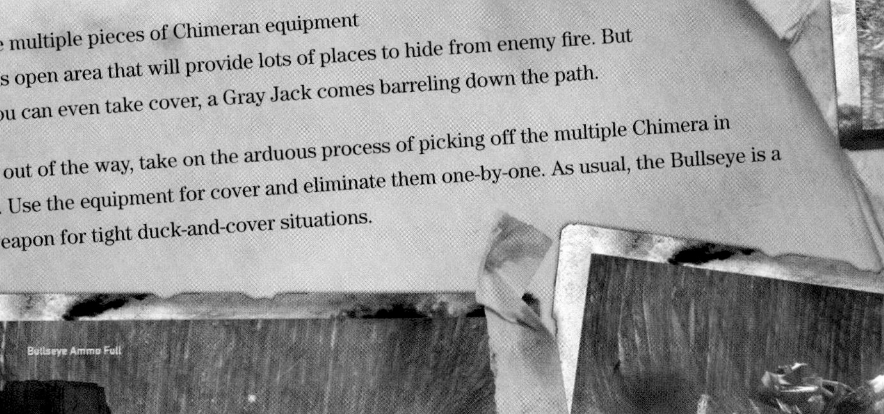

At the opposite end of this open area, some Leapers and a sprinting Gray Jack appear. Continue down the path and go around the corner. Cartwright then barks out a warning regarding some Hedgehog mines. Quickly duck for cover before they detonate.

The path contains multiple Hedgehog mines, as well as some patrolling Chimera. Using cover is extremely important for survival. Go slow, stay down and pick off the enemies using a strong weapon, such as the Bullseye or Carbine.

Enter the structure through the opening at the end of the path. Inside, follow Cartwright's lead and pick off the Slipskulls hanging from the walls and machinery.

United States Army Rangers
1st Regiment

★ Escape the Gorge

Throw the switch at the back of the structure to open the large door to the right. Unfortunately, this exposes Hale and Cartwright to more Chimera. Pinpoint and eliminate the Auger-wielding Steelhead first, then concentrate on the remaining foes. A well-thrown Hedgehog grenade can work wonders here.

Before exiting the area outside the structure, scour the area for a dead soldier and another Intel Item. Proceed up the ramp to exit the gorge. Up top, Cartwright and Hale find their Lynx waiting.

DOCUMENT INTELLIGENCE #21

Tower Notes

This important map indicates the location of the Chimera tower at Cheddar Gorge. More importantly, it also notes that the tower was excavated—not built—which has far greater implications about the Chimera than anyone previously thought.

DEVIL AT THE DOOR

Southern Command

Bristol, England
13 July 1951—14:24 GMT

MISSION OVERVIEW

Hale and Cartwright discovered the key to the entire Chimeran strategy. The Tower they found had not been built—it had been excavated. That single fact changed everything we thought we knew about the Chimera. The walls of the gorge blocked all radio signals. The Chimera knew their secret would be safe as long as the pair of intruders didn't escape. However, escape they did. It was an hour's drive from Somerset to Southern Command, even with Cartwright at the wheel. Chimeran power conduits snaked in and out of the ground along the side the road. Hale must have noticed that the conduits led away from the Tower in all directions. After half an hour, Southern Command still wasn't responding on the radio. There could be only one explanation…

Bristol: Mission 1

START

Ammo	A
Health	+

FIELD REPORT

Enemy Intel
Hybrid
Steelhead
Howler
Titan

Hardware
M5A2 Carbine
Bullseye
Rossmore 236
Combat Shotgun
Auger
L23 Fareye
XR-005 Hailstorm
XR-003 Sapper
Hedgehog

Mission Objective

★ Eliminate the Chimera outside Southern Command.

★ Enter Southern Command.

ASSAULT ON SOUTHERN COMMAND

★ Eliminate the Chimera Outside Southern Command

When Cartwright and Hale arrive at Southern Command, they find that it's under attack. Cartwright drives ahead, concentrating on the Stalkers, leaving Hale to mop up the Chimeran foot soldiers.

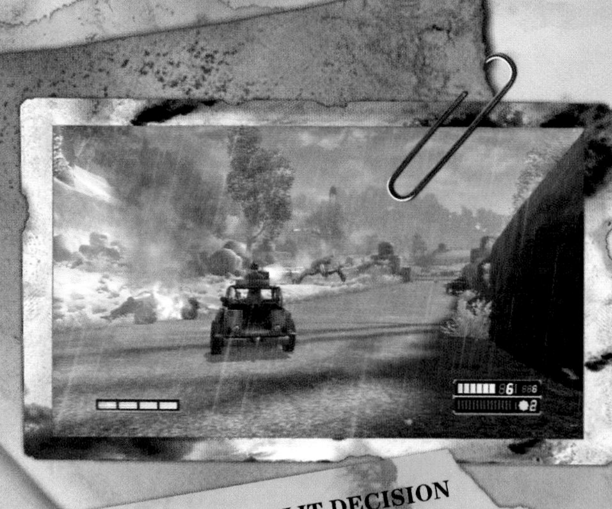

SPLIT DECISION

You can turn your weapons on the Stalkers in the area (the Power Core on the rear of their torsos is their weak spot), but they won't stick around for long. It may be more prudent to focus your attack on the nearby Hybrids before they can target Hale or wipe out the British soldiers fighting for their lives.

There are some sand bag bunkers here that provide a small amount of cover. Stay down and pick off the enemies as quickly as possible. Try tossing a Hedgehog Grenade to help even the odds.

Quickly take cover behind one of the metal barricades at the top of the small hill. There are multiple Hedgehog mines here that can cause instant death if you're not careful. There are some Howlers behind the mines and they come charging at Hale and the remaining soldiers. Equip the Rossmore and take evasive action while firing at the beasts.

HERO MOMENT!

Keep an eye on the surviving allies. It's entirely possible that a Howler will pin down at least one of them. If you're fast enough, you can save him from a grisly death.

After eliminating the Howlers, slowly move forward along the path, ducking for cover behind the metallic barricades every time you encounter more Hedgehog mines.

The battle wages on to the east. Head toward the explosions and locate a squadron of men who are making a stand against some Chimera at a nearby bunker. Take cover and stay back, then pick off the foes from afar. As always, toss in a few grenades to thin out their numbers.

GRAB AND GO

Before you proceed any further, enter the bunker and restock your munitions and Sym-Bac serum supplies.

United States Army Rangers
1st Regiment

★ Enter Southern Command

Head out for the north gate. Although it is currently locked, a blast from a lumbering Titan takes care of that. As before, unleash a barrage of grenades at the beast or hit it with fire from the Carbine. Remember to keep moving and stay out of its reach while also avoiding its weapon blasts.

Move through the open gate and slowly enter the next area. This area is laced with mines and the tall brush and undergrowth make spotting them extremely difficult. Be prepared at all times to take cover and, if no cover is available, quickly shoot the mines before they detonate.

RISK VERSUS REWARD

There is a small path on the opposite side of the barbed-wire fence. It's completely filled with Radial mines, which makes the path quite treacherous. The reward for making it through safely is the acquisition of ammunition stores and Sym-Bac serum. On a subsequent playthrough of the game, you will find the Arc Charger.

RETAKE THE COMMAND

Return to the minefield and carefully navigate through it to reach the path leading up the hill on the other side. Up top, Hale encounters more Chimeran resistance, as well as a few strategically placed missile rocket turrets.

Use the Fareye to pick off the Hybrids from a safe distance, or take cover and use the Bullseye and Frag grenades. Either way, eliminate the attacking Chimera and then destroy the turrets.

The path leads to a ridge that overlooks the entrance to Southern Command. Mitchell and Cartwright need Hale's help to stop the Chimeran assault so they can get inside. Dig in up here and use the Fareye to snipe as many enemies below as possible.

After eliminating the majority of the foes from your position above, join the British soldiers down near the entrance and help them finish off the remaining foes. There is one pesky Steelhead here that is using its Auger to blast through the blockades, making it difficult to target. Sneak around to the side and use the Hailstorm to flush it out.

Take out the final remaining Hybrid and join Cartwright at the base of the entrance. The Chimera are closing the blast doors and he needs Hale to get inside before it's too late.

FOOD, ARMS AND FUEL **MUST** COME FIRST

EVACUATION

Southern Command

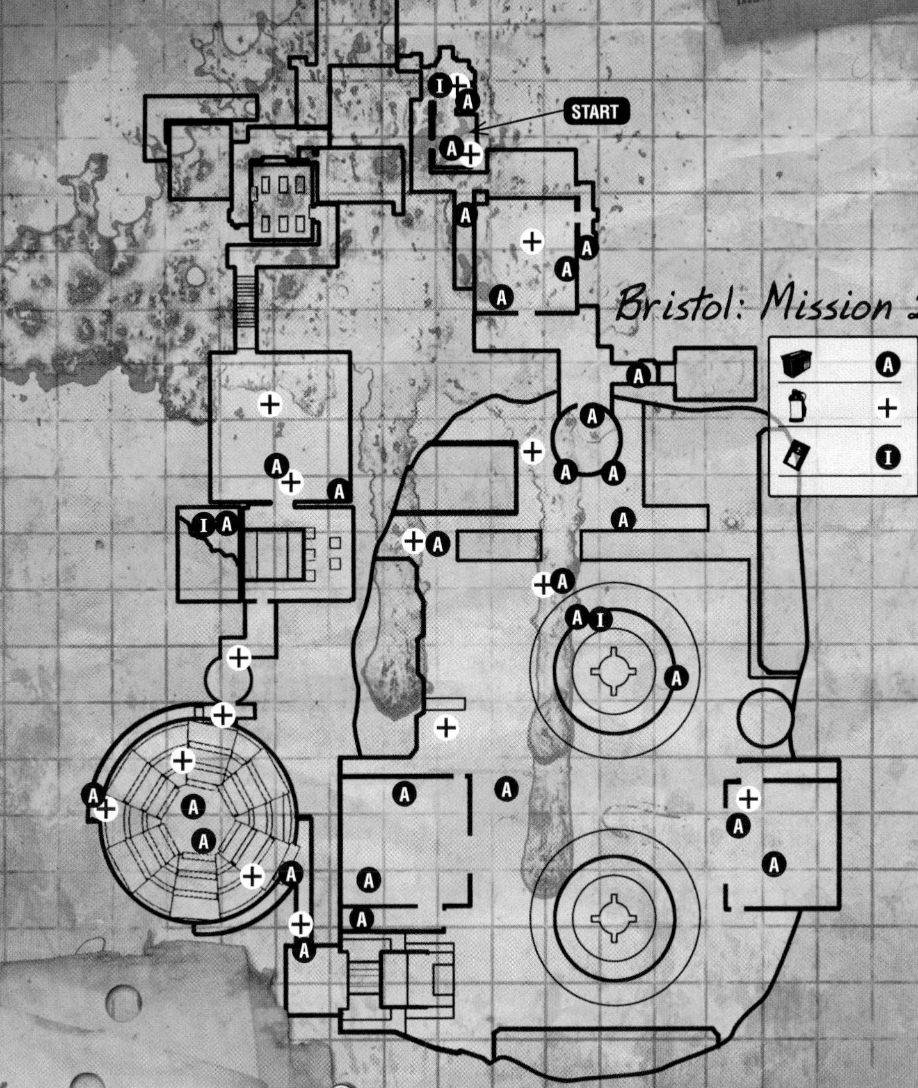

Bristol, England
13 July 1951—15:59 GMT

MISSION OVERVIEW

Southern Command wasn't just our last command base. It was the last piece of ground in all of England that the Chimera didn't control. The soldiers fought off the worst of the attack on the Northern entrance, but we then faced a graver threat. The Chimera had infiltrated the hangar on the south side. We knew they would launch Spires at any moment. If we didn't get the planes out safely, then all of England would truly be lost.

FIELD REPORT

Enemy Intel
Hybrid
Steelhead
Slipskull
Leaper
Titan
Hardfang

Hardware
M5A2 Carbine
Bullseye
Rossmore 236
Combat Shotgun
Auger
L23 Fareye
XR-005 Hailstorm
XR-003 Sapper
Frag Grenade
Hedgehog
Air-Fuel Grenade

Mission Objective

- ★ Get to the hangar.
- ★ Eliminate the Chimera attacking Parker's transport.
- ★ Evacuate Southern Command.

United States Army Rangers
1st Regiment

DEADLY SILENCE

★ Get to the Hangar

Hale is the only one to make it inside the south entrance of Southern Command. It's up to him to make it to the hangar and get the VTOLs free before a Spire strike wipes out everyone. Inside, it is deathly quiet and almost pitch black, making things even tougher for the lone soldier. To reach the hangar, you must first deal with the approaching Slipskulls, Hybrids, and Steelheads in the stairwell. Start with the Bullseye and tag and bag the Slipskulls on the wall, ducking behind the doorway for cover. Next, toss a grenade or two into the stairwell to eliminate the remaining Chimera below. Or, position Hale at the top of the stairs and let loose with the Hailstorm, as the reflective bullets have less ground to cover..

Finish off any remaining Chimera at the bottom of the stairwell, then take a right into the hallway to the red lit alcove. Hale is witness to a disgusting sight—a pack of Leapers feasting on the carcass of a fellow soldier. Show him some mercy, then collect the ammo and Intel Item next to the dead body.

DOCUMENT INTELLIGENCE #23

Crates

Dated January 15th, this document details a soldier's account of witnessing heavily guarded mysterious crates being offloaded from VTOLS, some of them stamped with the American flag. The strange thing is that up until Hale's team was sent to Britain, the Americans were not supposed to have been involved in the war.

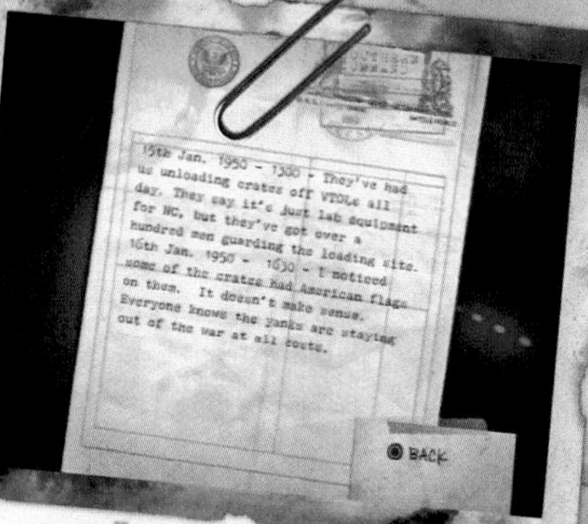

Return to the hallway and take the left path. Some powerful foes protect the room around the corner. If the Steelhead's back is toward Hale, take this opportunity to perform a quick kill. Use the Auger in conjunction with a few force shields to pick off the rest of the foes.

The adjoining hallway leads to the Mess Hall. Inside, Hale meets more Chimeran resistance, but it's nothing the Auger or Hailstorm can't handle.

HELL BREAKS LOOSE

★ Eliminate the Chimera Attacking Parker's Transport

The Mess Hall leads to the Storage area. The large doorway at the end of the Storage area opens to a lift. Throw the switch on the left to activate it, then throw the switch inside to go down into the hangar.

The lift opens up to a bloody and brutal battle between British resistance fighters and a large group of Chimera, including a massive Titan. Quickly get out of the lift and make for cover, avoiding the beast's blasts while shooting it with the Bullseye and circle strafing, or follow the strategy mentioned below in the "Quick Kill" tip box.

QUICK KILL

Hale is under siege from both the Titan and a large number of Hybrids. To quickly eliminate the Titan, switch to Air-Fuel grenades and throw at least two or three of them. Since they can attach to any surface, they may stick on its hide and detonate with deadly results.

With the Titan out of the way, run for cover and turn your attention to the surrounding Hybrids. Look for easy kill opportunities, such as explosive barrels. If not, rely on some Frag Grenades or equip the Fareye to pick them off. Take a moment to pick the area clean of ammunition, grenades, and Sym-Bac serum, then move toward the first VTOL lift.

Before moving on, take the ramp down into the first lift. There are some grenades and ammunition at the bottom, as well as an Intel Item.

Parker and her team are pinned down at the second VTOL lift. Before they can take off, Hale must eliminate the Chimera in this area. Since they're not going anywhere, take some time to explore the expansive hangar, collecting munitions and supplies in the process.

DOCUMENT INTELLIGENCE #24

Preparations

Dated July 12th, 1951, this page is from the journal of a British soldier who is preparing for the inevitable Chimeran attack on Southern Command.

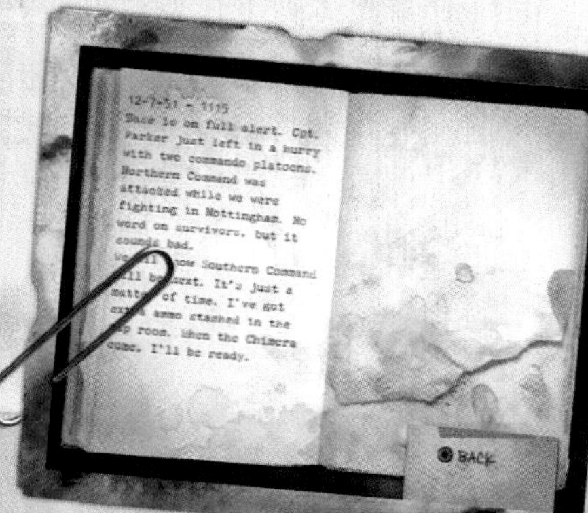

FREE AT LAST

Now stealthily make your way over to the east side of the hangar and locate the foes near the turret nest in the back corner that are focusing firing at Parker's VTOL.

Head into the garage on the right, then go into the adjoining hallway. The exit is much closer to the turret nest, making it all but impossible for the Chimera to turn the turrets on Hale. This provides a much easier—and safer—opportunity to eliminate them.

United States Army Rangers
1st Regiment

ESCAPE ALIVE

★ Evacuate Southern Command

After securing the turret, Parker takes off with the VTOL and leaves Hale and the remaining soldiers to fend for themselves. Locate the lift ramp in the southwest corner of the hangar, step onto the platform, then throw the switch and ride it up to ground level.

Hale must escape from Southern Command alive, which isn't going to be an easy proposition. The moment he steps foot into the dark auditorium beyond the ramp, all hell breaks loose.

There are lots of foes around the auditorium's perimeter. The small brick wall provides very little in the way of cover, especially from Hedgehog Grenade attacks. Therefore, you must improvise with the Auger's force shield and the Fareye and its focus capability. Each time focus runs out, duck behind the wall to let the meter refill, then go at it again. When all of the enemies are gone, explore the area and exit through the opposite doorway.

The gruesome sound of an incoming Leaper attack indicates another tense battle. Look toward the top of the ramp and prepare for battle. Lay down some Sapper rounds; some well-placed globs is all it takes to knock out the Leapers. When the onslaught is over, take the lift at the top of the ramp down into the lower portion of the facility.

Now wind your way through Southern Command's corridors and rooms. Look for a red-lit alcove, which is located just before the large Map Room. Search the room to find another Intel Item.

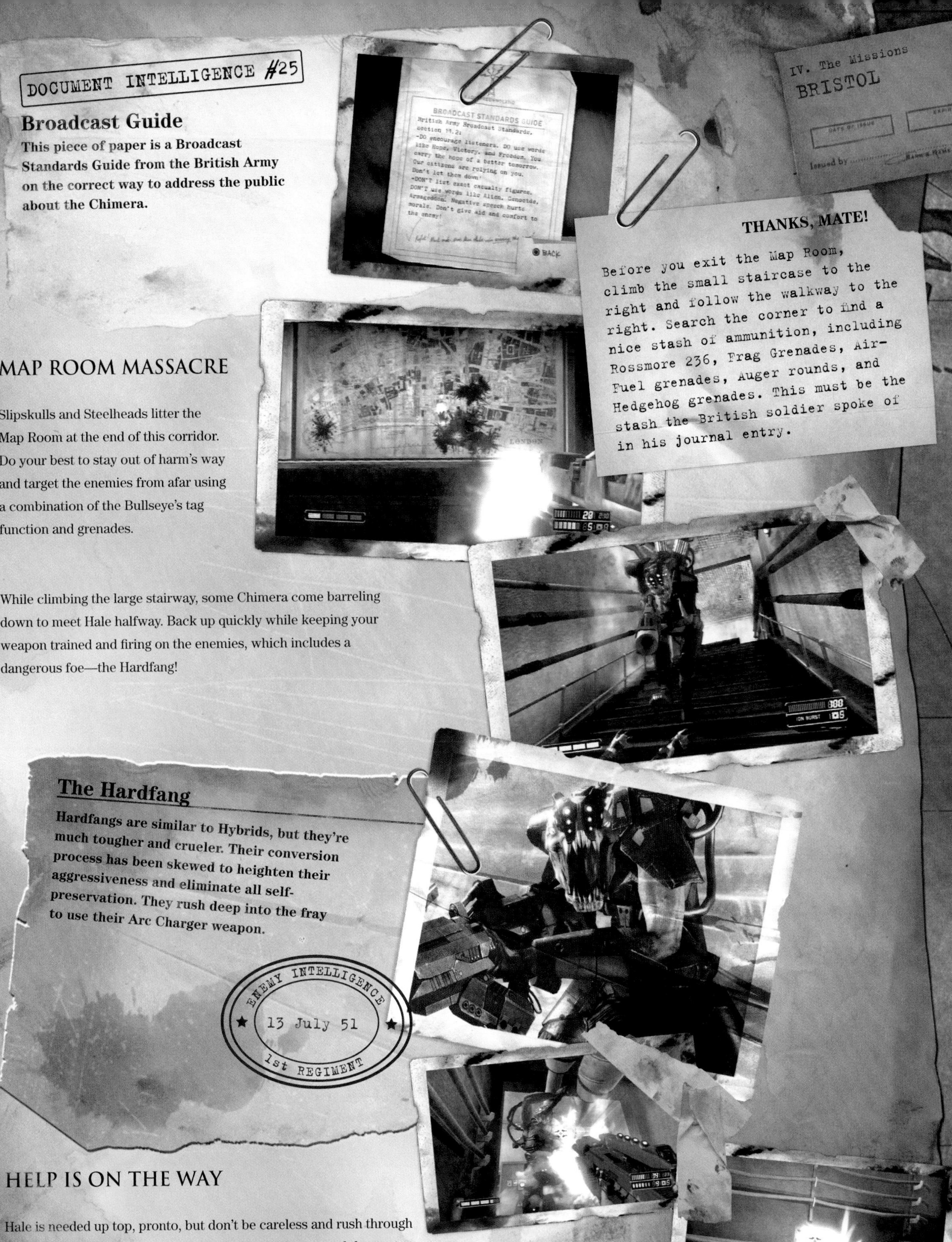

DOCUMENT INTELLIGENCE #25

Broadcast Guide

This piece of paper is a Broadcast Standards Guide from the British Army on the correct way to address the public about the Chimera.

THANKS, MATE!

Before you exit the Map Room, climb the small staircase to the right and follow the walkway to the right. Search the corner to find a nice stash of ammunition, including Rossmore 236, Frag Grenades, Air-Fuel grenades, Auger rounds, and Hedgehog grenades. This must be the stash the British soldier spoke of in his journal entry.

MAP ROOM MASSACRE

Slipskulls and Steelheads litter the Map Room at the end of this corridor. Do your best to stay out of harm's way and target the enemies from afar using a combination of the Bullseye's tag function and grenades.

While climbing the large stairway, some Chimera come barreling down to meet Hale halfway. Back up quickly while keeping your weapon trained and firing on the enemies, which includes a dangerous foe—the Hardfang!

The Hardfang

Hardfangs are similar to Hybrids, but they're much tougher and crueler. Their conversion process has been skewed to heighten their aggressiveness and eliminate all self-preservation. They rush deep into the fray to use their Arc Charger weapon.

ENEMY INTELLIGENCE
13 July 51
1st REGIMENT

HELP IS ON THE WAY

Hale is needed up top, pronto, but don't be careless and rush through the rest of the facility. There are plenty of enemies around the next corner and inside the infirmary. Use the Auger to shoot through the wall, then head inside and clean up the rest.

PARTING WAYS

Southern Command

NORTHERN COMMAND

Bristol, England
13 July 1951—17:01 GMT

Bristol: Mission 3

Mortar

START

MISSION OVERVIEW

The soldiers were finally able to fight off the Chimera in the hangar. We sent the survivors to a rendezvous point in Cardiff, 20 miles northwest. I stayed at the base to finish loading what supplies we could. There was no way to tell how long we could last in Cardiff. Chimeran Behemoths were already approaching Southern Command. A spire attack was inevitable.

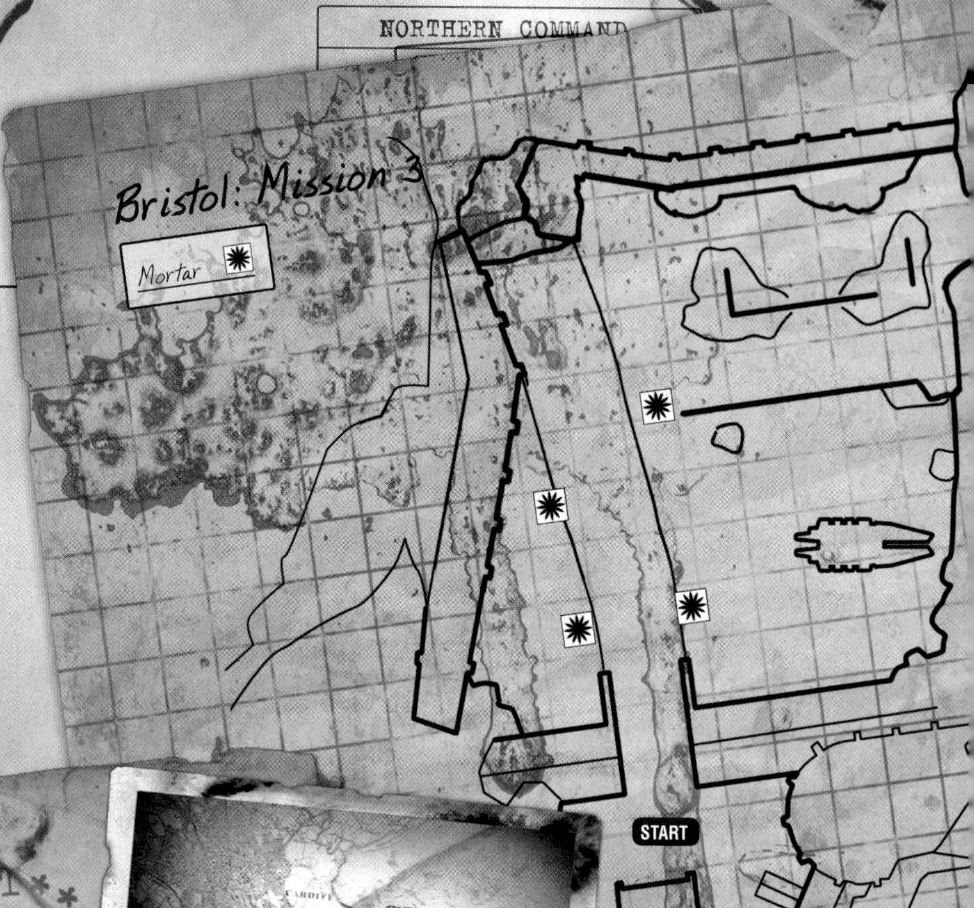

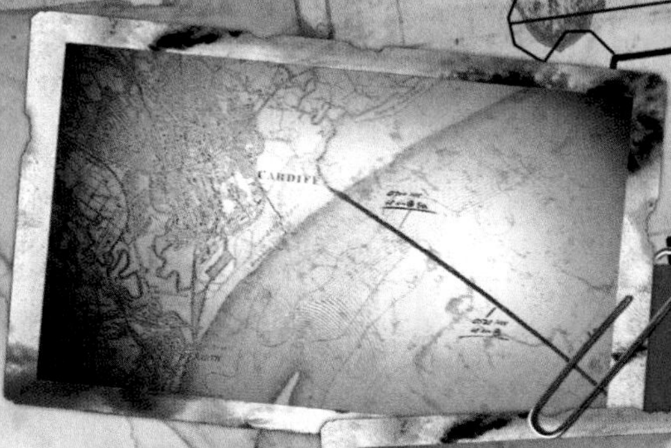

FIELD REPORT

Enemy Intel
Titan

Hardware
Stalker

Mission Objective

★ Hold off the Chimera until the evacuation is complete.

United States Army Rangers
1st Regiment

SENTINEL

★ Hold Off the Chimera Until the Evacuation Is Complete

At the outset, a huge Stalker confronts Hale. As he prepares to fight it off, the hatch opens to reveal Cartwright at the controls. The two must use the Stalker on the battlefield and stave off the Chimeran threat until the evacuation is complete.

Mission success depends upon Hale and Cartwright eliminating the Titans terrorizing the British troops. From the starting position, locate the first two mortars on the west side of the battlefield. Unleash a combination of missile and cannon fire to destroy them.

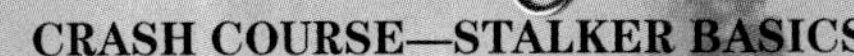

CRASH COURSE—STALKER BASICS

Like the tank, the Stalker's machine guns can overheat with extended use. Keep an eye on the overheat meter located on the bottom-right corner of the screen. Just above the overheat meter is the Stalker's cannon reload meter. It takes approximately three seconds to reload the cannon between shots. Finally, the Stalker's armor meter is located above Hale's health meter. When this runs out, the Stalker will explode with Hale in it.

Next, move the Stalker to the left while still maintaining the position up on the ramp and eliminate the third mortar on the east side of the battlefield. With all four of the mortars out of the way, turn your attention to the Titans. Move onto the battlefield and start chipping away at their thick hides with a combination of missile and autocannon fire. Stay on the move and use the "dash maneuver" to avoid the Titans' blasts. Don't stop firing until they both explode.

INTO THE DEPTHS

Chimeran Tunnels

Bracknell, England
13 July 1951—18:14 GMT

MISSION OVERVIEW

I had no idea what Hale was planning to do. Cartwright told me about the Tower they found in the gorge, but we didn't have even a fraction of the soldiers it would take to mount an assault. Whatever Hale was planning to do, he was on his own.

FIELD REPORT

Enemy Intel
Menial
Gray Jack
Leapers
Hybrid
Steelhead
Hardfang

Hardware
M5A2 Carbine
Bullseye
Rossmore 236
Combat Shotgun
Auger
L23 Fareye
XR-005 Hailstorm
XR-003 Sapper
Frag Grenade
Hedgehog
Air-Fuel Grenade

Mission Objective

★ Follow the Chimeran tunnels to their origin.

★ Escape the Tower.

United States Army Rangers
1st Regiment

TUNNELS AND CAVERNS

★ Follow the Chimeran Tunnels to Their Origin

Hale goes solo on this mission, as he travels deep within the Chimeran tunnel system. Down at the ground level, some Menials go about their tasks. Once they sense Hale's presence, they turn their full attention on him. Stay put and use the Carbine to pick them off from above.

The next area is a breeding ground of Leaper Pods. The Pods hatch if they sense movement, so stay still. Stay back and use any type of grenade (hold off on using any Air Fuel Grenades) to destroy the pods before they can do any harm. There are four sets of pods: one to the immediate left, one near the back, and two off to the right. Explore the pit to the right, as there is an Intel Item to find.

DOCUMENT INTELLIGENCE #26

Conduits

This important piece of information is a map from the British Intelligence Corps that displays the number of known and suspected Chimeran conduits spreading underground from Bristol and Bracknell to London.

GRAY JACK SURPRISE

Don't get complacent inside these tunnels; there are Chimera everywhere. One can jump out at Hale at any moment, as evidenced by the charging Gray Jack that comes barreling around the corner.

Locate the metallic walkway bridge at the back of this area and take it to reach the next bridge. Scout the area and listen for more Leaper Pods, as the next batch is just inside the doorway.

Follow the small tunnel until it turns into a large underground cavern. Hold your position near the dead body and stay back. There are Menials and some Gray Jacks here. These foes remain hidden until Hale moves farther into the cavern.

Pick off the Menials first, then focus on the Gray Jacks. Use a fast weapon against these nasty creatures, such as the Hailstorm. If you haven't used the Sapper yet, then lay down a trap of globules and lure the Gray Jacks in the same direction as the trap.

Clean the area of all the foes (there is a Leaper Pod nest off to the left), then get onto the platform at the back of the cavern and move through the tunnel opening.

Follow the tunnel as it slopes down at a steep angle, taking out any Hybrid resistance along the way. Beware of more Menials at the bottom of the tunnel.

United States Army Rangers
1st Regiment

TRAPPED!

★ Escape the Tower

Chimera assault Hale the moment he enters this large, circular cavern. The foes rise up on small lifts from the chasm below. It's a brutal fight that seems to last for an eternity, but one that you can survive with the right tactics.

Start the fight by dashing across the platform, picking up the Hailstorm, Rossmore and Fareye ammo in the center. Next, run across the small bridge to the right to access the perimeter on the opposite side.

Once on the other side, turn around and face the platform. Now equip the Hailstorm and shoot an Auto-turret to start mowing down the first wave of foes. You should only use the Hailstorm if you have plenty of ammo. If not, fight from the center using double-barrel Rossmore rounds or go at it from afar with Air Fuel Grenades.

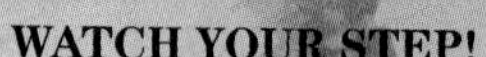

WATCH YOUR STEP!

Be very careful when walking, as there are gaps between the walkways around the platform. One misstep will result in instant death.

If necessary, shoot another Auto-turret or dispose of the second wave of Chimera. After doing so, dash back across the platform and eliminate the next wave of Menials. Now cross over to the opposite walkway, but look for more Gray Jacks along the way.

If you run out of Hailstorm ammo, switch to the Auger and use its force shield to protect Hale from enemy fire while picking off the last wave of Steelheads.

Before exiting this area, explore the perimeter for another Intel Item. It is located along the northern portion of the outer walkway.

DOCUMENT INTELLIGENCE #27

Surrounded

This journal entry, dated July 15th, details the events of a poor soldier who was being stalked and hunted by the Cloven.

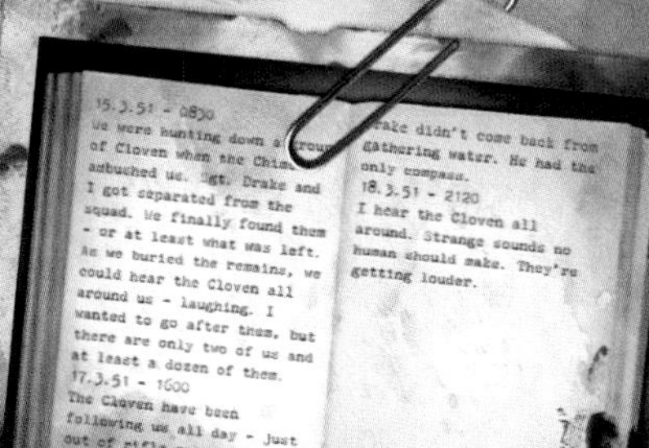

15.3.51 - 0830
We were hunting down a
of Cloven when the
ambushed us. Sgt. Drake and
I got separated from the
squad. We finally found them
- or at least what was left.
As we buried the remains, we
could hear the Cloven all
around us - laughing. I
wanted to go after them, but
there are only two of us and
at least a dozen of them.
17.3.51 - 1600
The Cloven have been
following us all day - just
out of rifle range. They're
toying with us.
18.3.51 - 1840
didn't come back from
gathering water. He had the
only compass.
18.3.51 - 2120
I hear the Cloven all
around. Strange sounds no
human should make. They're
getting louder.

HIGHWIRE

A different kind of Leaper foe attacks Hale inside the next tunnel. Use the Carbine and back up as they swarm nearby; try to knock out several of them while avoiding their acidic discharge.

The Roller

Rollers are adult Leapers that have developed a faster, trundling locomotion. As they near the end of their life cycle, internal decomposition results in venting of a corrosive spray. Rollers use this as an opening attack, blinding their prey before closing to strike with their claws and teeth.

Drop into the hole to continue deeper into the tunnel system. Another Leaper Pod nest bars Hale's progress, but a well-tossed grenade should take care of the problem. At the end of the tunnel, Hale emerges inside a massive cavern with conduit cables intersecting in virtually every direction.

Tread along the first cable. At the other end, drop down onto the walkway, take cover, and eliminate the Slipskulls attached to the cavern walls. The Bullseye's tag function is best put to use against these fast-moving Chimera.

VENTILATION DUCTS

These air vents siphon the hot air out of the cavern in order to keep the interior cool enough for the Chimera to operate. However, the hot air they emit creates an updraft that can temporarily lift a human body into the air. Use these updrafts to leap from one cable to the next.

Ride the air vent up to the next cable, then climb its length to reach the walkway high above. There are more conduit cables inside the next portion of the cavern. Hop into the air draft from the next air vent to access another cable, then walk across its length toward the next set of vents.

These vents send Hale onto a metallic platform where a few Menials are waiting for their next victim. Use the Rossmore or Carbine to quickly eliminate them. There are also two nasty Hardfangs at the opposite end of the walkway. Use the Fareye to pick them off or target the nearby Power Cores to take them down.

As you continue to ascend, scan the cable below and to the left to locate an Intel Item. To collect it, you must drop down from the cable above.

DOCUMENT INTELLIGENCE #28

Stranger

This journal entry reveals more information about these bizarre and mysterious men called Cloven. Apparently, they are Russian men who devoutly follow an even more mysterious leader. His picture was found in their mouths; they hanged themselves and cut out their tongues.

AUGER ACCESS

The cable in between the two sets of air vents has a cache of Auger ammo at its end. Grab it if you are low on ammo.

GETAWAY

You need to backtrack quite a bit to return to the previous cable near the Intel Item. When you're ready, follow the tunnel opening to a new area. Inside, more enemies attempt to attack from the platform above. Lob a Hedgehog Grenade or use the Carbine to cut down their numbers.

Take the next tunnel and follow the path as it winds between the Chimeran technology and cavern walls. More Hybrids, Steelheads, and even a Hardfang attempt to stop Hale from reaching the exit. Continue to use the environment for cover and employ grenades and your weapons' secondary functions to safely reach the lift at the end of the path.

IN A DARKER PLACE

Chimeran Tunnels

IV. The Missions
BRACKNELL

Bracknell, England
13 July 1951—22:33 GMT

MISSION OVERVIEW

We set up a makeshift camp at a cove in Cardiff. The Chimera usually steer clear of the coast because they can't burrow through sand. I tried again to radio the Americans, but it was no use. We were on the Atlantic coast, and they were in the North Sea… if they were still there at all. Several hours had passed when I received a brief radio message from Hale. It was filled with static, but I could make out the words "power conduits" and "dead end." Beyond that, we only have speculation. But I believe he followed the conduits from within the Chimera's own underground tunnels.

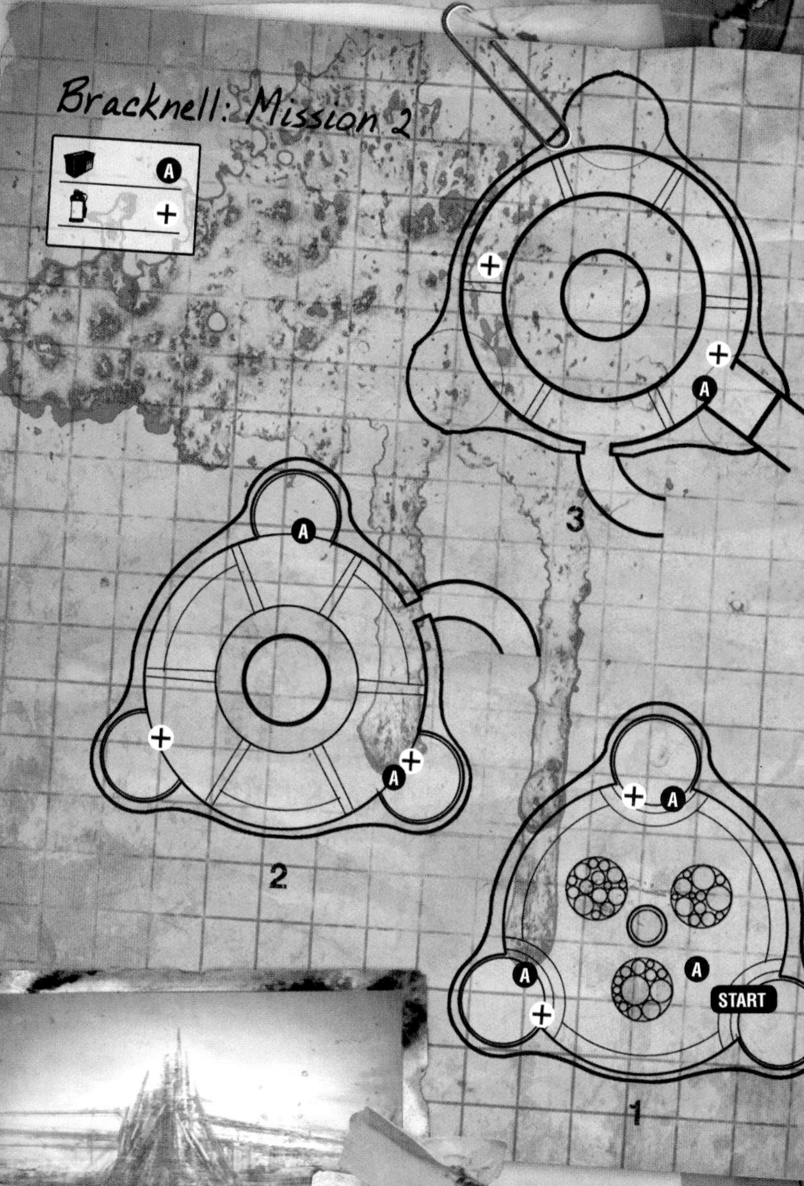

FIELD REPORT

Enemy Intel
Menial
Hybrid
Steelhead
Titan
Leaper
Gray Jack
Stalker

Hardware
M5A2 Carbine
Bullseye
Rossmore 236
Combat Shotgun
Auger
L23 Fareye
XR-005 Hailstorm
XR-003 Sapper
L209 LAARK
Frag Grenade
Hedgehog
Air-Fuel Grenade

Mission Objective

★ Escape the Tower.

United States Army Rangers
1st Regiment

THE ASCENT—TOWER AREA LEVEL #1

★ Escape the Tower

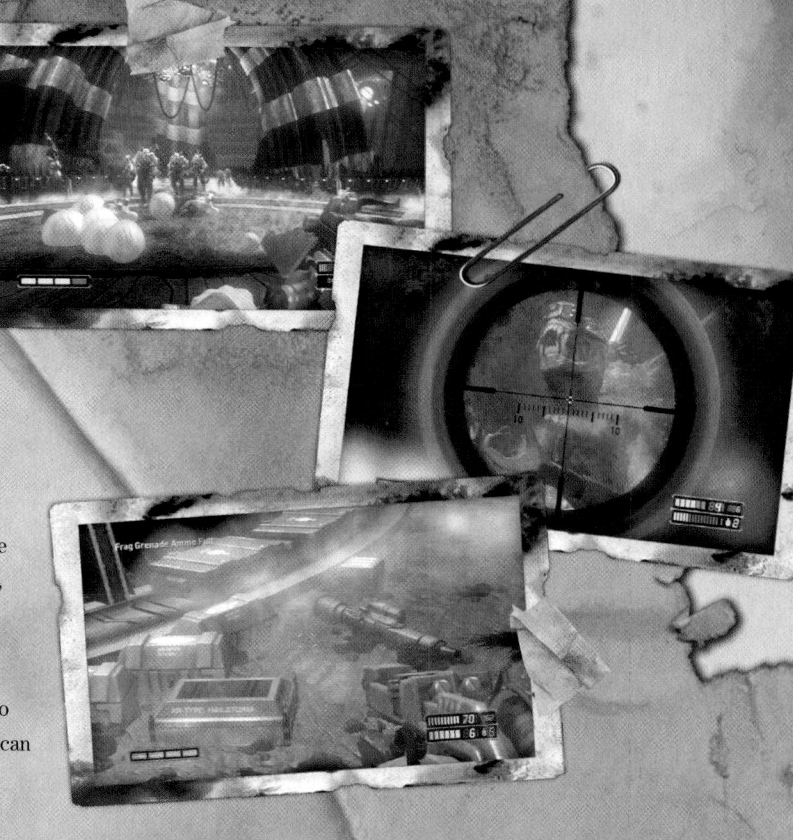

To escape the tower, Hale must endure one final push through its uppermost levels. You can think of this next area as a deadly gauntlet where survival is the ultimate goal.

The tower's upper-most level is comprised of three connecting areas, one on top of the other. The first one is overflowing with menacing Menials, so back into a corner to avoid an unforeseen attack from behind. Also, the XR-003 Sapper is a lot of fun to use on these mindless drones. Lay down a line of pulsating globules, then stand back and watch them fly.

Some Hybrids and Steelheads (they all drop from the platforms above) follow the Menials. This area doesn't have much cover, so quickly dispose of them. The Fareye, in conjunction with focus, can help your cause.

When all of the foes are history, pick up the items strewn about the area. In addition to various kinds of munitions, there is a new weapon here—the L209 LAARK. When you're ready to move on, locate the switch in one of the alcoves and turn it on to activate the lift.

L209 LAARK

WEAPON INTELLIGENCE

The L209 LAARK (Light Anti-Armor Rocket) was originally designed for use against Russian armored divisions. Since the Chimeran invasion, it has been successful against the Stalker and other heavy vehicles. Once fired, LAARK rockets are capable of user-guided maneuverability.

THE ASCENT—TOWER AREA LEVEL #2

The second level of the tower seems way too quiet. The only potential hostiles in view are the nests of Leaper Pods along the walkway. Suddenly, though, some Hybrids and Auger-wielding Steelheads emerge. The best defense here is to employ a variety of strong weapons and some grenades.

POD PERIL

Make sure you destroy the Leaper Pods with an explosive before getting too close. These creatures are faster and more aggressive than the earlier ones.

Continue to creep along the walkway and proceed slowly to avoid a potential Leaper assault. Some Steelheads stand between Hale and the exit, which leads to the tower's final level.

THE ASCENT—TOWER AREA LEVEL #3

This tunnel ramps upward toward the tower's uppermost level. Of course, it's lined with Leaper Pod nests that erupt if you get too close.

It's definitely slow going, as there are more Chimera waiting for Hale at the top of the ramp. Stay back and continue to use everything in your arsenal to fight them.

As soon as Hale pokes his head inside this area, he is already being targeted for elimination by the Hybrids inside. Tag and bag with the Bullseye, then take cover and pick them off from cover. Watch out for the Gray Jacks coming from the right side of the perimeter, too.

MORE FUEL FOR THE FIRE

There is a second L209 LAARK at the top of the ramp. Definitely grab it if you missed the first one in tower area #1.

STALKER SHOCKER

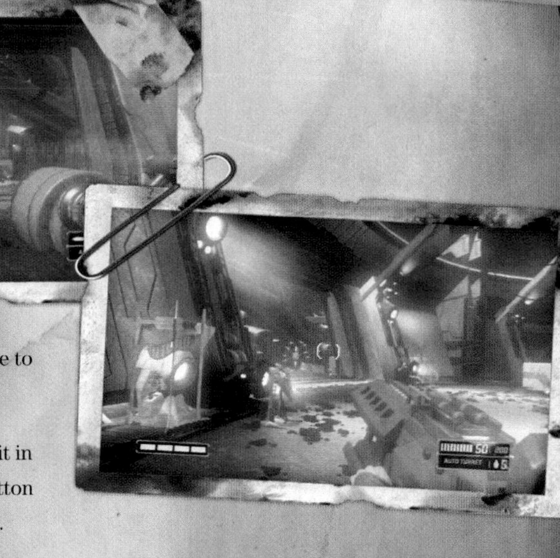

As soon as the perimeter is enemy-free, locate the doorway with switches on both sides. Activate each switch to open the door and get ready for a hardcore battle with a Chimeran Stalker.

Use a shot from the LAARK before the Stalker has a chance to return fire. Follow that up with regular rounds from the Hailstorm. Shoot at the Stalker's legs, or ground below them, and most shots will hit the power core. Also, try using a grenade to weaken the Stalker even more.

Next, switch back to the LAARK and discharge a rocket, then press and hold L1 to suspend it in mid-air. Next, aim the barrel of the LAARK in the direction of the Stalker and release the button to send the rocket into the mechanical monster. A direct hit should rip the Stalker to shreds.

A DESPERATE GAMBLE

City Outskirts

London, England
14 July 1951—05:05 GMT

MISSION OVERVIEW

It was several hours before I heard from Hale again. He told me he was in London and he asked if snow was normal for July. He described a Tower in the middle of London. It was one far bigger than what they had found in Somerset, with power conduits emerging in all directions. He said if we destroy the Tower, we destroy the Chimera. I didn't know what to make of it. For all I knew, Hale was completely mad. And, even if what he was saying was true, we had no idea how to destroy the Tower. But there was one new factor working in our favor. I had contacted the Americans and they had joined forces with us in Cardiff. I decided to gamble that Hale was right. I convinced the Americans to help launch a full assault on the Tower. We were bringing everything we had to London. I was counting on Hale to clear out a landing zone. If he couldn't take out the Stalkers, the mission would be over before it began.

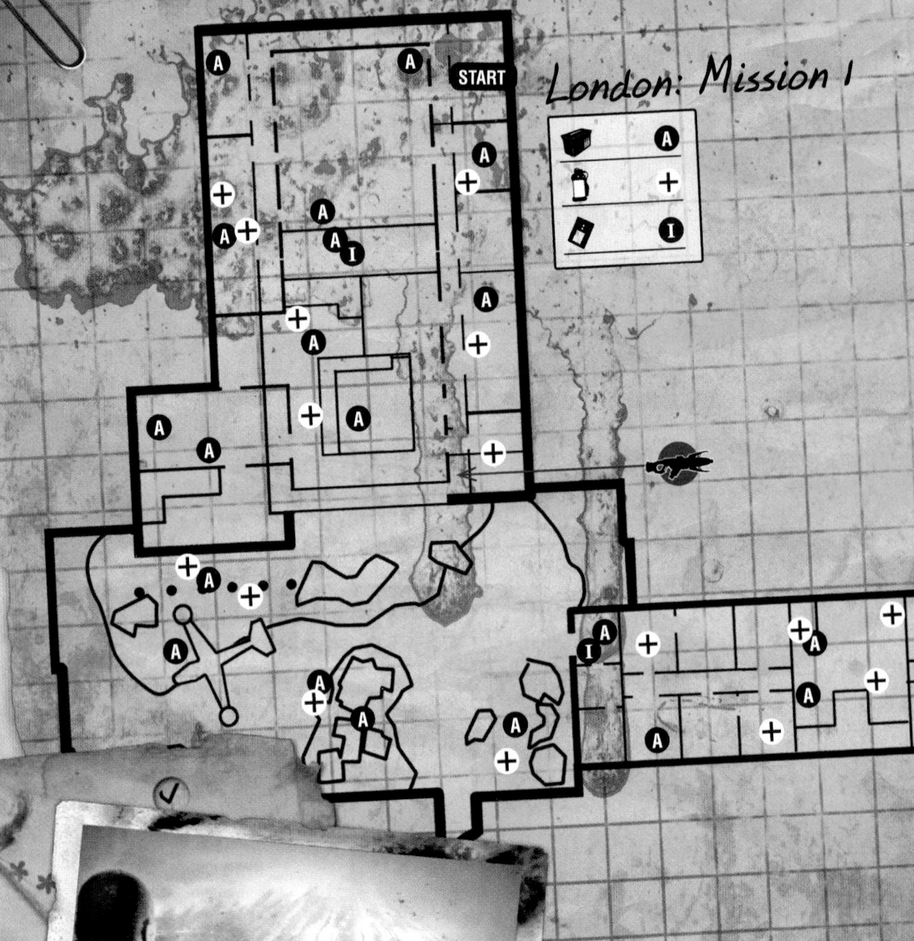

FIELD REPORT

Enemy Intel
Hybrid
Steelhead
Roller
Hardfang
Slipskull

Hardware
M5A2 Carbine
Bullseye
Rossmore 236
Combat Shotgun
Auger
L23 Fareye
XR-005 Hailstorm
XR-003 Sapper
L209 LAARK
Frag Grenade
Hedgehog
Air-Fuel Grenade

Mission Objective

★ Get to the Central Tower.

★ Find a landing zone for the transport.

United States Army Rangers
1st Regiment

LONDON BRIDGES

★ Get to the Central Tower

Hale starts off in a central station on the outskirts of London. For the allied forces to launch an assault on the tower, he must clear a landing zone for them. At the moment, his primary objective is to make it to the central tower in one piece.

The station seems abandoned and deserted, but that is far from the case. Stay alert and at the ready while exploring the various rooms and storefronts on either side of the station, stockpiling ammunition along the way.

Before you leave this portion of the station and enter the next area, locate the small grate along the back wall near a set of vending machines. Use a melee attack to break the rusted bars; now Hale can crawl inside the ductwork and retrieve an Intel Item.

DOCUMENT INTELLIGENCE #29

Weather

This co-pilot's log details how his VTOL went down due to the strange weather patterns. His leg was broken in the crash and he managed to drag himself into this crawlspace where he died alone, but at least with dignity.

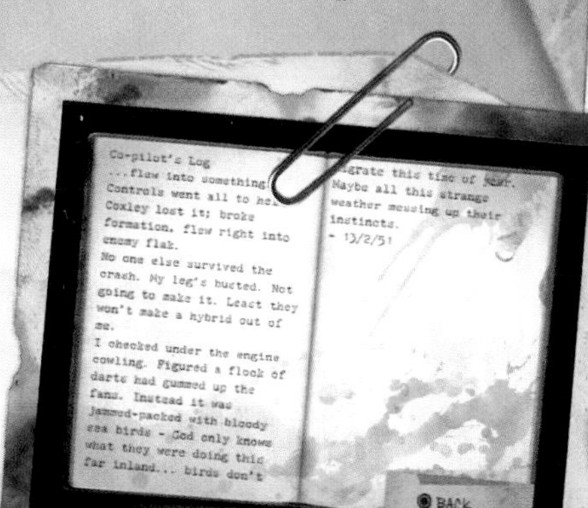

Back out in the station proper, and locate the arched entryway leading to the next area. As Hale approaches, the all too familiar sound of a Leaper onslaught is heard. This time, it's the ultra aggressive Rollers. Before entering the archway, throw an Air Fuel Grenade at the arch, get close enough to make the Rollers and Steelhead attack, then back up and let them hit the fire.

To make things interesting, an Auger-wielding Steelhead joins the fray. You can't hide or take cover from his fire, so flush him out using the Bullseye's tag function or launch an Auto-turret with the Hailstorm.

KILL OR BE KILLED

It's extremely important to eliminate the Hardfang as quickly as possible. Look for it to emerge from the platform in the center of the station. If it reaches Hale's location, its Arc Charger will slice him to pieces in seconds. If you can't snipe the foe with the Fareye, switch to the Auger and launch a force shield to protect Hale from its blasts.

KINGS CROSS

Things get even tougher in the next section of the station. As soon as Hale sets foot in this area, some Chimera come down the path and attack. Their ranks include Hybrids, Steelheads and a Hardfang.

Continue to stay back and snipe the remaining Hybrids on the walkways. When the shooting stops, do a thorough search of the storefronts, as well as the rooms on the opposite side. You need to locate the stairs near the dividing wall.

Upstairs, the Chimera launch another assault. Have a strong weapon at the ready and be prepared to return fire. The Auger is a good weapon to use in this area, as you can return their fire through the walls and eliminate them while dodging their attacks.

Things don't stay quiet for long. At the walkway along the back wall, a second Roller attack occurs. On the other side, a Hardfang and his Hybrid brethren launch an ambush from inside the storefronts. Stay focused and use the appropriate weapon for each. Use the Hailstorm's regular ammo or a well-placed Hedgehog Grenade to blow them to pieces. To exit the area, take the stairs down to the area outside.

SNIPING IN THE SNOW

When Hale reaches these windows, equip the Fareye and pick off the advancing Chimera on the snowy banks outside. There are quite a few Hybrids patrolling the area, as well as one operating a turret, which is preventing the allied forces from landing.

THE WEATHER OUTSIDE IS FRIGHTFUL

The only way to continue is through the downed VTOL in the center of the square. Look for a roving pack of Rollers that attempt to stop Hale's progress, as well as more Hybrids and Steelheads on the other side.

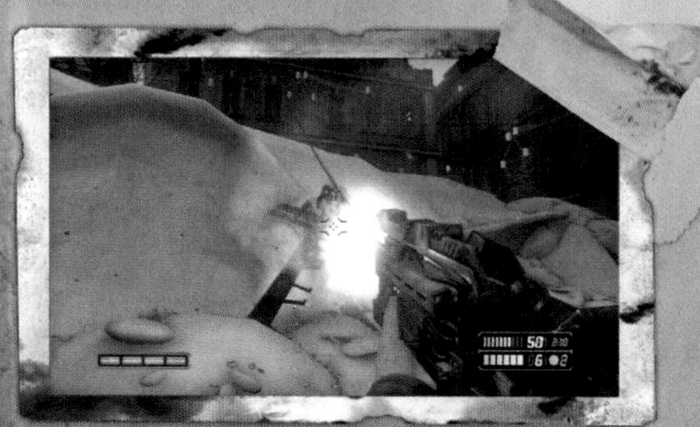

THE MAKESHIFT BUNKER

When it's safe to do so, enter the makeshift bunker in the center of the square and stock up on various munitions and Sym-Bac serum.

United States Army Rangers
1st Regiment

ROOM FOR ONE

★ Find a Landing Zone for the Transport

The ultimate destination is the tunnel that is burrowed into the snow bank located near the southeast corner of the square. The tunnel leads into a Chimera-infested hotel.

Inside the hotel, proceed through the dark hallways until you locate the room with a pile of stacked furniture and debris in the back corner. Crawl through the opening underneath the debris to enter the room, then search for the Intel Item next to a dead soldier.

DOCUMENT INTELLIGENCE #30

Drowned

This scrap of paper, accompanied by a map, chronicles a soldier's desperate fight for survival against the cunning Chimera. When they couldn't find a way to burrow into Central Command, these creatures flooded it by burrowing a tunnel to the River Thames.

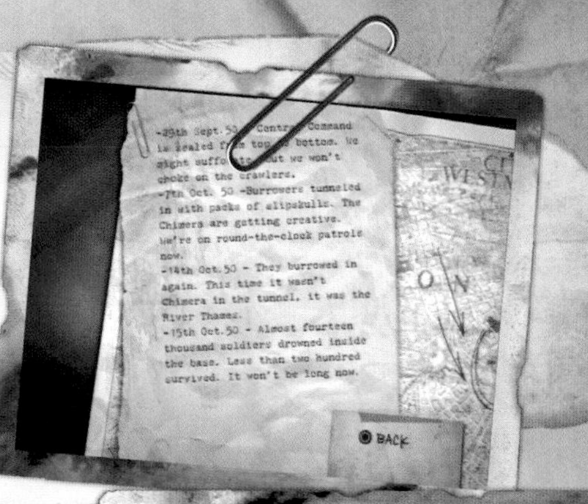

-29th Sept. 5[illegible] Centr[illegible] Command is sealed f[illegible] top [illegible] bottom. We might suffo[illegible] but we won't choke on the crawlers.
-7th Oct. 50 -Burrowers tunneled in with packs of slipskulls. The Chimera are getting creative. We're on round-the-clock patrols now.
-14th Oct. 50 - They burrowed in again. This time it wasn't Chimera in the tunnel, it was the River Thames.
-15th Oct. 50 - Almost fourteen thousand soldiers drowned inside the base. Less than two hundred survived. It won't be long now.

Back in the main portion of the hotel, all hell breaks loose. Hybrids and a Hardfang attack from the holes in the walls, attempting to catch Hale in their crossfire. Take cover and quickly pick them off.

The assault continues near the lobby in the form of some crafty Slipskulls and a pack of Rollers. Use the Carbine on the Rollers, then turn the Bullseye on the Slipskulls, tagging them first.

Stay near a wall or corner for cover and use the Fareye to pick off the next foes. After defeating the final Chimera, take the stairs to the upper floor and move through the final rooms to exit the area.

ICE AND IRON

City Outskirts

London: Mission 2 Floor 1

START

London, England
14 July 1951—07:42 GMT

MISSION OVERVIEW

Hale had cleared a landing zone, but an unexpected squad of Stalkers hampered our plans. We needed Hale to destroy the Chimeran anti-aircraft defenses—and quick. We couldn't have another landing like in York. Once again, we put our faith and very lives in this man's hands—it was up to him to clear out the Stalkers. I sent in some heavy equipment to his position, but he needed to make a clearing first. A big clearing.

***FIELD REPOR

Enemy Intel
Stalker
Titan
Hybrid
Widowmaker
Steelhead

Hardware
M5A2 Carbine
Bullseye
Rossmore 236 Combat Shotgun
Auger
L23 Fareye
XR-005 Hailstorm
XR-003 Sapper
L209 LAARK
Frag Grenade
M-12 Sabertooth
Frag Grenade

Mission Objective

- ★ Destroy the Stalker.
- ★ Destroy all Stalkers in the area.
- ★ Hold off the Chimera until reinforcements arrive.

CAT AND MOUSE

★ Destroy the Stalker

This suicide mission pits Hale against a Stalker. Unfortunately, there are no other soldiers to lure its attention, making targeting its weak spot very tough. It's not impossible, however; you need to be patient and careful, making use of the many makeshift bunkers placed around the battlefield for cover. Kick things off by using the LAARK and launching a rocket at the Stalker as it advances on the battlefield.

As soon as the shot is off, quickly run and duck into the bunker for cover. Almost all of these bunkers have a few canisters of Sym-Bac serum and ammunition, including a 40mm grenade for your Carbine.

COVER IMPERFECT

Even though these bunkers provide protection, they are not foolproof. There are many holes and open areas that expose Hale to the Stalker's weapons. Whenever you're inside a bunker, stay crouched, keep an eye on the Stalker's location, and make sure there is a solid object between Hale and the Stalker's fire.

The Stalker mainly uses its autocannon, which fires in bursts. Listen for it to temporarily stop for a second or two in between its attacks—this is your opportunity to retaliate. When you hear the Stalker stop firing, quickly jump out from cover, equip the Hailstorm (if you have any ammo) and aim at the legs or directly beneath the Stalker.

During this battle, it's possible to catch the Stalker from behind. This doesn't happen very often, as it does its best to keep facing Hale no matter where he is on the battlefield. But if you manage to stealthily get behind it by sneaking around or staying put long enough for it to walk away, you can duck out and target the Power Core set in its torso on its back side.

Once you've used the Carbine to launch a grenade, quickly run out from cover during a lull in the attack and run to the next bunker to collect another 40mm grenade or more Sym-Bac serum. Wait for the next lull and then duck back out and launch another. If you get caught within its fire, take quick evasive action and dive back into the nearest bunker.

After one or two direct hits, the Stalker mixes up its attacks and launches a barrage of missiles. Move out from under the bunker (if you're in one) and keep moving to avoid taking damage from their explosions.

GRAB AND FRAG

At some point, you need to scavenge for more powerful ammunition. There is a cache of Frag Grenades along the sidewalk near the small bunker to the north. Grab them and keep moving to avoid the Stalker's fire.

Continue to chip away at the Stalker using everything in your arsenal. If you run out of grenades, switch to a strong weapon and do your best to target it from behind. Although its weak spot is the Power Core, this doesn't mean you can't destroy it from the front. Continue to shoot at it from any angle until it blows up.

THE BIG GUNS

Don't celebrate just yet—your mission is far from over. Once the Stalker has been destroyed, a Titan appears on the battlefield. Switch to the Bullseye and tag it, then keep moving and strafing around it to stay out of range and avoid its fire. This tactic works exceptionally well and can take out a Titan in no time flat.

United States Army Rangers
1st Regiment

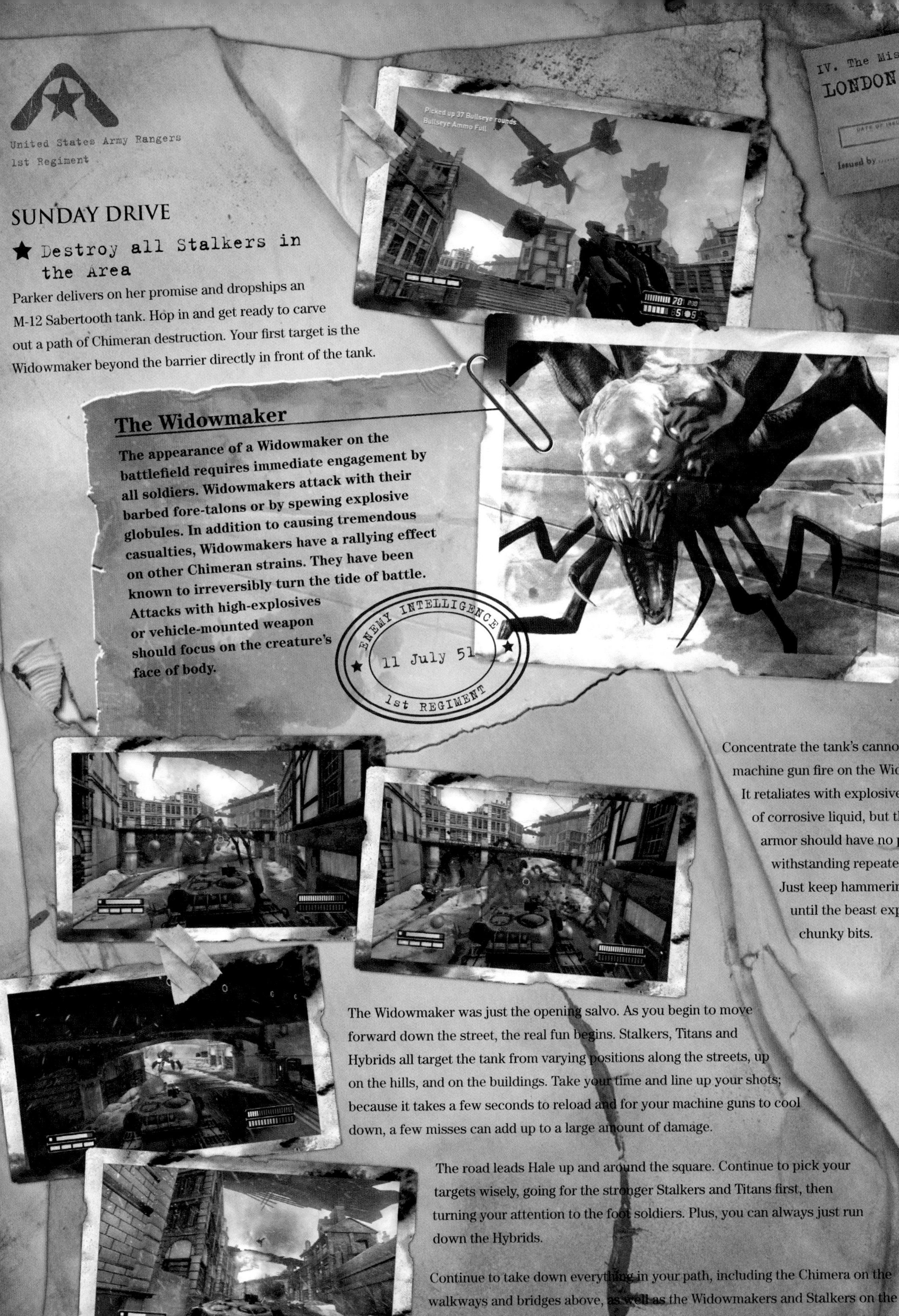

SUNDAY DRIVE

★ Destroy all Stalkers in the Area

Parker delivers on her promise and dropships an M-12 Sabertooth tank. Hop in and get ready to carve out a path of Chimeran destruction. Your first target is the Widowmaker beyond the barrier directly in front of the tank.

The Widowmaker

The appearance of a Widowmaker on the battlefield requires immediate engagement by all soldiers. Widowmakers attack with their barbed fore-talons or by spewing explosive globules. In addition to causing tremendous casualties, Widowmakers have a rallying effect on other Chimeran strains. They have been known to irreversibly turn the tide of battle. Attacks with high-explosives or vehicle-mounted weapon should focus on the creature's face of body.

Concentrate the tank's cannon and machine gun fire on the Widowmaker. It retaliates with explosive globules of corrosive liquid, but the tank's armor should have no problem withstanding repeated attacks. Just keep hammering away at it until the beast explodes into chunky bits.

The Widowmaker was just the opening salvo. As you begin to move forward down the street, the real fun begins. Stalkers, Titans and Hybrids all target the tank from varying positions along the streets, up on the hills, and on the buildings. Take your time and line up your shots; because it takes a few seconds to reload and for your machine guns to cool down, a few misses can add up to a large amount of damage.

The road leads Hale up and around the square. Continue to pick your targets wisely, going for the stronger Stalkers and Titans first, then turning your attention to the foot soldiers. Plus, you can always just run down the Hybrids.

Continue to take down everything in your path, including the Chimera on the walkways and bridges above, as well as the Widowmakers and Stalkers on the ground. Eventually, the road leads to a bridge where you can exit the tank.

United States Army Rangers
1st Regiment

A DAY AT THE OFFICE

★ Hold off the Chimera Until Reinforcements Arrive

On foot, make your way to the office building at the base of the bridge. Once inside, Hale must hold off the remaining Chimera until the allies arrive. The lower floor is quiet and unoccupied. Take this time to explore and seek out an Intel Item. Its location is behind the counter in the room with the boarded up windows to the left.

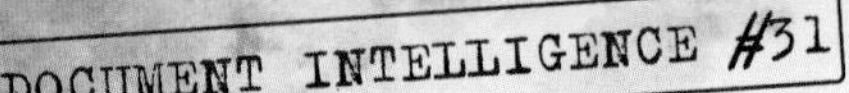

DOCUMENT INTELLIGENCE #31

Goliath

This journal entry, dated May 1st, details what it's like to encounter a Goliath and how the soldier and his rag tag team were able to bring it down.

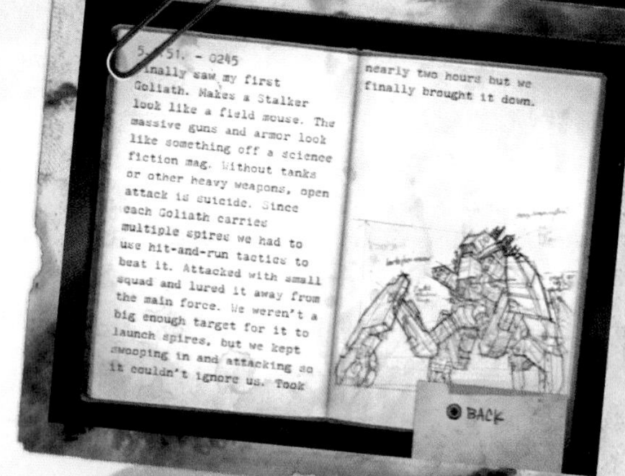

51. - 0245
inally saw my first Goliath. Makes a Stalker look like a field mouse. The massive guns and armor look like something off a science fiction mag. Without tanks or other heavy weapons, open attack is suicide. Since each Goliath carries multiple spires we had to use hit-and-run tactics to beat it. Attacked with small squad and lured it away from the main force. We weren't a big enough target for it to launch spires, but we kept swooping in and attacking so it couldn't ignore us. Took nearly two hours but we finally brought it down.

BACK

There are a few other rooms and hallways down on the bottom floor, but the real action is on the higher floors. Locate the staircase next to the elevator and head on up.

Upstairs, a cave-in blocks Hale's path from returning down to the first floor. The Chimera pick this loud distraction to launch their attack. Equip the Auger and pinpoint their location, which is the next set of stairs leading to the third floor. You should be able to kill a few through the wall; if any make it out into the open, use a force shield for protection.

When it's safe, head upstairs and continue to sweep the floor for more Chimera. Up here, Hale encounters a few more Hybrid, including one in the billiards room. Once they've been eliminated, the mission is complete.

BURNING BRIDGES

River Thames

London, England
14 July 1951—08:49 GMT

MISSION OVERVIEW

Our forces arrived in London nearly unscathed. It was difficult not to stare in awe at the Tower. We had only fled London six months earlier, and now it was almost unrecognizable. London was covered in snow, just like Hale said. I knew the Chimera thrived in cold weather, but it was hard to fathom they were somehow altering the climate. Even so, the power conduits, the snow and the Tower had to be related. I just had no idea how. There was no time to think about it. Chimeran armies were already guarding the Tower and more would be coming. We set up the tanks in assault formation and started across the Tower Bridge. The last tanks were crossing the bridge when scouts reported Goliaths approaching from behind. We had to destroy the Tower Bridge before they caught up to our tanks. Hale and a few other soldiers took up defensive positions while we set the charges.

London: Mission 3

START

FIELD REPORT

Enemy Intel
Hybrid
Steelhead
Stalker
Widowmaker
Roller
Leaper
Hardfang
Gray Jack

Hardware
M5A2 Carbine
Bullseye
Rossmore 236
Combat Shotgun
Auger
L23 Fareye
XR-005 Hailstorm
XR-003 Sapper
L209 LAARK
Frag Grenade
M-12 Sabertooth
Air-Fuel Grenade

Mission Objective

- ★ Hold back the Chimera until the bridge is destroyed.
- ★ Rendezvous with Cartwright's team.

United States Army Rangers
1st Regiment

KITCHEN SINK

★ Hold Back the Chimera Until the Bridge Is Destroyed

The resistance is planning to blow up the Tower Bridge to keep the Chimeran Goliaths, huge mechanical destroyers, from crossing to the other side. Start this mission by equipping the Fareye and picking off the Hybrids from a safe distance.

VANTAGE POINT

Don't spend a lot of time trying to eliminate every Hybrid. If you linger for too long, Hale will have a Stalker for company. When your allies retreat, quickly abandon low ground and make a dash for the second story of the burned out building to the east or the building to the southwest.

There are some nice supplies on the second story, so pick them up. Stock up on LAARK rockets and equip this weapon, then fire at the Stalker down on the street. Two or three shots should take it down.

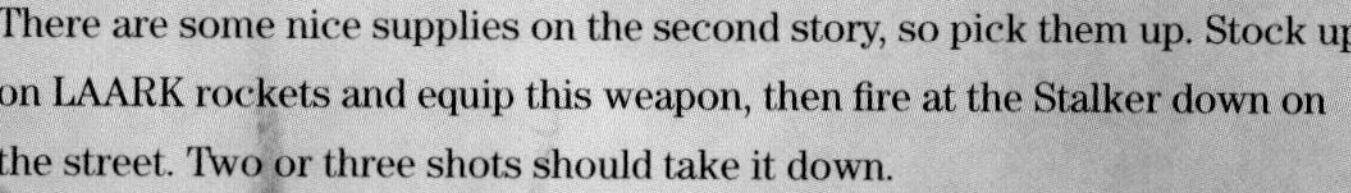

Shortly after the first strike, a second Stalker appears on the battlefield. Before it arrives, take cover and use the Fareye with focus to pick off as many Hybrids as possible.

The second Stalker appears from the east. Use the building's walls for cover, then pop out and fire off a rocket. Try to save at least one or two rockets for what comes next, if possible. A good alternative to use is the Hailstorm's Auto-turret, as well as Air-Fuel grenades. Using the Auger's force shield is also a good idea for extra protection.

The grand finale appears in the form of a massive Widowmaker. This vile, disgusting creature spews pulsating, acidic blobs that burst in deadly corrosive mist.

WATCH YOUR BACK!

There is a lot to deal with down on the street. However, don't forget to check your back once in a while, as a crafty Hybrid may sneak up the stairs.

Hold your position on the second story and begin the last assault by launching an Auto-turret at the Widowmaker, followed by any remaining LAARK rockets.

Grenades also work well in this situation, including the Hedgehog and Air-Fuel Grenades. Continue to avoid the acidic sacs while unleashing your arsenal of strong weapons and grenades against the Widowmaker until it explodes.

THE TIDES OF WAR

With the Chimera held in check, the resistance can blow up the Tower Bridge and hamper the Goliaths' approach. Could this be the turning point of the war?

United States Army Rangers
1st Regiment

ROOFTOPS—PART #1

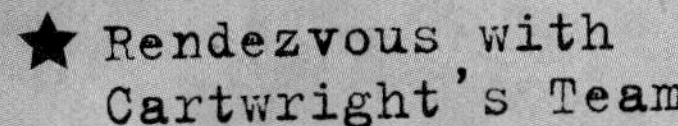

★ Rendezvous with Cartwright's Team

After the dust settles, return to the street and survey the carnage while restocking Hale's munitions stores. When you're ready, locate the opening between the buildings along the west side of the street.

There are two paths on this street. The left path leads down a snowy alleyway that converges with the next street over. Take this path first and use the Fareye to eliminate the patrolling Hybrids and the Steelhead at the end of the street. Also note that mines line the street, hidden by the debris and rubble.

The reason for this detour becomes clear when you arrive at the small, rubble-filled alcove on the right. Jump onto the debris to grab the ammo and the Intel Item.

STEALTH KILL

You may have noticed that it is possible to sneak up on enemies from behind and execute a crippling one-hit kill. Utilize this technique when the opportunity arises.

DOCUMENT INTELLIGENCE #32

Construction

This journal has entries starting from October 10th through November 1st. Its author survived long enough to witness the construction of the massive tower.

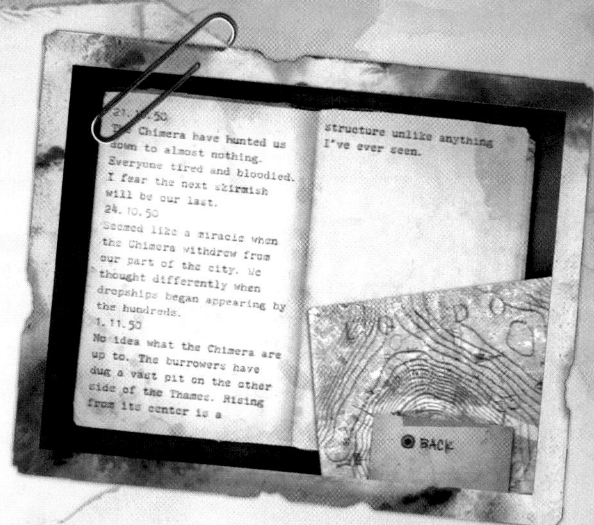
21.10.50
The Chimera have hunted us down to almost nothing. Everyone tired and bloodied. I fear the next skirmish will be our last.

24.10.50
Seemed like a miracle when the Chimera withdrew from our part of the city. We thought differently when dropships began appearing by the hundreds.

1.11.50
No idea what the Chimera are up to. The burrowers have dug a vast pit on the other side of the Thames. Rising from its center is a structure unlike anything I've ever seen.

Return to the main path and enter the burned out building on the right. Take the stairs to the second floor. The building across the way is just close enough that Hale can jump to it. Hop onto the wooden pallets and jump. After a successful jump, two Hybrids come charging at Hale with weapons blazing.

To reach the next rooftop, you need to make another leap. First, though, use the Auger and scan the area for enemies on the other side. When the coast is clear, jump across to finish what you started.

Drop a few grenades on the Steelheads below, or hop down from the roof and blast them with a strong weapon like the Hailstorm. Next, follow the street to the north through the archway and into the small courtyard.

Crawl through the hole in the wall to exit the courtyard, but stay on high alert at all times. In this case, a couple of Leapers and a Gray Jack are looking for someone to fight.

The path continues on the fire escape, which is located along the side of the left-most building. However, before taking this staircase, head to the end of the alleyway to collect another Intel Item.

DOCUMENT INTELLIGENCE #33

Demolitions

These schematics illustrate how Southwark Bridge was rigged with explosives. The question is, who already did this?

Southwark Bridge
Charges placed here.
Abutments are iron-reinforced concrete.
Single simultaneous detonation at marked locations should result in total collapse.

ROOFTOPS—PART #2

Climb the fire escape to return to the rooftops. More foes target Hale from strategic positions, so use the Fareye to deal with some of the foes and switch to another weapon for any close-range fighting.

Locate the top of the archway that connects the building you are on with the one across the way. Walk across the archway to reach the other side, but prepare for more resistance. Use the high elevation point to your advantage and toss a Frag or Air-Fuel Grenade at any enemies.

Back out on the street, a final squad of Chimera attack from the Electric Railway entrance. Use the Fareye to eliminate one or two of them—especially the Steelhead—then finish off the remaining enemies with the Auger and a force shield. To exit this area, take the stairs into the Electric Railway.

ON THE ICE

River Thames

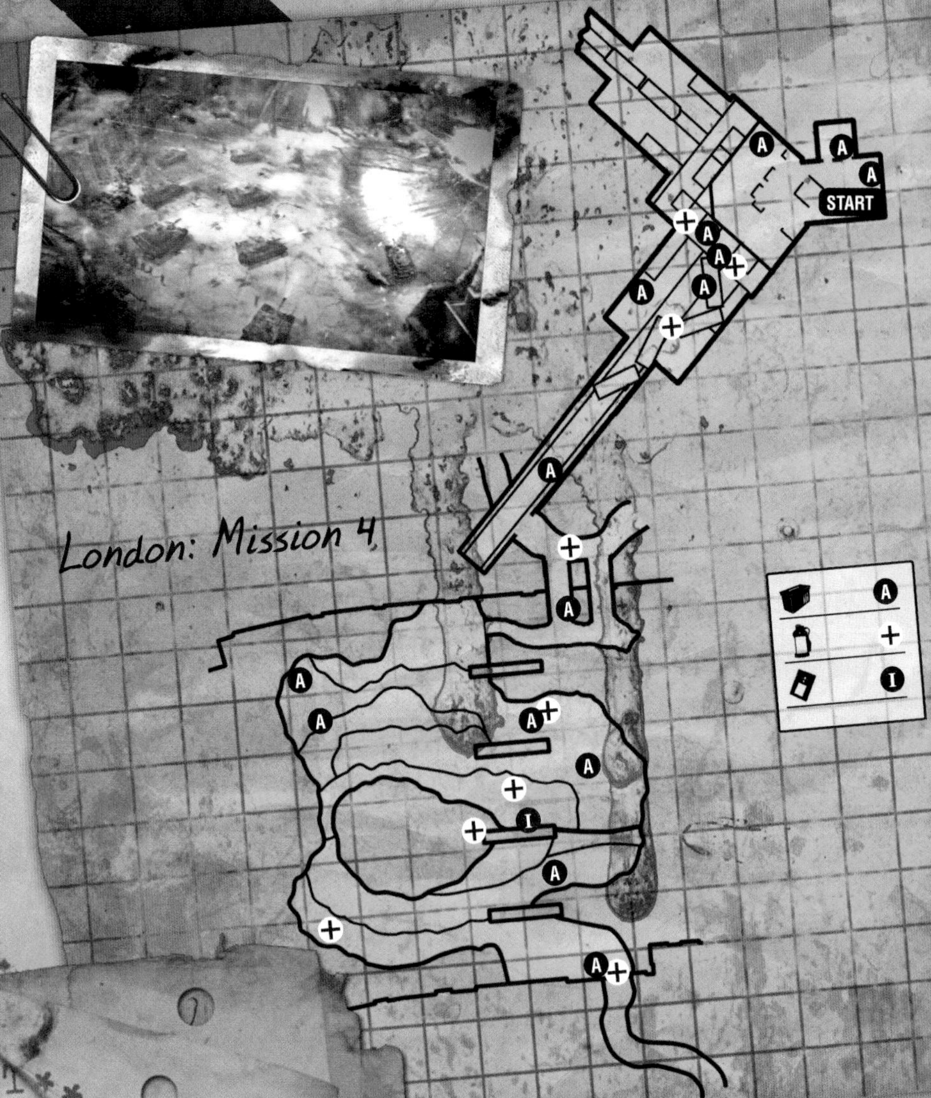

London, England
14 July 1951—09:38 GMT

MISSION OVERVIEW

The outlook of the battle was becoming grimmer by the second. Our tanks had killed legions of Chimera, but they still poured out of the Tower. The Chimeran forces were holding us in check while their Behemoths closed in on Southwark Bridge. With Tower Bridge destroyed, there was no possibility for retreat. The team I sent to destroy Southwark Bridge was not responding. It would only be a matter of time before we heard the spires in the air.

London: Mission 4

START

FIELD REPORT

Enemy Intel
Hybrid
Steelhead
Leaper
Hardfang
Slipskull
Menial

Hardware
M5A2 Carbine
Bullseye
Rossmore 236
Combat Shotgun
Auger
L23 Fareye
XR-005 Hailstorm
XR-003 Sapper
L209 LAARK
Frag Grenade
M-12 Sabertooth
Air-Fuel Grenade
Hedgehog Grenades

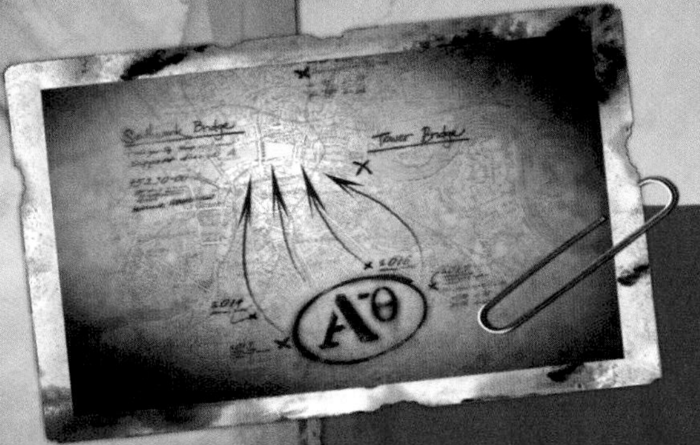

Mission Objective

★ Destroy Southwark Bridge.

A TRIP WORTH TAKING

★ Destroy Southwark Bridge

Hale must destroy the second bridge leading to the tower. To reach it, he must journey through the Electric Railway station, which is brimming with Chimera. After turning the corner inside the first tunnel, use the Auger to create a force shield for protection, then quickly switch to the Fareye and start picking off the multiple Hybrids and Steelheads in the room beyond.

AUTO AID

There are several enemies inside this room. If you're not careful, they will overwhelm Hale in a matter of seconds. For extra protection during this battle, use the Hailstorm and launch an Auto-turret.

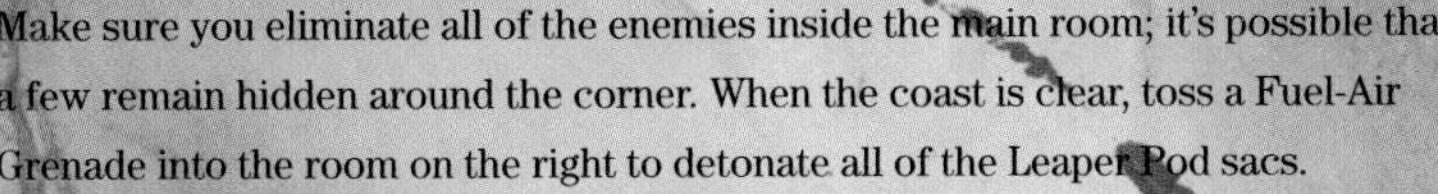

Make sure you eliminate all of the enemies inside the main room; it's possible that a few remain hidden around the corner. When the coast is clear, toss a Fuel-Air Grenade into the room on the right to detonate all of the Leaper Pod sacs.

The stairs on the left lead to a dead end, but the extra Sym-Bac serum and Bullseye ammo make it worth the short trip.

The stairs on the right lead to a hornet's nest of Chimera. Use the Auger and stay at the top of the stairs, then scan the area below through the floor and wall to dispose of a few enemies. Use a strong weapon, such as the Hailstorm, to blast back the Steelheads running up the stairs.

CLOSE-RANGE COMBAT

If a few foes manage to breach your defenses, quickly switch to the Rossmore and take them down as they approach.

There are still a few enemies down by the train tracks. Sprint down the stairs to avoid any Auger fire and launch an Auto-turret to quickly dispose of these beasts.

Take the stairs on the opposite side of the train tracks around to the next section of the station. Hold your position at the top of the stairs and use the Fareye to locate and target the Chimera below.

At this point, some Slipskulls join the fray. Stay as far back as possible (preferably near the top of the stairs) and use the Bullseye to tag and bag them. You can lay down an Auger force shield for extra protection if Hale's health gets low.

Now travel from one derailed train car to the next one to find a tunnel at the other end. Of course, a few Steelheads are waiting for Hale when he arrives. Toss a Hedgehog or Frag Grenade into the tunnel or launch an Auto-turret to get rid of them.

IN THE COLD

The tunnel leads to a frozen riverbed near the Southwark Bridge. Enemy resistance continues to be fierce, so use everything in your arsenal to stay alive. Use the Auger force shield to keep Hale's health at a maximum.

Eliminate the Hybrids along the icy path, but don't forget about the enemies near the boulders. Things go from bad to worse when Hale reaches the end of the path. There are two Auger-wielding Steelheads on the rigde. Avoid their blasts and toss a Hedgehog Grenade toward their position.

Next, get onto the ridge and follow it to the right until you hear the sound of a turret. Stay back and pinpoint its location, then toss an Air-Fuel Grenade at the turret's operator.

Double back the other way and head underneath the bridge's second arch, then grab the extra LAARK rockets on the other side. Also, don't forget to pick up the Intel Item at the top of a snow bank underneath the fourth arch.

DOCUMENT INTELLIGENCE #34

Loved Ones

This sad letter, dated September 12th, 1950, is from the British Department of Civil Defense sent to a Lt. Sean Wickham. It was sent to inform him that his beloved wife Emily was not included in the first tier evacuation plans and sent to holdover camp in London. Included with the latter is a picture and her locket.

12th September, 195

Dear Lt. Sean Wickham,

We regret to inform you that your wife, Emily Wickham, has not been designated for inclusion in the preliminary stage evacuation. Mrs. Wickham has been transported to a holdover camp in London to await passage on the next available vessel. It is our hope to save every British soul.

Thank you for your understanding this most dire hour.

Lt. Col. Hamish Robson
Regional Commissioner,
Department of Civil Defence

Go underneath the third arch and proceed up the path. Continue up the path and prepare to fight a few more Hybrids. These foes are tossing Hedgehogs Grenades like they're going out of style, so stay on the move.

All that stands in Hale's way now are a few Menials. If you're still on the ridge above them, shoot them from this vantage point, then drop down and follow the path until you reach a dead soldier and a detonator.

Hale then blows up the bridge, but not before a Goliath makes it safely across. It's up to Hale and Cartwright to take down the Goliath the hard way.

GIANT SLAYER

River Thames

NORTHERN COMMAND
CLASSIFIED

London, England
14 July 1951—10:55 GMT

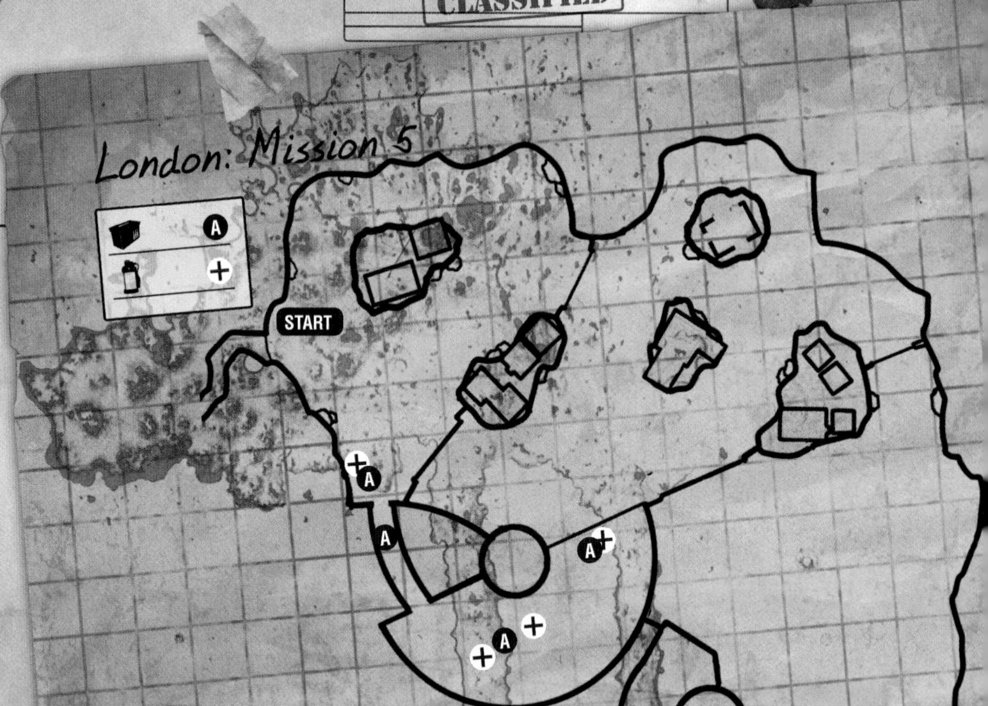

MISSION OVERVIEW

It was up to Hale and Cartwright to eliminate the Goliath that made it across the bridge. We know from earlier reports that fighting one of these beasts without the aid of heavy artillery is a death sentence. All they had was the weapons they were carrying and the use of a LU-P Lynx. If they were going to bring it down and reach the tower, they would need to find some much heavier firepower.

London: Mission 5

START

FIELD REPORT

Enemy Intel
Stalker
Hybrid
Steelhead
Goliath
Widowmaker

Hardware
M5A2 Carbine
Bullseye
Rossmore 236 Combat Shotgun
Auger
L23 Fareye
XR-005 Hailstorm
XR-003 Sapper
L209 LAARK
Frag Grenade
M-12 Sabertooth
Air-Fuel Grenade
Hedgehog Grenades

Mission Objective

★ Commandeer a Stalker. ★ Join the Assault on the Tower.

FIRST ENCOUNTERS

★ Commandeer a Stalker

With Hale at the wheel and Cartwright operating the Lynx's turret, the duo must eliminate the roving Stalker and then get inside the tower to secure one of their own. The best strategy to take against the Stalker is to stay inside the Lynx and constantly drive around it in circles.

HEAVIER FIREPOWER

With the Stalker out of the way, drive south and locate the entrance to the tower. There is a Hybrid welcoming committee waiting for Hale and Cartwright. You can attempt to mow them down with the Lynx, or hop out and pick them off from afar.

Enter the tower and continue to pick off the Chimera inside from afar using the Fareye. Watch out for the Auger-wielding Steelheads and make them your top priority. An empty Stalker waits for Hale and Cartwright at the end of the path. Eliminate the few remaining Steelheads and then get inside the Stalker.

CARBINE + GRENADE LAUNCHER = QUICK KILL

Don't hesitate to use the Carbine's M200 40mm Grenade Launcher. Although this an older weapon, it is still extremely useful to use when fighting clusters of Chimera.

TO DESTROY A GOLIATH

★ Join the Assault on the Tower

Once inside the Stalker, break through the small barrier and proceed to the snowy landscape. The Goliath is fast approaching; this will be a difficult battle. The Goliath appears from the northwest, so get in position and start firing as soon as it appears.

The Goliath

Goliaths are massive devices that the Chimera use to subjugate entire cities. They employ concussion mortar batteries to soften up opposition. Entire companies have broken under mortar barrages, forcing them to run for their lives. This exposes them to the Goliath's most fearsome weapon—the Spire. Spires are biological warfare missiles that deliver payloads of Chimeran Crawlers. A single Spire can infect thousands and Goliaths always have more than one.

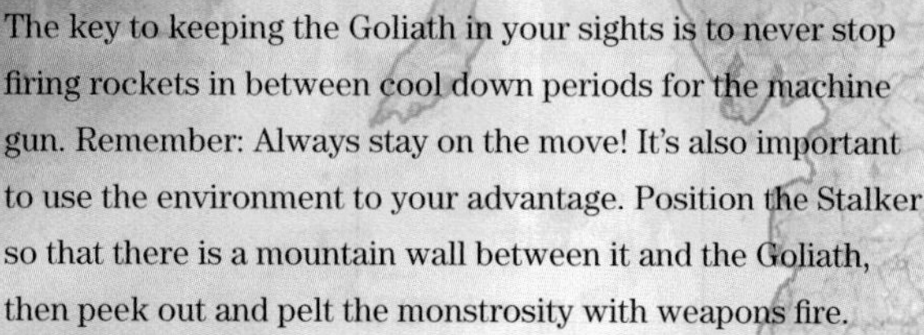

The key to keeping the Goliath in your sights is to never stop firing rockets in between cool down periods for the machine gun. Remember: Always stay on the move! It's also important to use the environment to your advantage. Position the Stalker so that there is a mountain wall between it and the Goliath, then peek out and pelt the monstrosity with weapons fire.

It's also important to quickly get a burst of speed (press ⊗) and take evasive action when the Goliath launches a rocket. Doing so should enable you to avoid a direct hit. Unfortunately, this fight is just the beginning. The battle wages on and Hale's attention is required at the base of the tower, where the allied assault is taking place.

ASSAULT ON THE TOWER

The tower entrance is due south. There are some more Stalkers to battle along the way, too. It's important to note that these Stalkers are a bit more mobile, which makes them quite dangerous. There are also some Hybrid foot soldiers located near the tower entrance. Wipe them all out, then approach the entrance to dismount the Stalker and head inside.

BELLY OF THE BEAST

Inside the tower, things go from bad to worse—much, much worse. A Widowmaker breaks through the wall and is looking for lunch. The key to surviving this battle is to stay on the move and avoid the Widowmaker's acidic globules while continually unleashing a barrage of heavy firepower and grenades. You can use the LAARK, but make sure you are far enough away from the Widowmaker (and clear of obstructions) to avoid taking splash damage.

ANGEL'S LAIR

Chimeran Tower

IV. The Missions
LONDON

NORTHERN COMMAND
CLASSIFIED

London, England
14 July 1951—12:08 GMT

MISSION OVERVIEW

Hale made it into the tower. Lt. Cartwright was gravely injured in the battle against the Widowmaker, so Hale was on his own once again. We didn't know what we would find inside, but whatever was in there, destroying it was the only way to win this war. We found massive exhaust vents outside the tower. We figured if Hale could follow the power conduits, he would find the source.

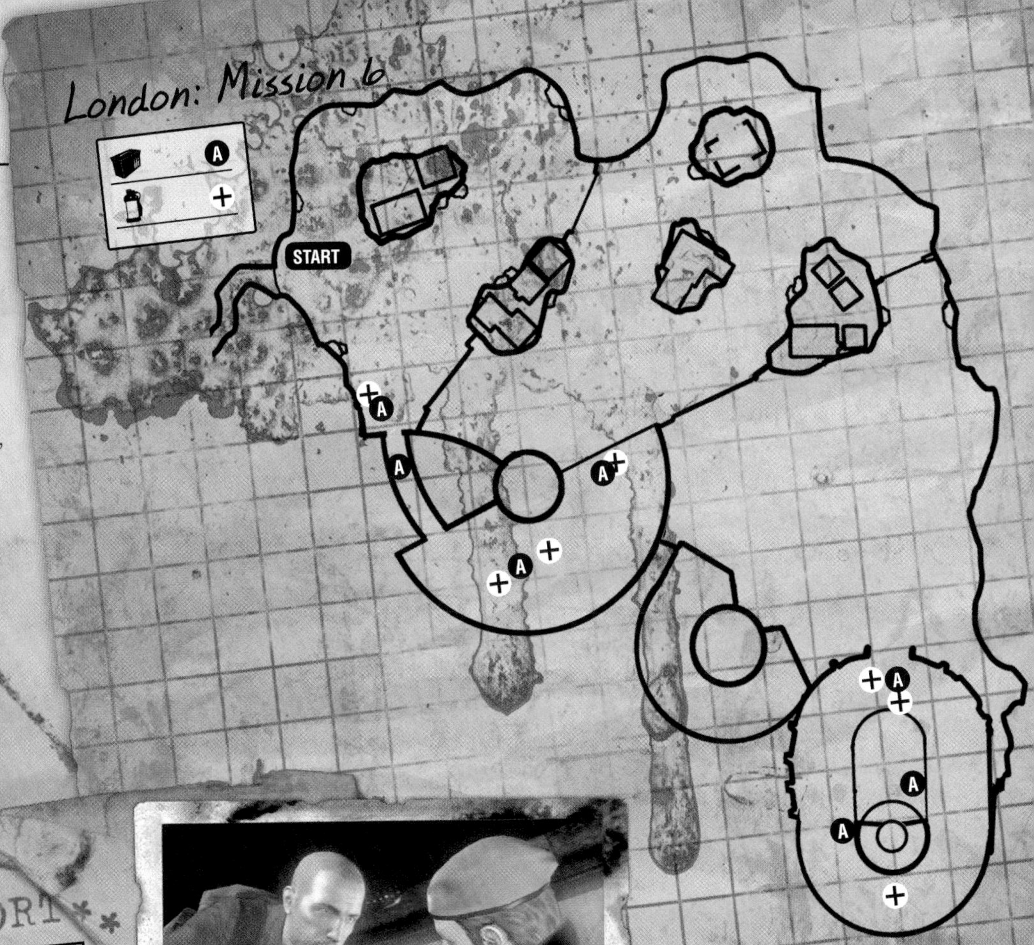

London: Mission 6

A
+
START

FIELD REPORT

Enemy Intel
Angel
Hybrid
Steelhead
Menial
Slipskull

Hardware
M5A2 Carbine
Bullseye Mark II
Rossmore 236
Combat Shotgun
Auger
L23 Fareye
XR-005 Hailstorm
XR-003 Sapper
L209 LAARK
Frag Grenade
M-12 Sabertooth
Air-Fuel Grenade
Hedgehog Grenades

Mission Objective

★ Follow the Power Conduits to their Source.

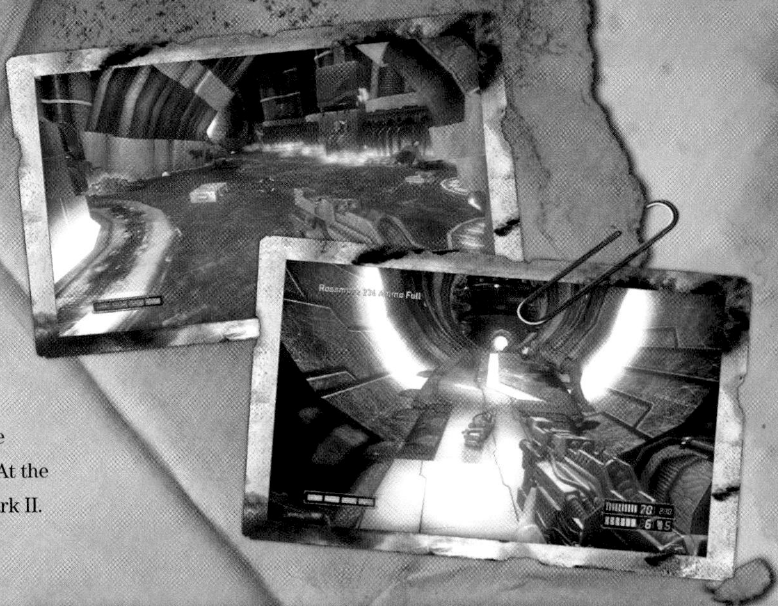

BELLY OF THE BEAST

★ Follow the Power Conduits to Their Source

To destroy the Chimera once and for all, Hale must locate the source of their power. His objective is to follow the power conduits that run through the tower. With all of the dead soldier's everywhere, it looks like he's not the first to attempt this mission. First, continue down the path. At the base of the ramp, Hale finds a new weapon, the Bullseye Mark II.

Bullseye Mark II

WEAPON INTELLIGENCE

The Bullseye Mark II is an upgraded version of the Chimeran service rifle. It has the same functionality of the standard model, but uses a supercharged power cell to develop significantly more firepower. Slugs fired from the Mark II create massive holes in victims. Fatal blood loss is inevitable without immediate medical attention. Because of this, the Mark II is referred to simply as "blue death."

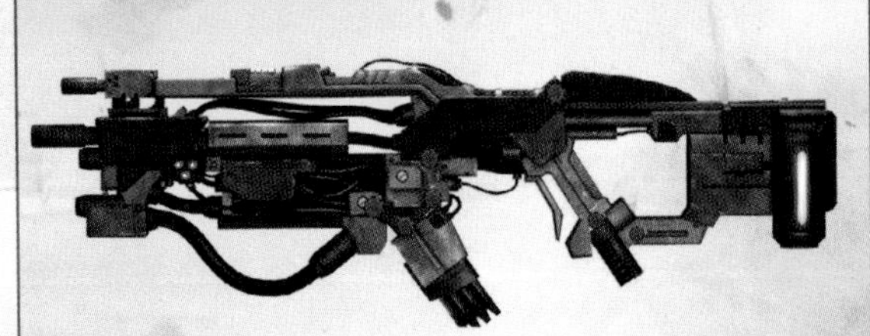

As Hale is about to drop into the vast chamber beyond the ramp, an Angel suddenly appears at the entrance. To say it is horrifically frightening is an understatement. The good news is that it disappears as quickly as it appears. The bad news is that this is definitely not the last you'll see of it.

The Angel

It is believed that Angels are the most advanced Chimeran strain currently operating in Britain. Angels are usually found near Chimeran strongholds, although there have been some battlefield sightings. Initial observations indicate that Angels exert a command influence over other Chimeran strains. The extent of this connection is unclear. As leadership units, Angels don't directly participate in combat. The extent of their offensive capabilities is unknown.

The ramp to the left leads into a Hybrid ambush. These advanced foes are stronger than the typical Hybrids, plus they carry Bullseye Mark IIs. Equip the Auger and lay down a force shield when they appear, or use the Fareye and pick them off from a distance. It doesn't hurt to lob a grenade or two as well.

The Advanced Hybrid

Advanced Hybrids are the fanatical defenders of the Chimeran Towers. Every aspect of their physiology is tuned to grant them extreme levels of performance. They are outfitted with specialized cooling units to ensure their core body temperature doesn't climb uncontrollably during the heat of combat.

Use the Fareye to eliminate the remaining Advanced Hybrids at the top of the ramp, then activate the switch to open the gateway in front of it.

YOU'VE GOT COMPANY

The Angel has returned and this time it's not going away without some encouragement. Take cover from its acidic projectiles and stay on the move. Use the LAARK against this beast; one or two direct hits is all it takes to knock it down from its perch.

TAKE THE LOW ROAD

Locate the ramp on the side of the bridge to go below it. There are a few canisters of Sym-Bac serum down here, as well as various other ammunition supplies.

It looks like the Chimera don't take kindly to Hale killing their Angels, so some Menials are dispatched to right this wrong. Use the Rossmore to cut down these foes with ease. Don't forget about the Advanced Hybrid near the back, who is probably peppering Hale with Mark II fire.

DEEPER STILL

As Hale crosses the next bridge, a few Auger-wielding Steelheads make an appearance. Switch to the Fareye and quickly dispose of as many as possible. When the coast is clear, take the ramp leading down to the lower section and follow the walkway to the end. Search the area for an Intel Item; it's resting next to two dead soldiers.

Power Source

These documents indicate that the Chimeran power source may emanate from the central tower, thus providing power to the other towers through massive conduits.

Return to the bridge and take it to the opposite end. Use the Auger to beat back the Advanced Hybrids, then retaliate with a powerful weapon and grenades to wipe them out. When it's safe, step onto the lift and activate the switch to go to a floor high above.

IN A PICKLE

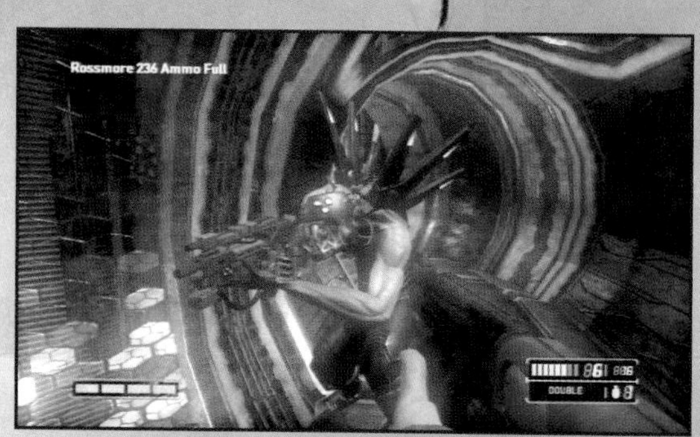

As Hale moves through the tunnel, some Advanced Hybrids ambush him. When they appear, spin around and take out the one from behind, then focus on the other one. Create a force shield in front or behind Hale to create a little breathing room.

The chamber beyond the tunnel can be a complete nightmare, because of the numerous Steelheads, Advanced Hybrids, Slipskulls, and Menials. Send in an Auto-turret first to lessen their numbers, then use the Bullseye Mark II to tag and bag the Slipskulls on the walls. The Fareye is also an ideal weapon to use to clean up any remaining enemies.

Next, take the ramp at the back of this chamber to access the next portion of the tower. There is a second Chimera-filled chamber at the end of the next tunnel, so dispose of them using any means necessary.

PROCESSING

Take the ramp into a tunnel to continue deeper into the tower. A switch-activated lift at the other end of the tunnel leads to a new area. This, in turn, leads to a huge chamber that is processing Chimera-filled cocoons.

Enter the walkway through the opening, don't enter the next small room. From this position, tag and bag the Slipskulls without taking any damage.

Wind through the chamber and head through the small connecting hallways to reach the next area. On the other side, eliminate the Advanced Hybrids by using any means necessary.

The final hallway leads to a long, ascending tunnel. All that stands in Hale's way now are a few Slipskulls. As before, use the Mark II's tag function to eliminate them. When the path is clear, activate the switch at the end to reach the tower's top tier.

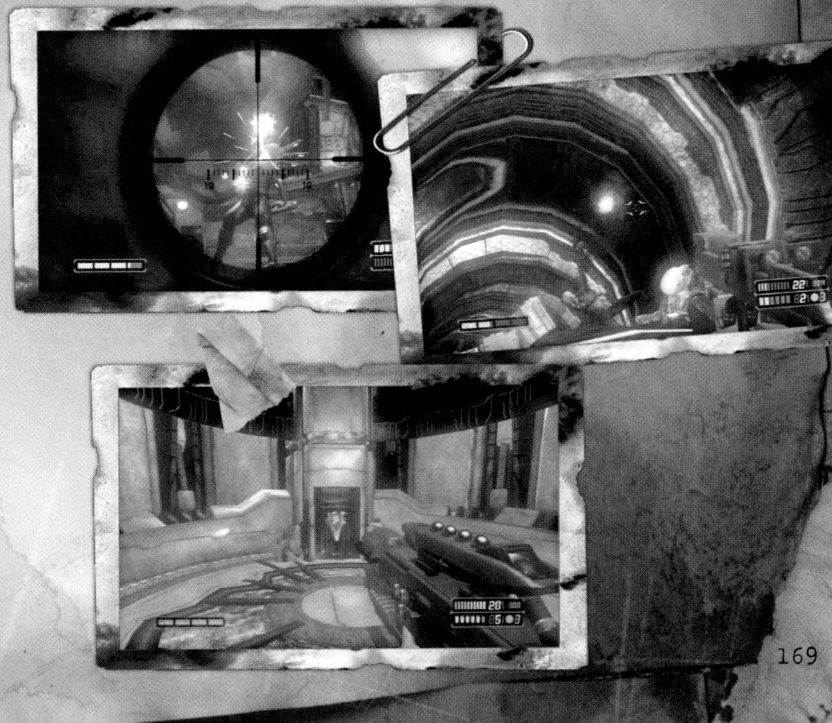

LAST HOPE

Chimeran Tower

NORTHERN COMMAND
CLASSIFIED

London, England
14 July 1951—15:13 GMT

MISSION OVERVIEW

FIELD REPORT

Enemy Intel
Leaper
Roller
Widowmaker
Advanced Hybrid
Steelhead
Angel
Slipskull
Titan
Hardfang

Hardware
M5A2 Carbine
Bullseye Mark II
Rossmore 236 Combat Shotgun
Auger
L23 Fareye
XR-005 Hailstorm
XR-003 Sapper
L209 LAARK
Frag Grenade
M-12 Sabertooth
Air-Fuel Grenade
Hedgehog Grenades

Mission Objective

★ Follow the power conduits to their source.

★ Destroy the reactor.

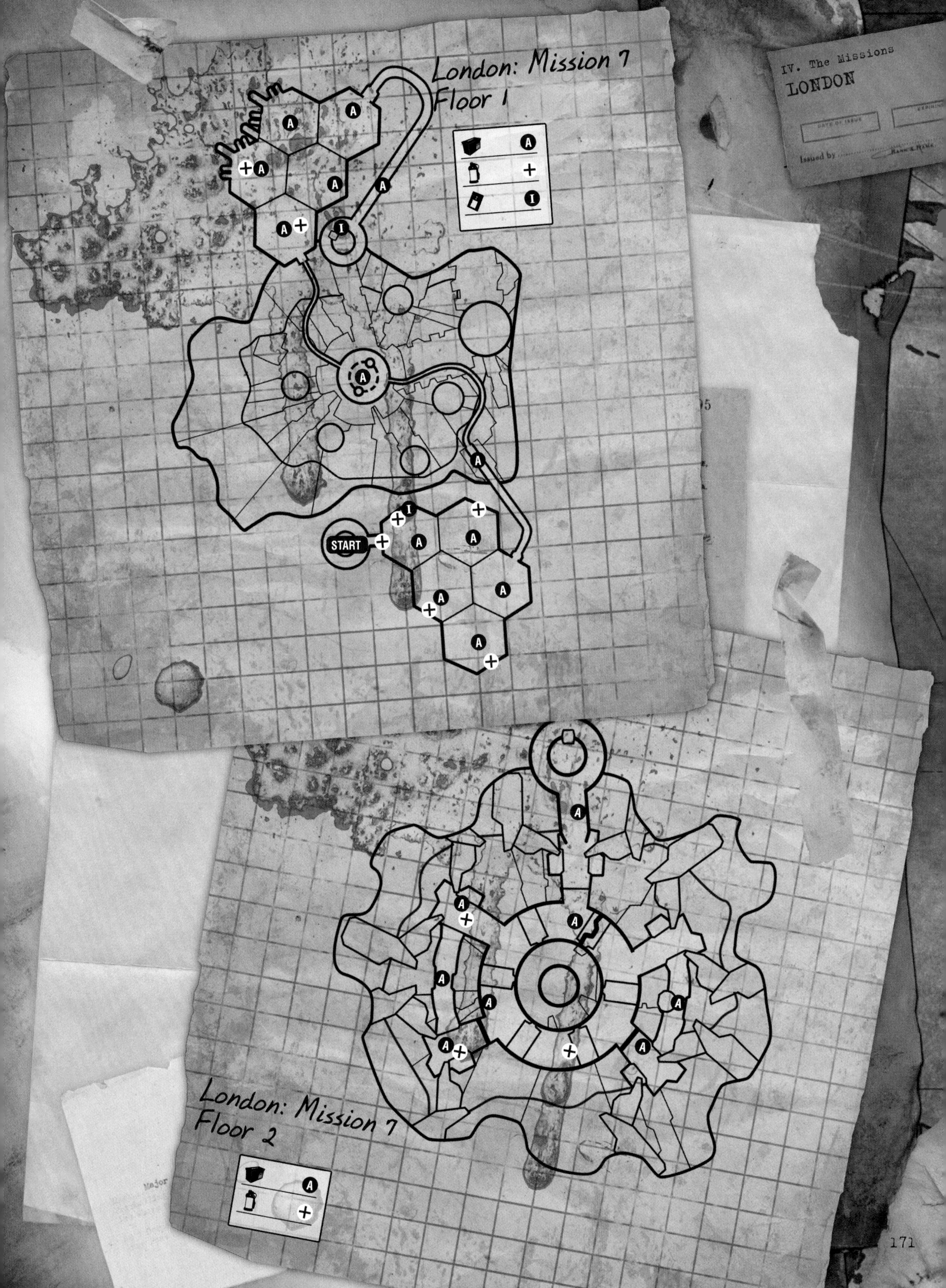
IV. The Missions
LONDON
London: Mission 7
Floor 1
START
London: Mission 7
Floor 2

United States Army Rangers
1st Regiment

THE BEGINNING OF THE END

★ Follow the Power Conduits to Their Source

This is it. Hale must make a final assault on the tower, with the mission objective to locate and destroy its power source. It's a safe bet that the Chimera will pull out all the stops to ensure that this doesn't happen.

Drop down into the first chamber, equip the Carbine, and mow down the Leapers and Rollers. Next, collect all of the ammunition in the area and locate the opening in the chamber wall along the right-hand side. Search the area for an Intel Item.

DOCUMENT INTELLIGENCE #36

Observations

Dated July 14th, this journal details the environment inside the tower, as well as observations and theories on how it works.

Inside the second portion of this chamber, Hale encounters a soldier in a desperate battle with a Widowmaker. Equip the LAARK and unload the entire payload into the beast before it retaliates.

There's no rest for the weary. After the Widowmaker battle, some Advanced Hybrids come calling. Use the Auger to launch a force shield, then switch to the Fareye and pick them off from a distance.

Explore the rest of the chamber, grabbing some supplies in the process, then exit via the tunnel entrance to the east. A few Rollers and Leapers inside the tunnel drop from the holes in the ceiling.

SNIPER ALLEY

Outside the tunnel, switch to the Fareye and use focus to eliminate the Auger-wielding Steelheads in the distance, then creep up the cable. When it's safe, follow the conduit through the exit to get outside.

AND ANGEL MAKES THREE

If you think it's been tough going so far, you're in for a rude awakening. Although the allies have located Hale's position and sent help, you must contend with two Angels and a pack of Advanced Hybrid snipers from above.

RIP UNIT SEVEN

There is a VTOL up in the sky carrying troops from Unit Seven. Before the troops can drop in, an Angel appears and latches onto the ship. It's a spectacular and horrific sight all at once.

Equip the LAARK and fire off its rockets into the beast. The Angel shoots acidic projectiles that burst into clouds of corrosive and noxious gas that linger for a few moments before dissipating. Avoid the gas at all costs, and take evasive action if it surrounds Hale.

A second Angel makes an appearance after the first one goes down. There are also a handful of Advanced Hybrids in sniper positions on the walkways. Take cover, switch to the Fareye, and concentrate on the snipers first. Keep moving to avoid the Angel's advances, as well as the snipers' Bullseye shots. When the battle ends, take a few moments to sweep the area clean of supplies, then locate proceed to the northwest and continue the ascent.

DOCUMENT INTELLIGENCE #37

Angels

This page, taken from a hastily put together British Intelligence Corps. field manual, offers a few details on the Angel and its relationship to the other Chimera.

British [illegible] Corps.
Chimera [illegible] Units
-Commonl[illegible]rred to as "Angels" due to exhaust plume from mechanical apparatus. Apparatus believed responsible for their flight ability.
-Angels capable of directing other Chimera through unknown means.
-Because of ability to summon reinforcements, they should never be considered to be alone.
-The loss of an angel will deny the enemy leadership. Potential for disruption to the Chimera makes the angel a priority. They should always be the primary target.

BACK

INTO THE CORE

Hale and the surviving soldiers run into light Chimeran resistance in the next area. As you approach the exit, keep an eye on the ground for an Intel Item—the last one in the game! If you found all 37 items, you receive a Skill Point. For the complete list of Skill Points, what they are, and how to achieve them, see the "Top Secret" section in the back of this guide.

Take the lift at the end of the tunnel to the next chamber. Hale finds the Chimeran power source inside. His ultimate goal is to destroy it, but he must first take part in one more bloody battle.

Start the battle by taking cover toward the end of the walkway, then equip the Fareye to pick off the Advanced Hybrids fighting the allies around the massive Titan.

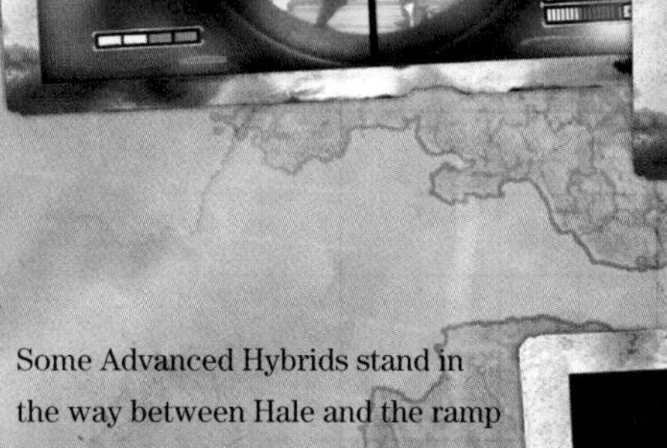

Continue to hold your position at the back of the walkway and equip the Mark II. Tag the Titan and strafe around it while unleashing your clip into the beast. A few Fuel-Air grenades can only speed up its death.

The battle is still far from over. Carefully move down the walkway until Hale encounters his next set of foes. Switch back to the Fareye and take them out before they can zap Hale with their Arc Chargers.

Some Advanced Hybrids stand in the way between Hale and the ramp leading to the reactor controls. Take cover and pick them off, then make an assault on the controls and take out the remaining Steelheads guarding the area. Lob a grenade or launch one from the Carbine to take them out quickly.

DESTROY THE REACTOR

★ Meltdown—Rod #1

Activate the switch on the ramp that overlooks the reactor. This begins the process of lowering its protective shielding. Next, shoot the first exposed rod to destroy it.

As usual, stick with the Fareye to pick off as many of the approaching foes as possible, then switch to a more up close and personal weapon for the ones who break through your line of fire.

MELTDOWN—ROD #2

Locate the next exposed rod, which is counterclockwise from the first one, and focus your weapon on it. Don't stop shooting until it's completely destroyed.

MELTDOWN—ROD #3

The shield that covers the rods goes down one at a time. You may need to wait for the third one to lower before you can access the rod. As soon as it is exposed, start shooting but watch out for more Advanced Hybrids attacking from either side of the perimeter.

HEALTH AND AMMO

Grab all of the Sym-Bac serum and ammunition in this area. This battle is so tough and intense that you will need all you can find.

MELTDOWN—ROD#4

Another Angel appears to protect the final rod. Eliminate the threat right away, then finish the job and blow up the reactor. The mission is a success and England is saved, but what of Hale, Russia, and the rest of the world?

Congratulations! Watch the final cinematic and the credits roll, then get ready for another tour of duty. There are still plenty of new things to see and do, including a host of new weapons that become available the second time through, new difficulty levels, Co-op and Multiplayer Modes. Plus, it wouldn't be an Insomniac Game if there weren't Skill Points to achieve. For more information and strategies on these items and modes, turn to their respective sections in this guide.

MULTIPLAYER

NO. 402-x-2

Getting Started

Even after you conquer the game's single-player experience, there is an amazing multiplayer mode to explore. To participate in some of this intense combat online and offline, select MULTIPLAYER from the Main Menu. Team up with other players and compete as an Allied Unit or Chimeran alien force.

There are several additional items that are required to get online, including a subscription to an Internet service provider, a network device, a WLAN access point (for wireless networks), and a PC.

Broadband Only!

The online game is broadband only! To play online, you must connect through a DSL, cable modem, high-speed Internet connection, a Local Area Network (LAN), or a Wireless Local Area Network (WLAN).

GETTING CONNECTED

Before you can play online, you must first set up your Network Setting via the PlayStation 3 cross bar menu, then sign up for the PlayStation Network. For further information and setting up details, please refer to the PlayStation 3 Instructional Manual.

Once you're good to go, there are just a few more steps before you can get online and start fragging!

1. **After choosing Multiplayer, select ONLINE GAME to login to the Resistance: Fall of Man's servers.**
2. **Please read the USER AGREEMENT and select YES if you agree to the terms. You must agree to the terms of the USER AGREEMENT to connect to Resistance: Fall of Man online.**
3. **Check out any Insomniac Games-related announcements and then highlight CONTINUE and press ⊗. You're now logged in!**

PLAYING THE ONLINE GAME

At the Online Main Menu, you can choose from Ranked and Custom games, create a Party, use the Community feature, and adjust the Online Options.

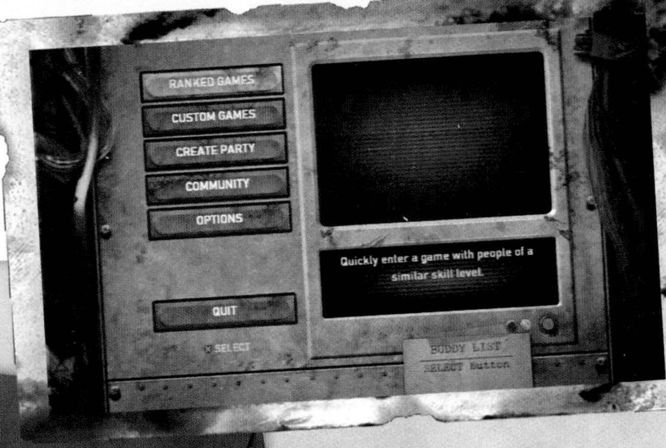

BRITISH INTELLIGENCE AGENCY
MULTIPLAYER INTELLIGENCE

RANKED GAMES

Choose RANKED GAMES at the Online Main Menu to play with and against other players. Choose from three Match Types: "Free-for-All," "Team-Based," and "Grab Bag."

Free-for-All: These are non-team game modes, such as Deathmatch and Conversion.

Team: These are team-based game modes, such as Capture the Flag and Meltdown.

Grab Bag: Leave it up to the computer to decide; what you get is anybody's guess.

MATCH SIZE

Choose the size of the map and the number of players competing in the match. Match sizes include: Small (up to 16 players) and Large (up to 40 players).

CUSTOM GAMES

Choose CUSTOM GAMES at the Online Main Menu and tailor your online games by manually setting up game filters, such as Game Type, Map and Max Players. After setting the game filters, you can choose to SEARCH and join a game in progress or CREATE and host your own.

CREATE PARTY

Create a Party and invite your friends to join by selecting CREATE PARTY from the Online Main Menu. When you choose to create a party, the game goes to the Party Room Screen. From here, you can find Ranked and Custom games, as well as create a custom game of your own. Note: Parties can only play on the same team and will be disbanded once the online game ends.

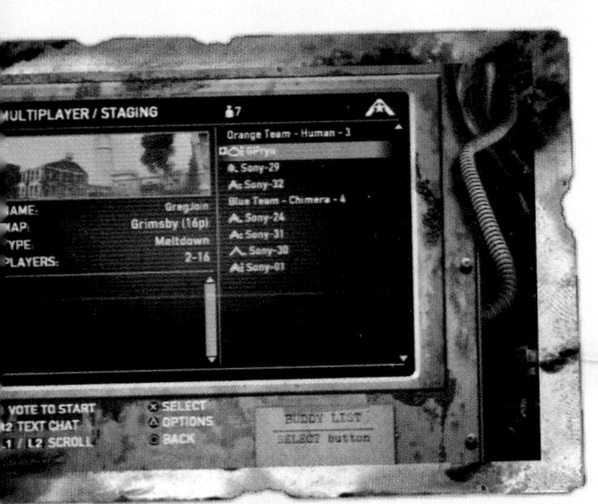

STAGING AREA

Whether you're hosting or joining a Ranked or Custom game, or creating your own Party, you will eventually get to the Staging Area. At the Staging Area, you can chat with other players, view the match information, and prepare for the next battle.

COMMUNITY

Check in daily to make sure you have the latest game info, or use the personal Message feature to schedule an online match with your friends or clan-mates.

Character Sheet: View your character appearance, online stats, ranking and medals, and ribbons.

Clan: Create or join a clan.

*Leaderboard: Check out the latest updates for Individual, Weekly, Monthly, and Friend Leaderboards. (*Only available on myresistance.net)*

BUDDIES/IGNORE LISTS

Adding someone to your buddy list gives you a quick way to contact that person. The status column indicates whether that person is online, creating a quick way to add them to a party if you choose to play with them. Ignore Lists are just the opposite. If someone is harassing you, or if you just don't want to play with or contact someone, add them to your Ignore List and the game will do its best to keep them at bay.

Buddies: Manage your Buddy and Ignore Lists.

Messages: Use the Message feature to communicate with your friends and schedule online matches.

CLANS

Clans are kind of a "buddy list extension." Joining a clan allows you to display that clan's "tag" (a three-letter word) next to your name, so everyone knows you're in that clan. Compete against other clans for high stats, or arrange wars and tournaments at www.myresistance.net.

OPTIONS

View and adjust the online game options, including Game Help, Controls, Skins and more.

MEDALS

Medals represent significant achievements. Although the ways to earn medals are secret (even we don't know!), you can see which ones you've earned by accessing your character sheet.

RIBBONS

Ribbons represent achievements during the course of a single match. Ribbons are presented for things like headshots, melee frags, fragging three people in a row without dying, and so on. You can view the ribbons you've earned by accessing your character sheet.

EXPERIENCE (XP)

As you play more Ranked games, you receive experience points (XP). As your XP total reaches certain thresholds, your player "level" also increases. Levels are expressed as military ranks, along with one, two, or three pips. The pips indicate how advanced you are within your military rank. Scoring higher than your opponents in ranked games will net you higher XP awards. For more information on Multiplayer unlockables, refer to the "Top Secret" chapter.

REWARDS

By increasing your player "level," you periodically gain rewards. These rewards can be things like Skins, as well as other interesting tidbits we're not allowed to reveal in this guide.

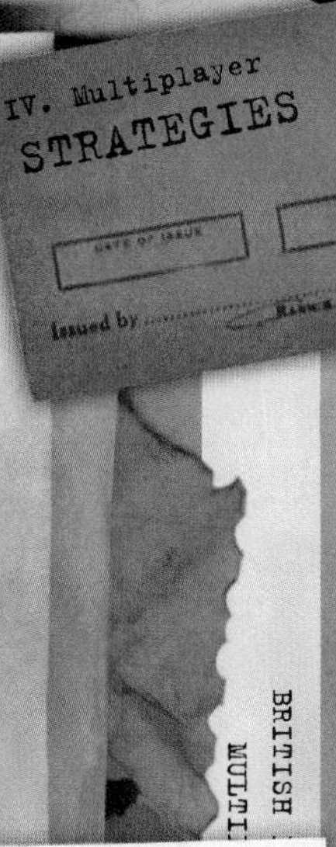

HUMANS VS. CHIMERA

The human allied soldiers and the Chimeran hybrids each have unique abilities to exploit on the battlefield.

Humans: The humans' special abilities include the ability to sprint (tap L2). Also, the humans have advanced radar abilities that enable them to see each other, as well as enemies (depending on the game mode and nodes captured).

Chimera: The Chimera's special abilities include the ability to go into Rage Mode (press L2). When in Rage Mode, Hybrids move faster and can see their enemies through walls, but they will also overheat and start to take damage. Hybrids are larger than the humans, making them bigger targets, and they lack the ability to crouch.

MULTIPLAYER OFFLINE

In addition to Multiplayer online, you can also play up to four-player multiplayer offline via split screen. To play multiplayer offline, select OFFLINE from the Multiplayer Menu. The multiplayer offline mode is similar to the online mode, except that you can not gain experience, medals, or ribbons.

ONLINE GAME MODES

MELTDOWN

★ **Objective: Two teams struggle for control of the coolant nodes placed around the map. By taking more coolant nodes than the enemy, a team can cause their opponent's reactor to overheat. Overheating causes a team's Meltdown Meter to drop. When it drops all the way, the game ends and the reactor explodes.**

Gameplay Information: Players can spawn at nodes captured by their team; players can achieve points by capturing nodes, recapturing nodes, and defending nodes.

Meltdown Basic Strategies

A straight rush for the reactor works the best, spawning as close to a target node as possible and attacking it relentlessly. This also helps for getting the most points, since capturing nodes nets 10 points per capture while defending a node nets one point for every defensive frag.

An alternate strategy that also works is to spawn away from the major conflicts and sneak "behind enemy lines" to capture unguarded nodes. This enables you to take over an enemy node, or cause your opponents to turn back and guard the node you attacked, thus allowing your team to capture the other nodes.

The weapon of choice for Meltdown is the Arc Charger—two secondary shots will capture a neutral node, and three secondary shots will capture an enemy node.

Frag grenades are another option for node capture. Frag grenades can take out an entire node with two grenades, but this does require precise aiming.

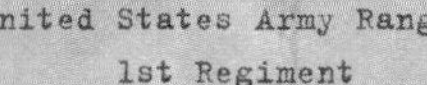

BREACH

★ **Objective: To win a Breach match, you must destroy the opponent's reactor. Destroying a reactor is similar to destroying a node, except that there are many more rods encased in each reactor. You can find the reactor by following the on-screen radar or checking the in-game map. Note: If a team owns all of the nodes on the map, its reactor's shields will not lower.**

Gameplay Information: Players can spawn at the nodes captured by their team; players can achieve points by capturing nodes, recapturing nodes, defending nodes, and attacking their opponent's home reactor; for every node a team captures, they are awarded a base defense.

- ★ *1 Node = Node-based radar*
- ★ *2 Nodes = Weapon pickups at home base*
- ★ *3 Nodes = Turrets aid in base defense*
- ★ *4 Nodes = Hedgehog mines around your base, increasing base defense*
- ★ *5 Nodes = Base reactor becomes invulnerable*

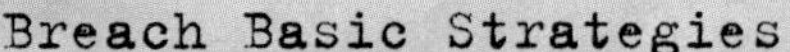

Breach Basic Strategies

A quick, decisive strike on the enemy base at the beginning of the round works the best. Have a player run toward the enemy base, pick up any weapons/grenades along the way, and then wait for the enemy players to leave their base. Once a majority—if not all—of the opposing team leaves their base, have the player infiltrate and make their way to the reactor. Even if the reactor isn't destroyed, you still have achieved a positive result. The reactor should be damaged or you have at least made your opponents panic, causing at least a few to return to their base.

The Arc Charger and/or grenades are the best choice of weapons to use to inflict damage to the reactor. These weapons enable the player to quickly attack the reactor, causing high damage before being fragged by any defenders.

Another route to pursue is to attempt to obtain all of the nodes in a quick fashion. This is both a good and bad situation because it will give one team all the defenses, allowing them to focus purely on their opponent's reactor. However, the team with no nodes is forced to spawn at their reactor, making it extremely difficult for the team with all the nodes to gain access to the reactor in an attempt to do damage.

BRITISH INTELLIGENCE AGENCY

CAPTURE THE FLAG (CTF)

★ **Objective: Your flag is stored at your home base, while your opponents' flag is stored on the other side of the map at their home base. Retrieve the flag to gain a point. The team with the most points after the timer runs out, wins!**

Gameplay Information: The player can only spawn at their flag; the maximum amount of players per team is eight, allowing only 16 players in any Capture the Flag Game; players obtain points by capturing the flag, fragging an enemy flag carrier, and recapturing a flag. Your flag must be on its stand in your base for your team to capture the enemy's flag and score the point.

CTF Basic Strategies

The recommended strategy for this match type is to have at least two players on defense, two players patrolling the area between the player's base and the enemy's base, and let the remaining four try to capture the flag. When a player takes the enemy's flag, the other attackers and the patrollers should escort the flag carrier back to the base to cap the flag.

TEAM DEATHMATCH

★ **Objective: To frag as many players on the opposing team as quickly as possible.**

Gameplay Information: Players obtain 10 points for every frag; players obtain 2 points for every assist; players lose 10 points for every suicide

Basic Team Deathmatch Strategies

The strategy is essentially the same as Deathmatch. Travel in groups to increase the chance of survival and frag enemies quicker.

CONVERSION

Objective: Conversion is a "Last Man Standing" type of match, in which your goal is simply to frag all of the other players before they frag you. You start out as a human, and if you die once, you respawn as a Chimera. If you die as a Chimera, you are considered out of the game and are placed into Spectator Mode.

Gameplay Information: Players continuously obtain points while they are alive; each player has a set number of Human and Chimeran Lives. By default, the player has one Human life and one Chimeran Life. When a player dies as a Human, he or she respawns as a Chimeran. When a player dies as a Chimeran, he or she enters the Spectator Mode until the round/game is over; the last player alive at the end of the round/game receives a 100 point bonus.

Conversion Basic Strategies

The stratefgy for Conversion is basically the same as Deathmatch, but with a twist. The same strategies apply, but with much more of an emphasis on survival as opposed to fragging randomly.

In large Conversion games, the first few moments are essentially a luck of the draw. If, however, you survive the initial spawn in, it's important to find a place and hide. Let the other players frag each other to increase your chance of survival. Dealing with five players is better than dealing with fifteen players.

MAPS

All of the multiplayer maps are in this section, complete with callouts for every weapon, flag, base, node and reactor so you can gain the upper hand on the opposition. The maps are labeled accordingly and have a size associated with the name. Maps labeled this way are sized based on the number of players each map allows.

- **Tiny = 8 Players**
- **Small = 16 Players**
- **Medium = 32 Players**
- **Large = 40 Players**

Please note that due to planned enhancements to the game, some items listed on the maps may change. Check out the server announcement page on myresistance.net for the most up-to-date information.

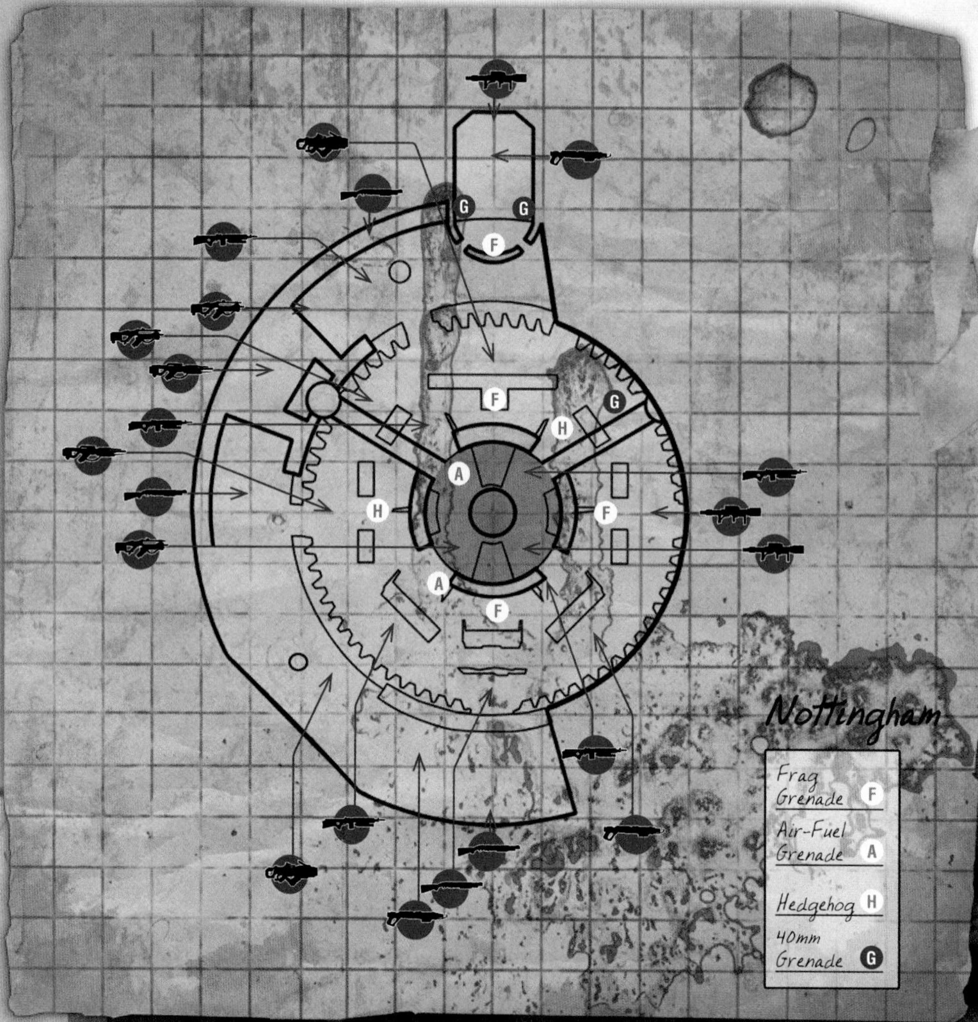

Nottingham

Frag Grenade	F
Air-Fuel Grenade	A
Hedgehog	H
40mm Grenade	G

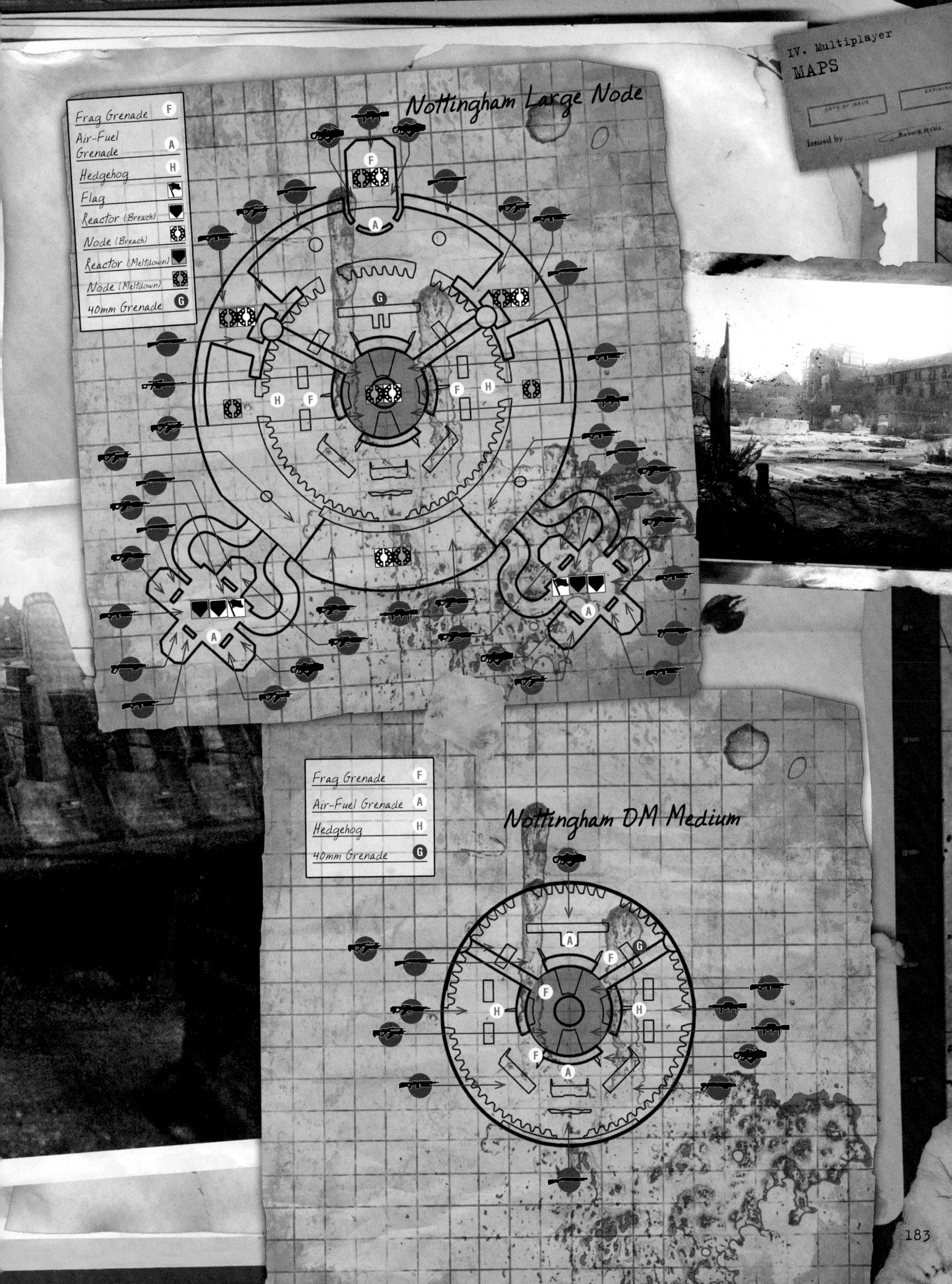
Issued by
Nottingham Large Node
Frag Grenade F
Air-Fuel Grenade A
Hedgehog H
Flag
Reactor (Breach)
Node (Breach)
Reactor (Meltdown)
Node (Meltdown)
40mm Grenade G
Nottingham DM Medium
Frag Grenade F
Air-Fuel Grenade A
Hedgehog H
40mm Grenade G

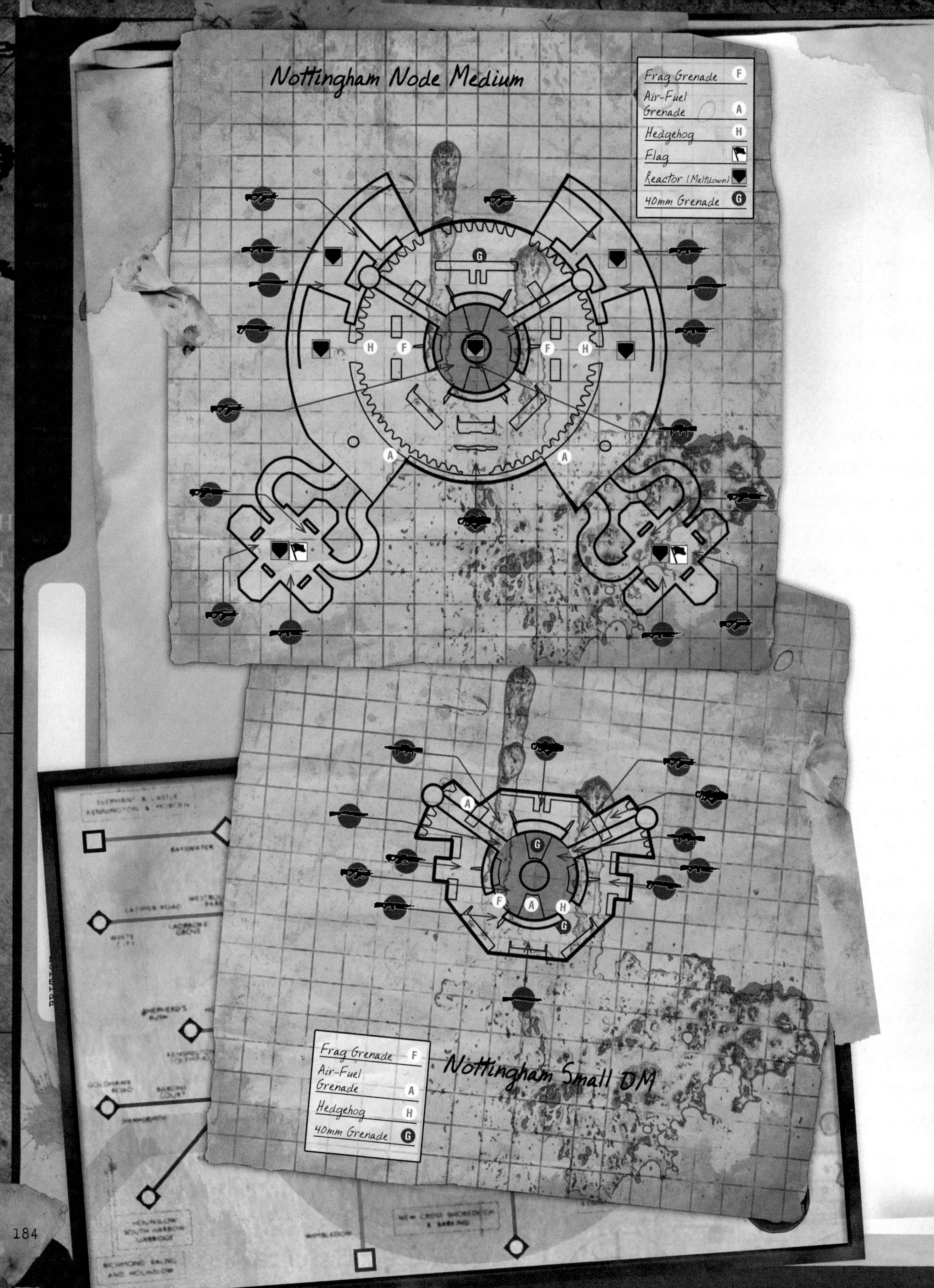

Nottingham Node Medium
Frag Grenade
Air-Fuel Grenade
Hedgehog
Flag
Reactor (Meltdown)
40mm Grenade
Nottingham Small DM
Frag Grenade
Air-Fuel Grenade
Hedgehog
40mm Grenade

Nottingham Small Node
Reactor (Meltdown)
Frag Grenade F
Air-Fuel Grenade A
Hedgehog H
40mm Grenade G
IV. Multiplayer
MAPS
Issued by
BRITISH INTELLIG
MULTIPLAYER
SEVEN SISTERS, Letchworth, Uxbridge
McMURPHY MORGAN JOHNSON
GRAVY TRAIN
Nottingham Tiny DM
Frag Grenade F
Air-Fuel Grenade A
Hedgehog H
40mm Grenade G
PRESENTS

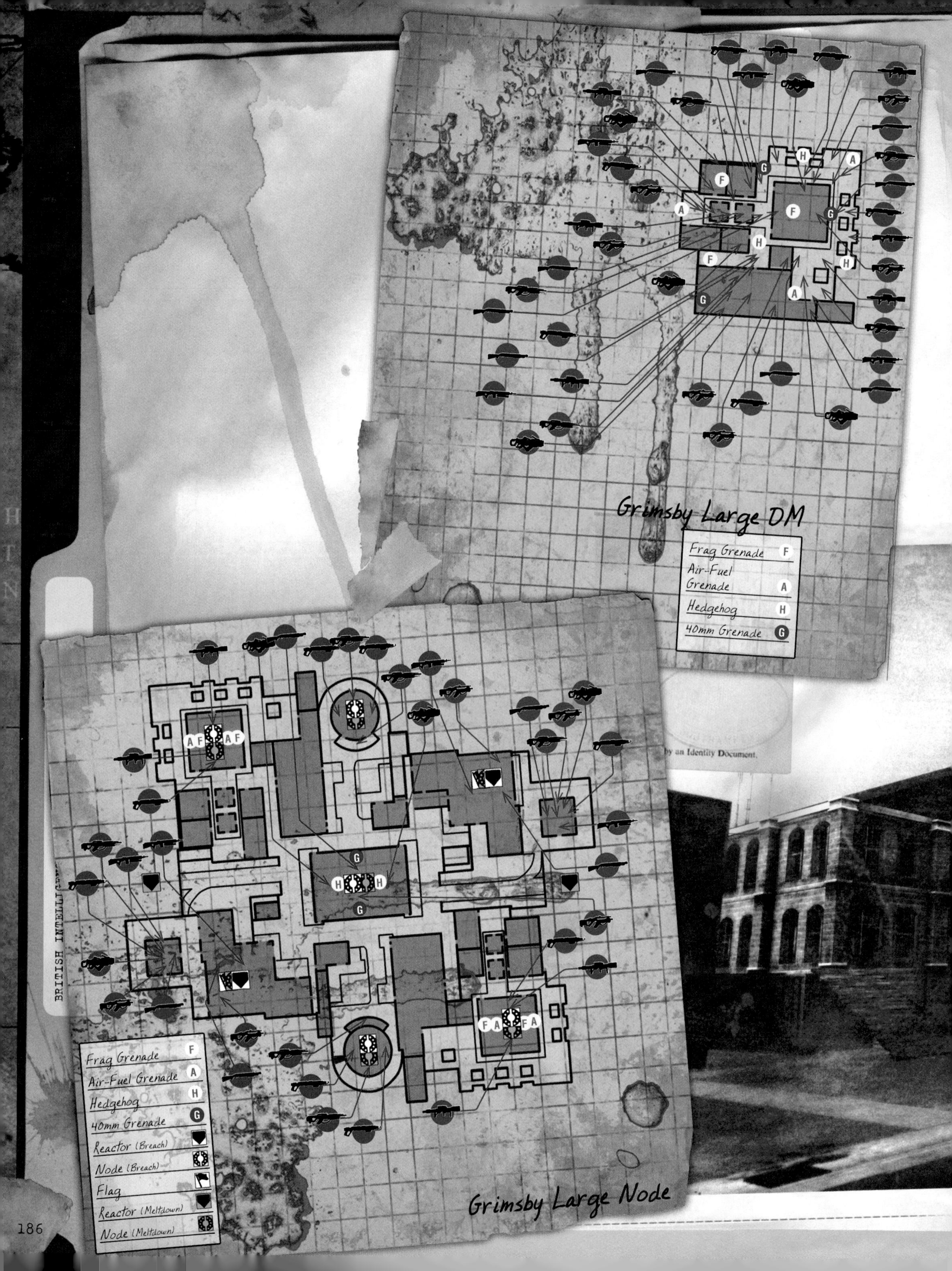

Grimsby Large DM
Frag Grenade F
Air-Fuel Grenade A
Hedgehog H
40mm Grenade G
Grimsby Large Node
Frag Grenade F
Air-Fuel Grenade A
Hedgehog H
40mm Grenade G
Reactor (Breach)
Node (Breach)
Flag
Reactor (Meltdown)
Node (Meltdown)
BRITISH INTELLIGENCE
by an Identity Document.

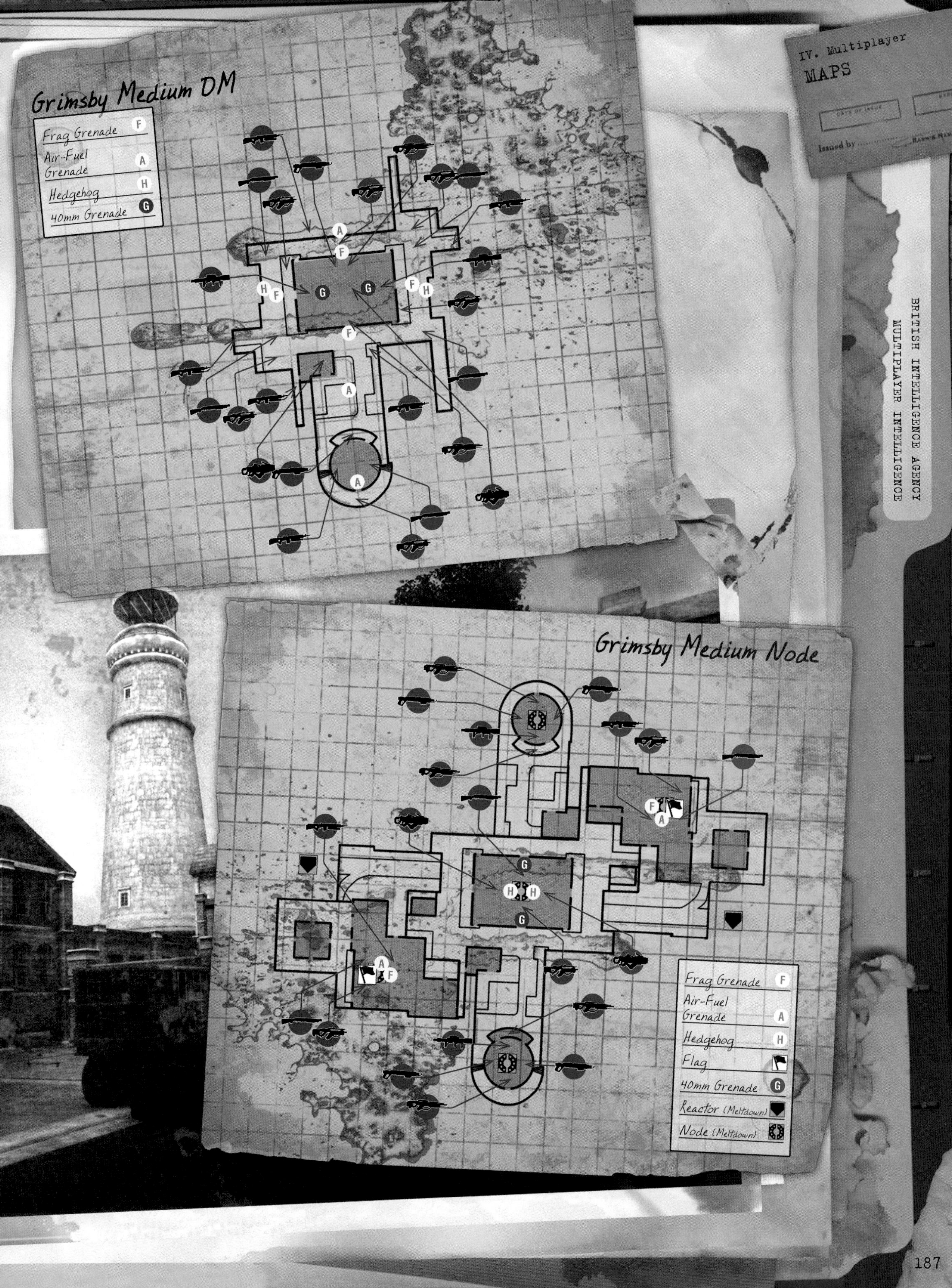
Grimsby Medium DM
Frag Grenade F
Air-Fuel Grenade A
Hedgehog H
40mm Grenade G
Grimsby Medium Node
Frag Grenade F
Air-Fuel Grenade A
Hedgehog H
Flag
40mm Grenade G
Reactor (Meltdown)
Node (Meltdown)
BRITISH INTELLIGENCE AGENCY
MULTIPLAYER INTELLIGENCE

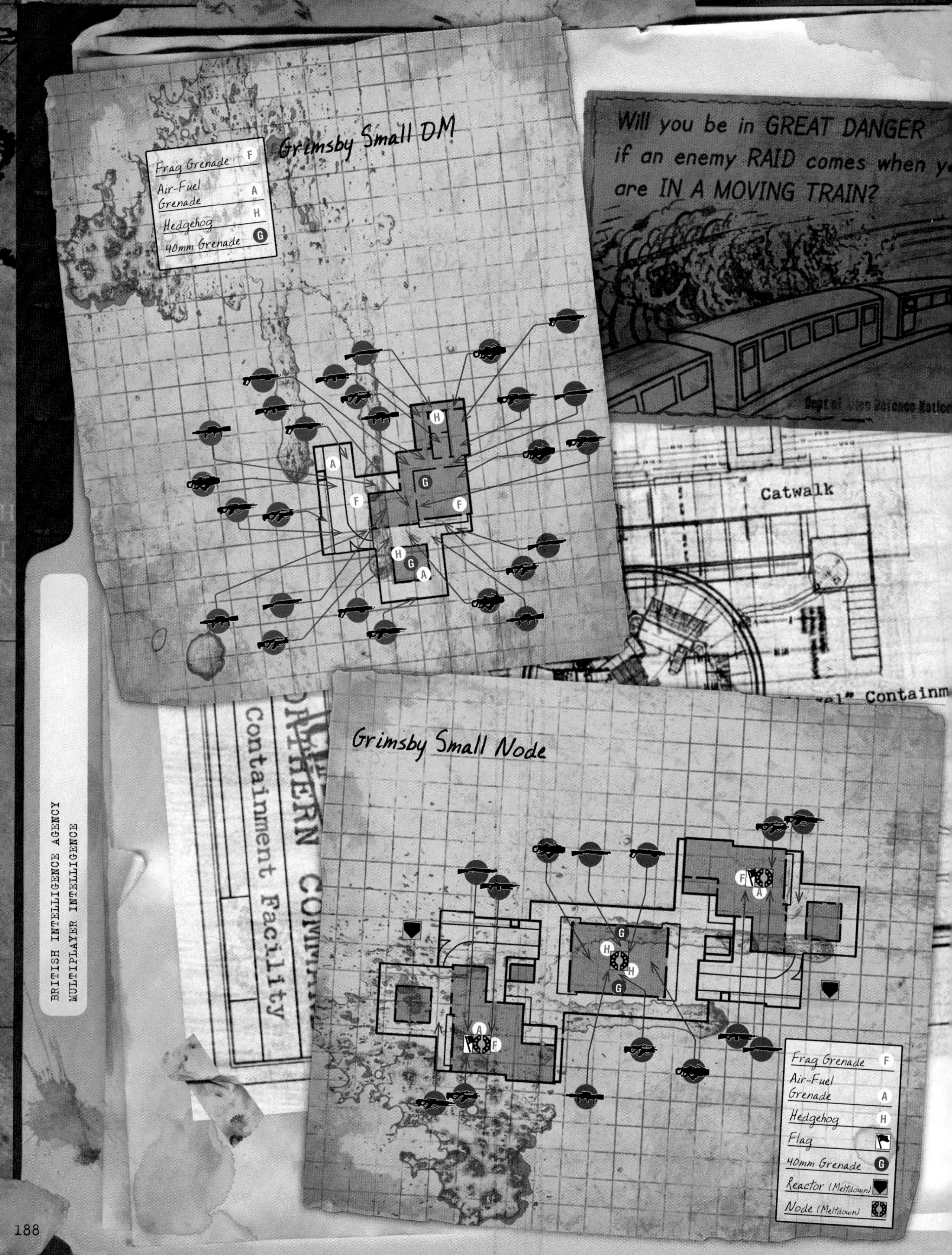

BRITISH INTELLIGENCE AGENCY
MULTIPLAYER INTELLIGENCE

Somerset Large DM
Frag Grenade F
Air-Fuel Grenade A
Hedgehog H
40mm Grenade G
Somerset Large Node
Frag Grenade F
Air-Fuel Grenade A
Hedgehog H
Flag
Reactor (Breach)
Node (Breach)
Reactor (Meltdown)
Node (Meltdown)
Grimsby Tiny DM
Frag Grenade F
Air-Fuel Grenade A
Hedgehog H
40mm Grenade G
BRITISH INTELLIGENCE AGENCY
MULTIPLAYER INTELLIGENCE

Frag Grenade F
Air-Fuel Grenade A
Hedgehog H
40mm Grenade G

Somerset Medium DM

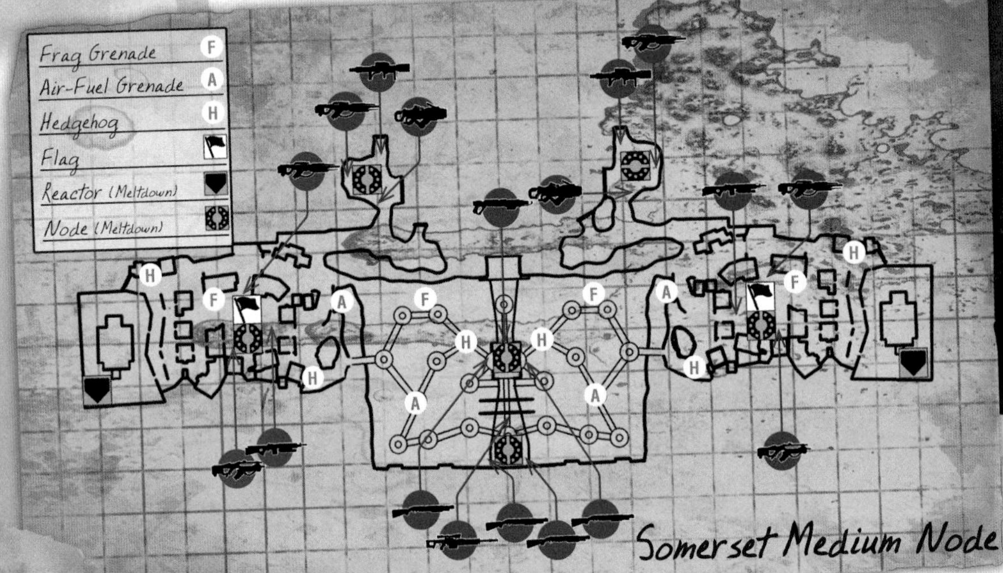

Somerset Small DM

Frag Grenade F
Air-Fuel Grenade A
Hedgehog H
40mm Grenade G

Issued by
Frag Grenade F
Air-Fuel Grenade A
Hedgehog H
Flag
Reactor (Meltdown)
Node (Meltdown)
Somerset Small Node
IN THE EVENT OF A RAID -
DO NOT RUSH, TAKE SHELTER CALMLY, THEN OTHERS WILL DO THE SAME.
Frag Grenade F
Air-Fuel Grenade A
Hedgehog H
40mm Grenade G
Somerset Tiny DM

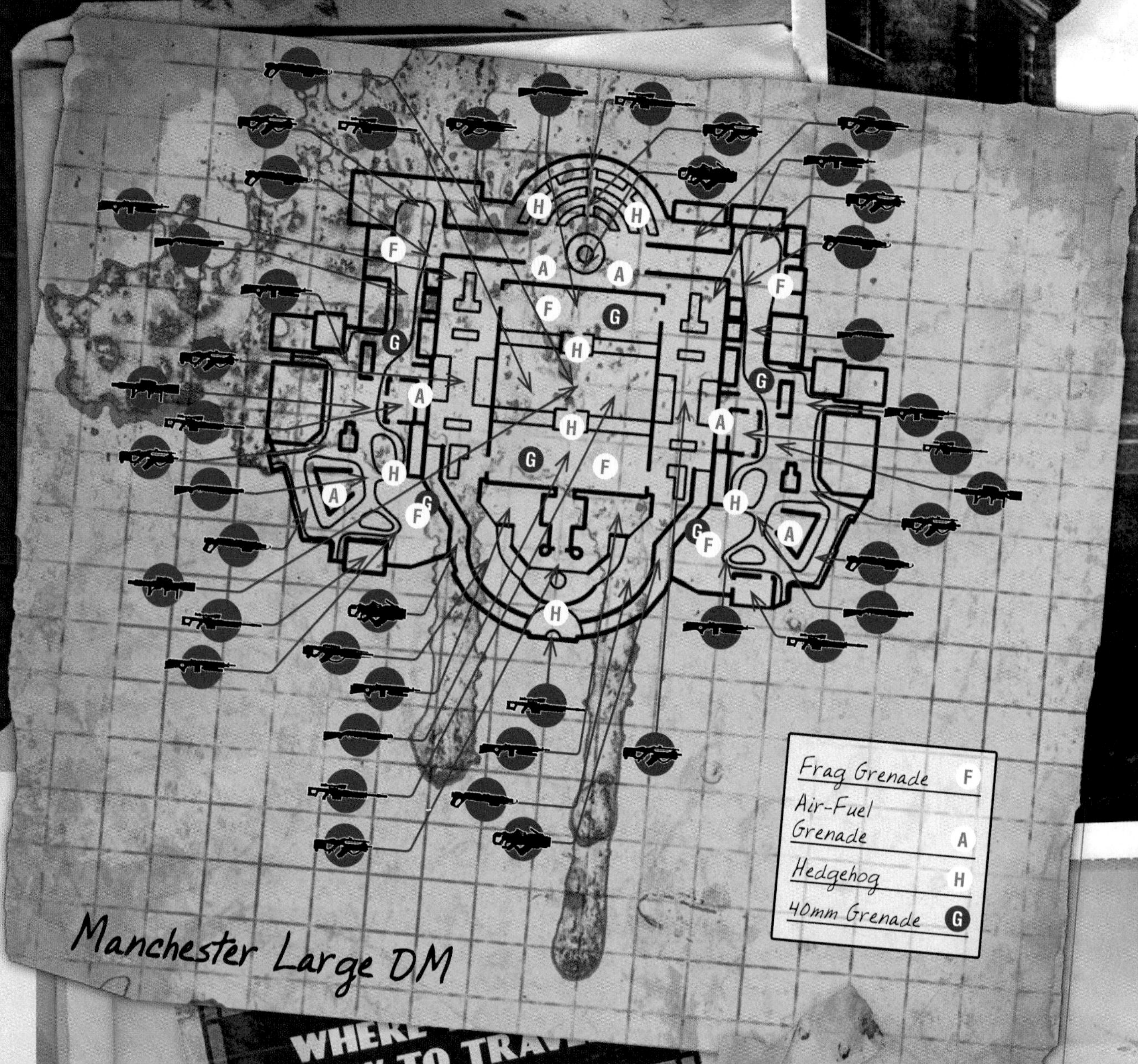
Frag Grenade F
Air-Fuel Grenade A
Hedgehog H
40mm Grenade G
Manchester Large DM

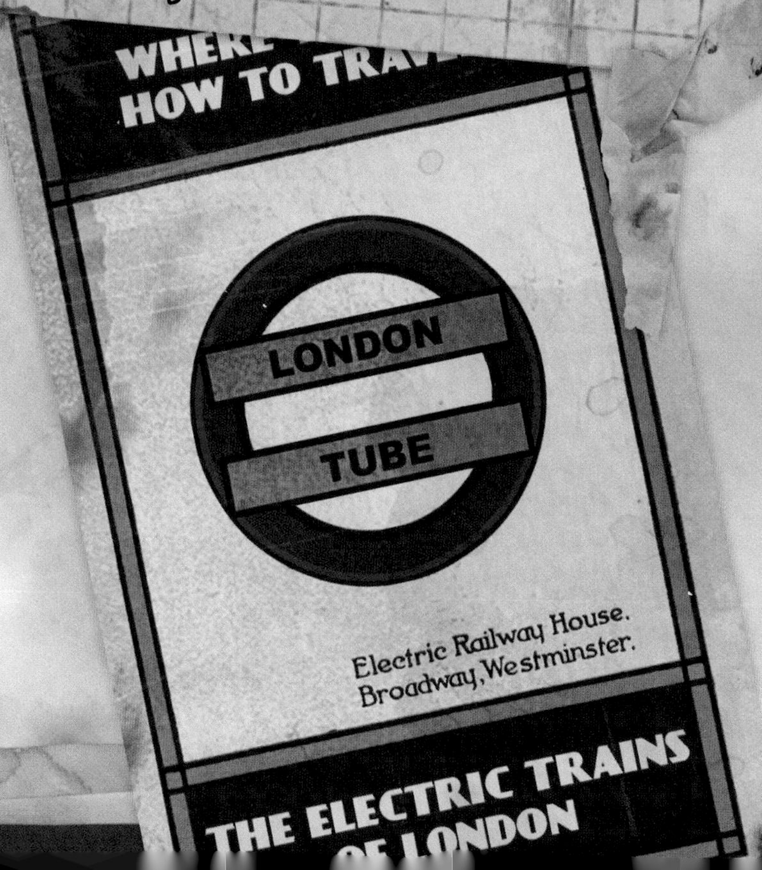
HOW TO
LONDON
TUBE
Electric Railway House.
Broadway, Westminster.
THE ELECTRIC TRAINS
OF LONDON

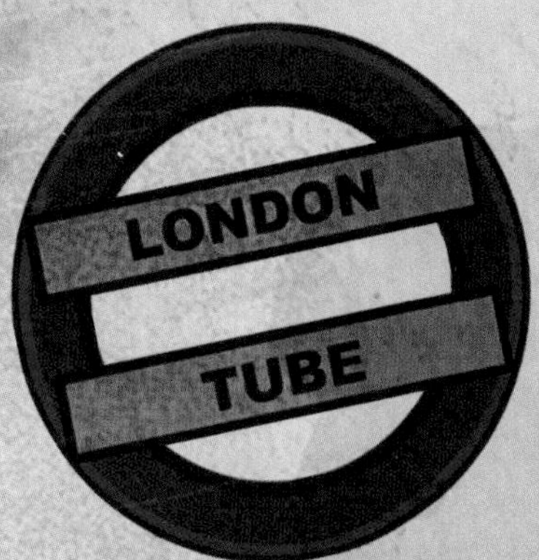

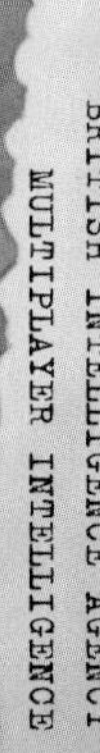

Manchester Large Node

Legend	
Frag Grenade	F
Air-Fuel Grenade	A
Hedgehog	H
40mm Grenade	G
Flag	
Reactor (Breach)	
Node (Breach)	
Reactor (Meltdown)	
Node (Meltdown)	

DON'T LET THEM SCARE YOU!
THEY ARE HARM-LESS WITH TEAMWORK!!
HELP US IN THEIR DESTRUCTION
ENLIST TODAY!
Manchester Medium DM
Frag Grenade F
Air-Fuel Grenade A
Hedgehog H
40mm Grenade G

United States Army Rangers
1st Regiment

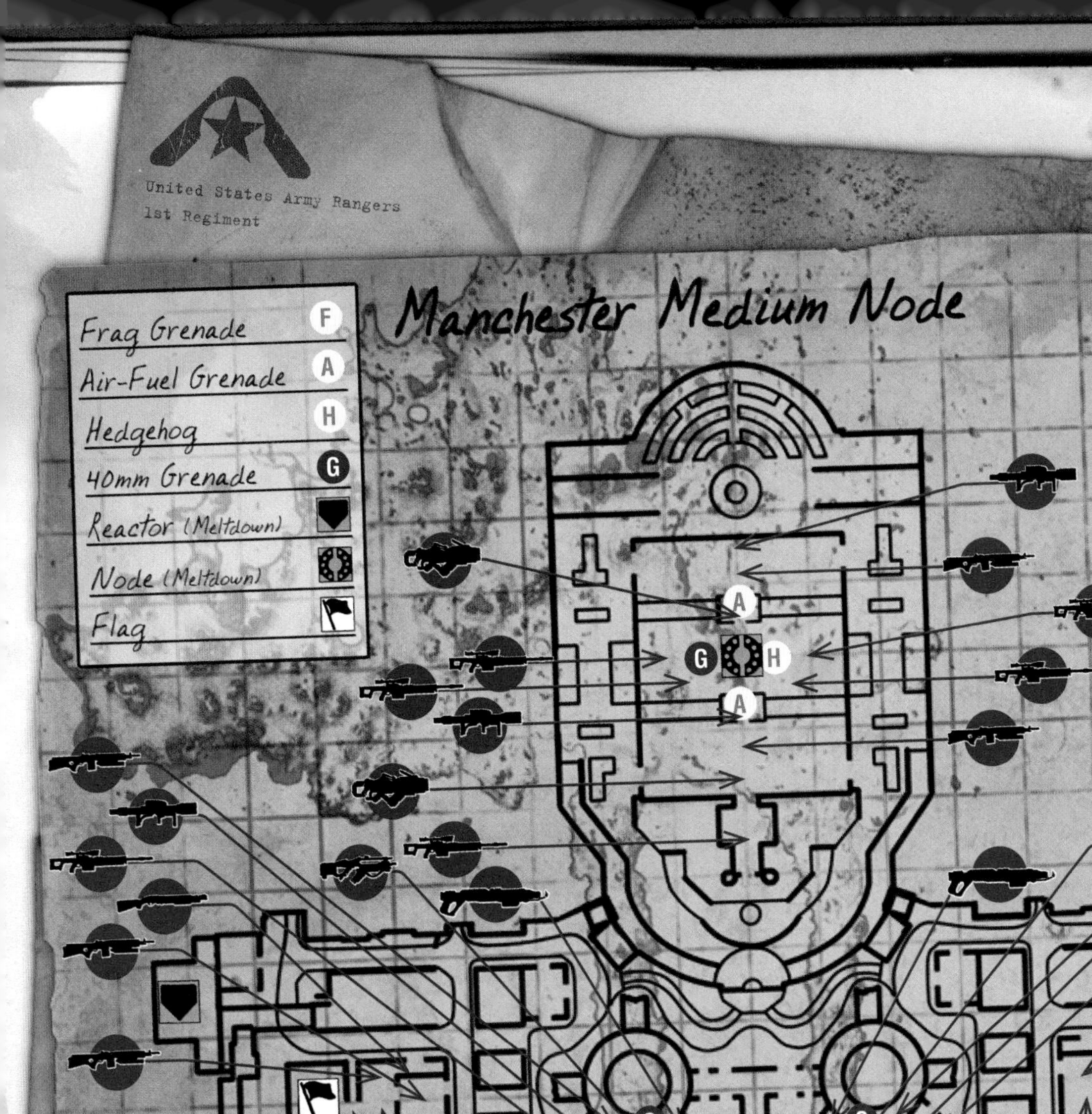

Frag Grenade F
Air-Fuel Grenade A
Hedgehog H
40mm Grenade G
Manchester Small DM
Manchester Small Node
Frag Grenade F
Air-Fuel Grenade A
Hedgehog H
40mm Grenade
Flag
Reactor (Meltdown)
Node (Meltdown)

Manchester Tiny DM

Frag Grenade F
Air-Fuel Grenade A
Hedgehog H
40mm Grenade G

JOIN THE FIGHT!

ENLIST NOW!

WE GIVE THUMBS UP FOR WARTIME EFFORTS

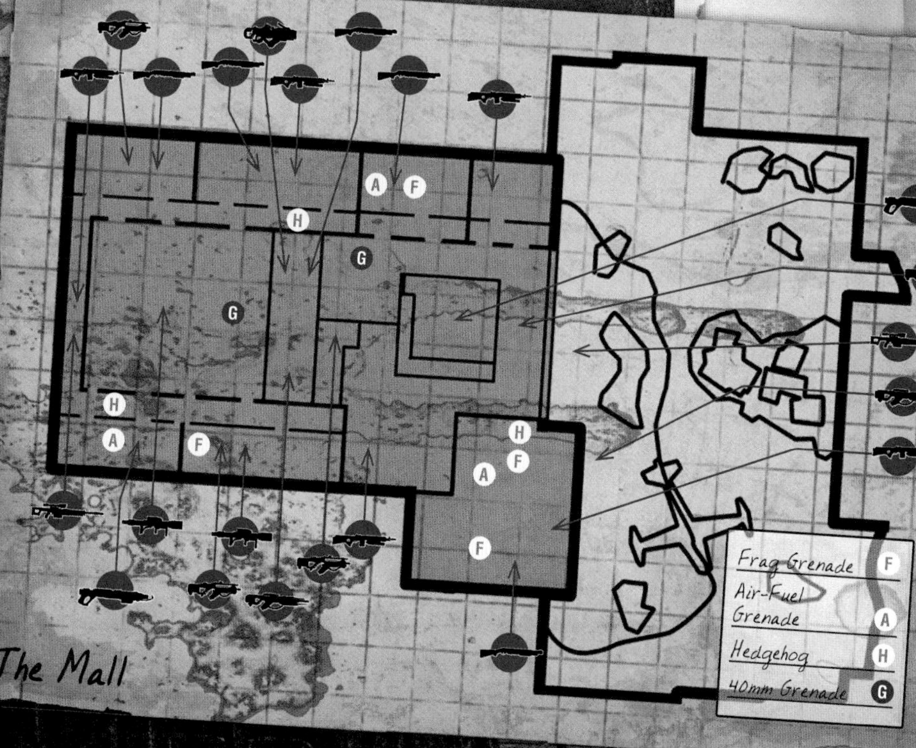

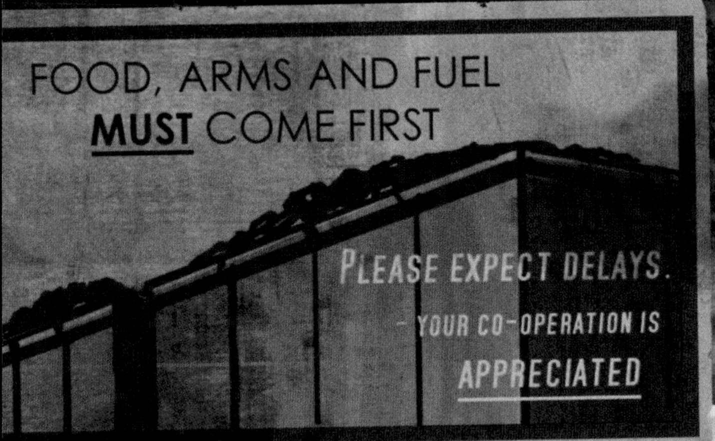

FOOD, ARMS AND FUEL
MUST COME FIRST
PLEASE EXPECT DELAYS.
- YOUR CO-OPERATION IS
APPRECIATED

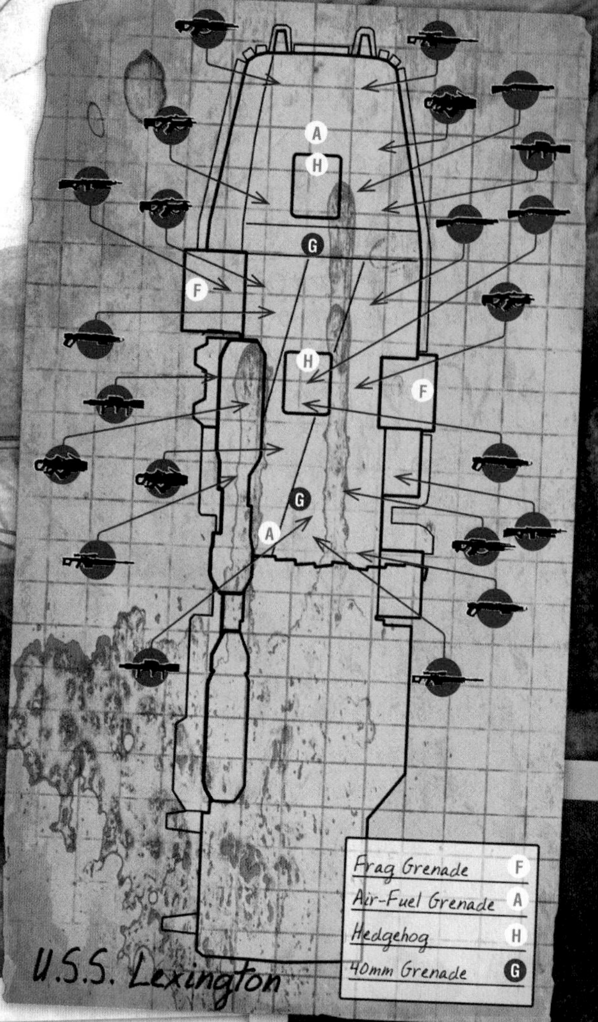

U.S.S. Lexington
Frag Grenade F
Air-Fuel Grenade A
Hedgehog H
40mm Grenade G

Rooftops
Frag Grenade F
Air-Fuel Grenade A
Hedgehog H
40mm Grenade G

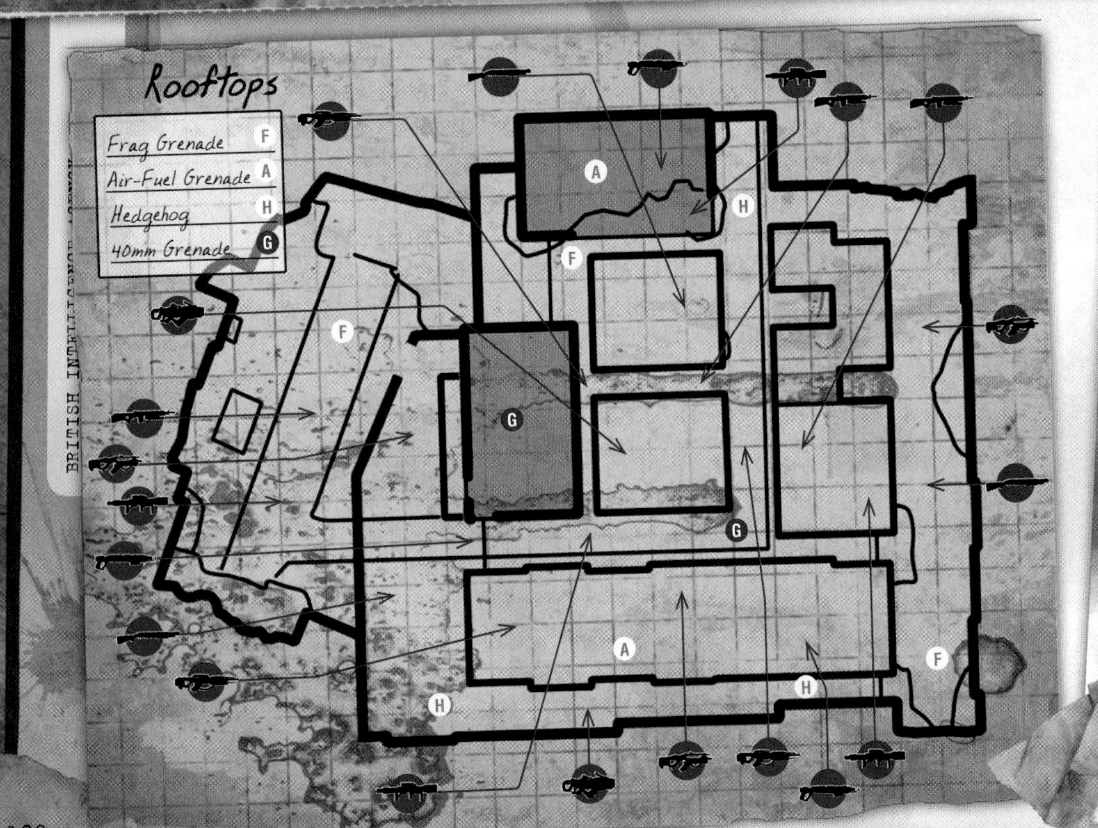

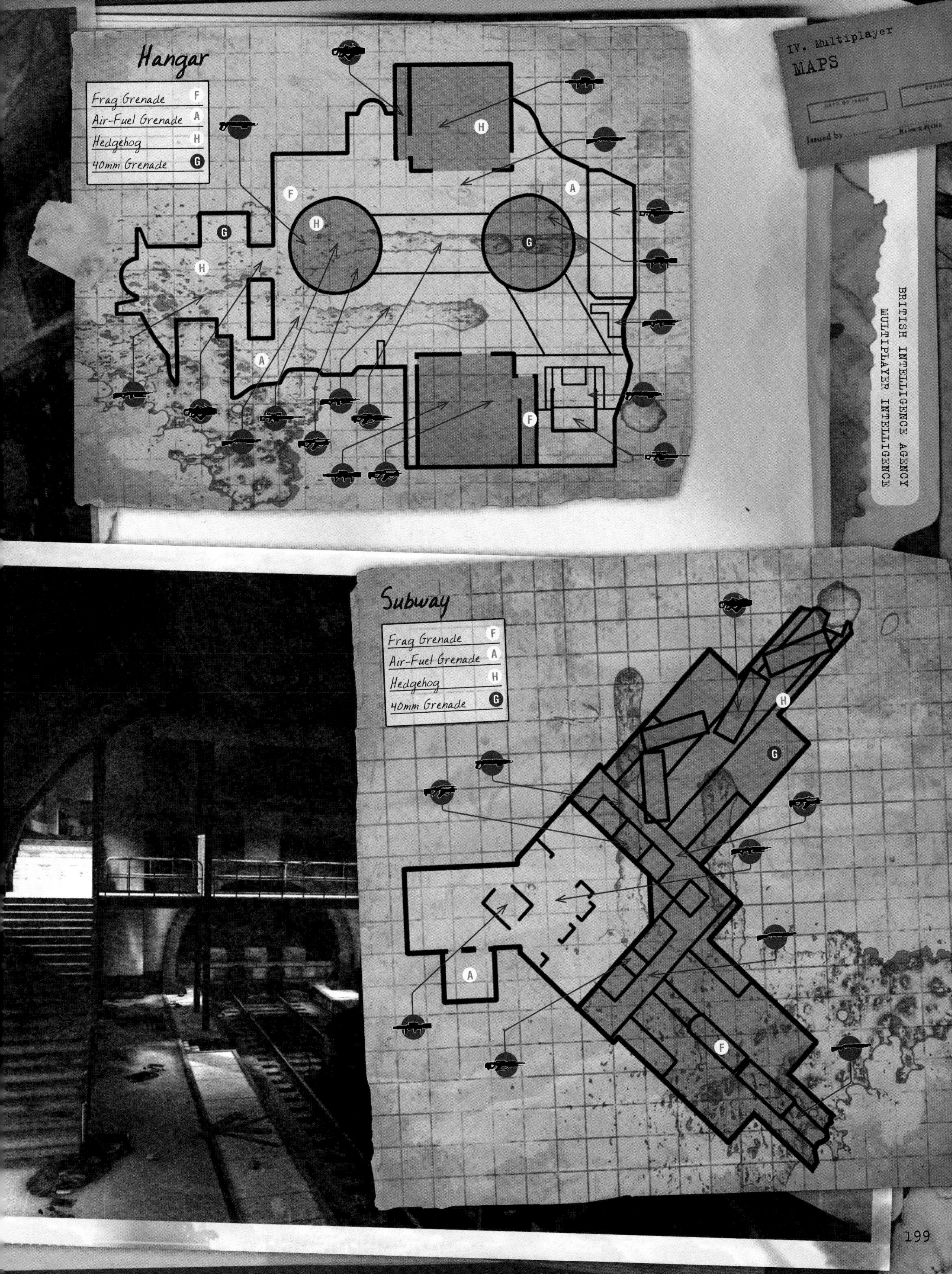

IV. Multiplayer
MAPS
Issued by
BRITISH INTELLIGENCE AGENCY
MULTIPLAYER INTELLIGENCE
Hangar
Frag Grenade F
Air-Fuel Grenade A
Hedgehog H
40mm Grenade G
Subway
Frag Grenade F
Air-Fuel Grenade A
Hedgehog H
40mm Grenade G

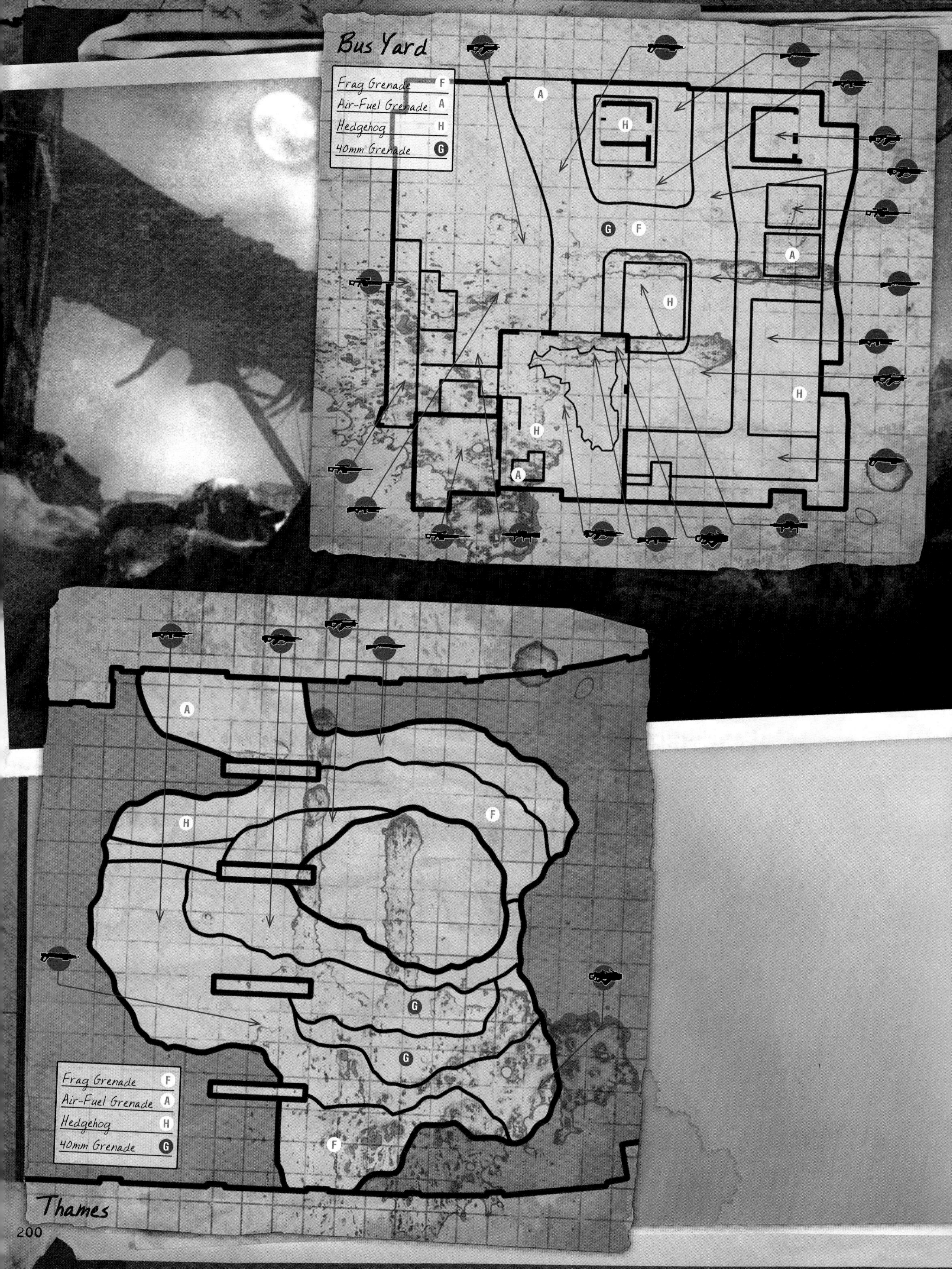

Bus Yard
Frag Grenade F
Air-Fuel Grenade A
Hedgehog H
40mm Grenade G
Thames
Frag Grenade F
Air-Fuel Grenade A
Hedgehog H
40mm Grenade G

VI. Top Secret

Date of Issue

Expiring

Issued by

CONFIDENTIAL

CONFIDENTIAL SECURITY BRIEF: A LEVEL ACCESS REQUIRED

After completing the game's Campaign Mode, there are still lots of things to see and do. Notwithstanding the amazing Multiplayer Mode, you can also play through the Campaign Mode a second and third time using much tougher difficulty levels *and* new weapons. How cool is that? This section details all of the game's awesome secrets. Read on only if you want them revealed!

Difficulty Levels

When you first play the game Easy, Medium, and Hard difficulty levels are available. If you somehow manage to beat the Hard difficulty level, Superhuman becomes available. If you complete Superhuman, well, you are a master gamer and should be touring the country showing off your shooter skills. Completing Superhuman also unlocks a new multiplayer skin. For more information on Skin unlocks, see the "Multiplayer Unlockables" at the end of this section.

More Vicious Foes Await!

On both Hard and Superhuman difficulty levels, there are more enemies to contend with and they sometimes appear in areas where there were no enemies previously.

New Weapons

If you defeat the game on the Easy, Medium, or Hard difficulty level, you will unlock five new weapons. However, you still have to locate them in their respective level; the weapons *are not* in your inventory when you start a new game. The location and level for each is listed in the following table.

Weapon	Level	Location
Reapers	1 - The Gauntlet	Inside the doorway of the house in front of the square.
Backlash Grenade	8 - Cathedral	Inside the house on the first room on the left after exiting the Cathedral.
Arc Charger	13 - No Way Out	At the end of the hallway near the officer's quarters.
L11-2 Dragon	20 - Evacuation	Inside the small bunker at the end of the Radial mine path.
Splitter	24 - A Desperate Gamble	On the second floor of the mall next to the vending machines by the windows.

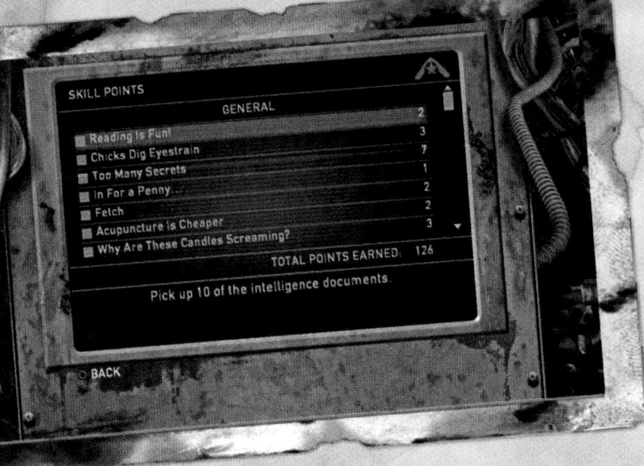

Skill Points

Anyone who has played a Ratchet & Clank game (and who hasn't) knows all about Insomniac's love for Skill Points. These are special feats that you must achieve during this game's Campaign Mode to gain points. You can then spend these points on Rewards, which are cool, unlockable bonuses. You can access the Skill Points and Rewards menus during gameplay by pressing START to access the Pause Menu, then selecting EXTRAS. We've taken the liberty of listing all of the Skill Points and the criteria for unlocking each on the following pages.

United States Army Rangers
1st Regiment

You can achieve the following skill points while playing the single-player or Cooperative mode.

Group; Global Skill Points

Name	Location	Description	Point Value
Mechanical Thumbs	Global	Defeat game on Hard difficulty	5
Reading is Fun!	Global	Pick up 10 log book items	2
Chicks Dig Eyestrain	Global	Pick up 20 log book items	3
Too Many Secrets	Global	Pick up all log book items	7
In For A Penny...	Global	Kill three Hybrids with a single grenade	1
Why Are These Candles Screaming?	Global	Kill 8 Hybrids with fire in 20 seconds	3
Lovely Parting Gifts	Global	Squat over 15 Hybrid corpses	2
Gasping For Air	Global	Kill 2 Hybrids in a level only after severing all their hoses	3
Fetch	Global	Kill a Pack Beast with a grenade	2
Tag, You're It	Global	Kill 5 enemies with the Bullseye in 30 seconds	2
Acupuncture Is Cheaper	Global	Kill 3 enemies at once with a Hedgehog	2
Nowhere to Hide	Global	Kill 5 enemies in a level by shooting them through a wall using the Auger	3
Twirly-Whirly	Global	Kill 5 menials with a Bullseye trap	3
Turrets Syndrome	Global	Use Chimeran turret to kill 6 enemies	3

Level Specific Skill Points

Name	Location	Description	Pt. Val.
Homing Beacons	York	Tag 4 hybrids with the Bullseye	3
Supersonic Meat Cubes	York	Kill 3 Leapers with a fragmentation grenade	3
Chimera Pate	York	Run over 10 enemies with the tank in Level 21	3
Don't Worry, Insurance Has It Covered	Grimsby	Break Chimeran Box in level 30	3
20th Sentry	Grimsby	Don't get hit by a laser mine	3
Personal Space Bubble	Grimsby	Don't let any menial grab you in Level 30	4
Lightfoot	Manchester	Take no damage from mines in level 41	3
This Is My Rifle, This Is My Gun	Manchester	Defeat the mech with only the assault rifle in Level 42	3
In One Ear, Out the Other	Nottingham	Get at least 5 headshot kills using the Fareye in Level 52	2
Mirror, Mirror	Cheshire	Destroy all glass objects in all 3 parts of the level	3
Passive Aggressive	Cheshire	Kill 4 Hybrids or Menials with non-weapon damage (barrels, cores, etc.)	3
We've Lost the Security Deposit Anyways	Cheshire	Break 10 medical lamps	2
Misplaced Aggression	Somerset	Blow up all cars in the town section of Level 70	2
Next Speed Trap, 50 Miles	Somerset	Make it through Level 71 in 7.75 (7:45) minutes	3
They Came From Behind!	Somerset	Run over 3 Hybrids while driving in reverse in Level 71	3
I Can See My House From Up Here	Somerset	Jump at least 50m while in the Lynx jeep in Level 71	2

Name	Location	Description	Pt. Val.
I Believe This Is Yours	Somerset	Use only Chimeran weapons to kill enemies in Level 72	3
One Eye Dog!	Bristol	Kill a Howler using the Fareye in Level 80	3
Pint in One Hand, Darts in the Other	Bristol	Shoot the center of 4 dartboards using the Fareye in Level 81	2
A New Kind Of Sourdough	Bristol	Kill every enemy in the kitchen using the Sapper in Level 81	4
Karma's a Bitch	Bracknell	Kill all enemies with their native weapon or the Backlash Grenade in Level 90	3
This is MY House!	Bracknell	Don't let any Chimera stand on the mining platform for more than 10 seconds in Level 90	4
Leapin' Lizards	London	Take no damage from Advanced Leapers in Level 100	3
Fast Like the Tortoise	London	Take no damage from Advanced Hybrids in Level 100	2
Le Parkour	Thames	Complete Level 110 in under 4 minutes	4
Vanilla Only, Please	Tower	Complete Level 120 without using alternate fires or grenades	4
What Would Hale Do?	Tower	Kill an Angel using only the Shotgun	2
Breakin' the Law	Tower	Destroy the Reactor without using the L200 LAARK	3
Return To Sender	Tower	Shoot five objects thrown at you by an Angel before they reach the player	3

Enemies

Name	Lev. Acquired	Description
Hybrid	The Gauntlet	After defeating first set of Hybrids.
Leaper	A Lone Survivor	After defeating first few Leapers.
Crawler	A Lone Survivor	After the cinematic and FPNICS.
Menial	Fate Worse Than Death	After the first room.
Cocoon	Conversion	At the third checkpoint.
Carrier	Fate Worse Than Death	At the window when you first see the Carriers.
Howler	Path of Least Resistance	After defeating the Howlers at the end of the level.
Steelhead	Cathedral	After defeating the first two Steelheads in the church.
Titan	Conduits	After defeating the Titan at the beginning of Level 51.

Name	Lev. Acquired	Description
Slipskull	No Way Out	After defeating all three Slipskulls in the burrower room.
Leaper Pod	No Way Out or Secrets	After finding the Leaper Pods for the first time.
Gray Jack	Angel	After the cryo room.
Hardfang	Evacuation	After defeating the first Hardfang in the cafeteria.
Roller	Into the Depths	After defeating the Rollers in the room with the tunnel in the floor.
Widowmaker	Ice and Iron	After defeating the first Widowmaker.
Hybrid 2.0	Angel's Lair	After the first wave of Hybrids in the node.
Angel	Angel's Lair	After defeating the first Angel on the bridge.

Vehicles

Name	Level Acquired	Description
Hawk	The Gauntlet	Player automatically starts with this.
Kingfisher	Path of Least Resistance	At the start of the level.
Sabertooth	A Lone Survivor	After getting inside the tank.
Dropship	Hunted Down	After spotting a Dropship in the parking lot area.
Stalker	Outgunned	After spotting the first Stalker in Level 42.
Burrower	No Way Out	After spotting the first Burrower in Level 60.
Lynx	Common Ground	After getting inside the Lynx.
Goliath	Giant Slayer	After spotting the first Goliath.

United States Army Rangers
1st Regiment

VI. Top Secret

BRITISH INTELLIGENCE AGENCY
CONFIDENTIAL DATA

Weapons—1st Playthrough

Name	Level Acquired	Description
M5A2 Carbine	The Gauntlet	Automatically unlocked at the start of the game.
Frag Grenade	The Gauntlet	Automatically unlocked at the start of the game.
Bullseye	The Gauntlet	In the alleyway after checkpoint 2.
Shotgun	Fate Worse Than Death or Hunted Down or Path of Least Resistance	Level 30: Behind the stairs in the outdoor area. Level 32: Behind the bar. Level 32: In the docks area. Level 40: Forced here on the stairs between hill 1 and 2.
Auger	Cathedral	After defeating the first two advanced Hybrids.
Sniper Rifle	Conduits	After defeating the large Hybrid and reaching checkpoint 1.
Hailstorm	Search and Rescue	After leaving the first area.
Sapper	A Disturbing Discovery	At the back of the first mech factory.
LAARK	In A Darker Place	On the ground in the first room.
Bullseye Mark 2	Angel's Lair	After leaving the first room and going into the node.

Weapons—2nd Playthrough

Name	Level Acquired	Description
Reapers	The Gauntlet	Inside the house at the bottom of the hill.
Backlash Grenade	Cathedral	After crossing the alley just past the cathedral; it's the first room on the left.
Arc Charger	No Way Out	At the end of the long hallway prior to the Burrower.
L11-Dragon	Evacuation	Before the first elevator leading to the hangar.
Splitter	A Desperate Gambit	At checkpoint 1, near the big windows.

Locations

Name	Level Acquired	Description
York	The Gauntlet	Unlocked at the start of the level.
Grimsby	Fate Worse Than Death	Unlocked at the start of the level.
Manchester	Path of Least Resistance	Unlocked at the start of the level.
Nottingham	Into the Fire	Unlocked at the start of the level.
Cheshire	No Way Out	Unlocked at the start of the level.
Somerset	Search and Rescue	Unlocked at the start of the level.
Bristol	Devil at the Door	Unlocked at the start of the level.
Bracknell	Into the Depths	Unlocked at the start of the level.
London	A Desperate Gambit	Unlocked at the start of the level.
Thames	Burning Bridges	Unlocked at the start of the level.
Tower	Angel's Lair	Unlocked at the start of the level.

Rewards

What do you get for all your hard-earned Skill Points? Head over to the Rewards menu and see for yourself. As you accumulate more points, new unlockable Rewards become available. In addition, there are a few more goodies to unlock by completing the game on the various difficulty modes.

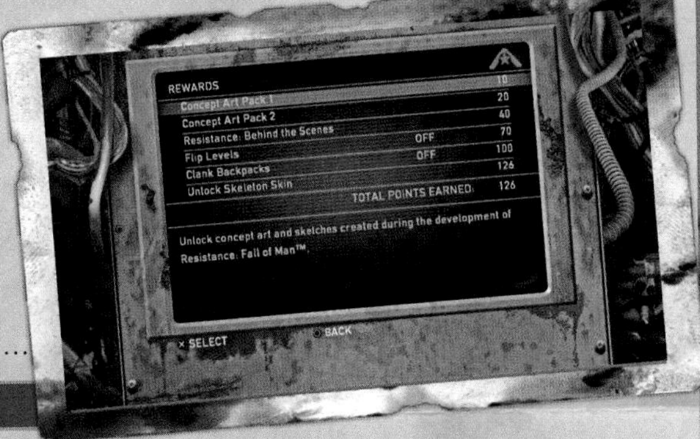

Rewards

Name	How to Unlock
Concept Art Pack 1	10 points
Concept Art Pack 2	20 points
The Mighty Wrench - Gives Allies Wrench	40 points
Flip Levels	70 points
Clank Backpacks	100 points
MP Mechanic Skin	126 points
MP Soldier Skin	Beat game on Superhuman mode.
MP Mechanic Head Skin	Beat game on Superhuman mode and collect all Skill Points.
Movie Player	Beat game once.

Multiplayer Unlockables

As you play more Ranked games, you are awarded experience points (XP). As your XP total reaches certain thresholds, your player "level" also increases. Levels are expressed as military ranks, along with one, two, or three pips. The pips indicate how advanced you are within your military rank. Scoring higher than your opponents in ranked games will net you higher XP awards. By increasing your player "level," you will periodically gain rewards. These rewards can be things like Skins, as well as other interesting tidbits. The complete list is below.

Unlockables

Rank	Type	Description
Level 1: ***Private***	Body	US Soldier
	Head	Head 1
	Head	Head 2
	Bangle	Small helmet
	Uniform	American standard
	Uniform	American dirty uniform
Level 4: ***PFC***	Body	UK Soldier body
	Uniform	British green
	Bangle	Canteen 2
Level 7: ***Corporal***	Uniform	British brick
	Bangle	Grenade pouch
	Bangle	Leather packs
Level 10: ***Sergeant***	Bangle	Pouches
	Bangle	Medic helmet 2
	Head	Head 3
Level 13: ***Gunnery Sergeant***	Bangle	Beret
	Uniform	American camo
	Head	Head 3
Level 16: ***Staff Sergeant***	Bangle	British goggles
	Bangle	Radio
	Bangle	Binoculars
Level 19: ***1ST Sergeant***	Body	Commando body
	Uniform	Commando standard
	Head	Head 4
Level 22: ***Sergeant Major***	Uniform	Commando camo
	Bangle	Belt knife
	Bangle	Backpack
Level 25: ***Sergeant Major***	Bangle	Chest pouches
	Bangle	Belt pouches
	Head	Head
Level 28: ***SGT Major of the Army***	Bangle	Medic helmet
	Bangle	Bedroll 1
	Bangle	Chute pack
Level 31: ***Lieutenant***	Head	Head 6
	Uniform	British desert
	SKIN	VTOL pilot
Level 34: ***Captain***	Bangle	Bedroll 2
	Bangle	Pouches
	Bangle	Pouch (fanny pack)
Level 37: ***Major***	Head	Head 7
	Bangle	British helmet
	Bangle	Backpack
Level 40: ***LT Colonel***	Uniform	Commando leather
	Bangle	Chest radio
	Complete skin	Shirtless
Level 43: ***Colonel***	Bangle	Camo helmet
	Bangle	Leather backpack
	Bangle	Back holster
Level 46: ***Brigadier General***	Head	Head 8
	Bangle	Canteen 1
	Bangle	Radio
Level 49: ***Major General***	Complete skin	Winters
	Uniform	American advanced
	Bangle	Hip bag
Level 52: **Lt. General**	Head	Head 9
	Helmet	American helmet
	Uniform	Commando arctic
	Bangle	Canteen
Level 55: **General**	Complete skin	Cartwright
	Bangle	Leather pouch
	Bangle	Canteen
Level 58: **Supreme Commander**	Uniform	British camo
	Bangle	Knife
	Head	Head 10
Level 60: **Supreme Commander Plus 2 PIPs**	Complete skin	Hale
	Bangle	Belt packs
	Bangle	Shovel
	Bangle	Backpack

Other Multiplayer Unlockables

	Complete skin	Surgeon
Unlocked Via MyResistance.Net Community	Complete skin	Cloven
Acquire All SP Skill Points	Complete skin	Mechanic
Finish SP In Superhuman Mode	Complete skin	Black OPS guy
All Skill Points & Superhuman	Complete skin	Bo flaming skeleton

RESISTANCE
FALL OF MAN™

OFFICIAL STRATEGY GUIDE

BradyGames Publishing
An Imprint of DK Publishing, Inc.
800 East 96th Street, 3rd Floor
Indianapolis, Indiana 46240

ISBN: 0-7440-0868-9

Printing Code: The rightmost double-digit number is the year of the book's printing; the rightmost single-digit number is the number of the book's printing. For example, 06-1 shows that the first printing of the book occurred in 2006.

09 08 07 06 4 3 2 1

Manufactured in the United States of America.

BradyGAMES Staff

Publisher
David Waybright

Creative Director
Robin Lasek

Editor-In-Chief
H. Leigh Davis

Licensing Manager
Mike Degler

Director of Marketing
Steve Escalante

Credits

Title Manager
Tim Cox

Book Designer
Keith Lowe

Screenshot Editor
Michael Owen

Production Designer
Wil Cruz

Author Acknowledgements

I would like to thank the following people for their help in making this guide happen: Ted Price, Ryan Schneider, James Stevenson, Greg Phillips, Caley Roberts, Connie Booth, Grady Hunt, Rob Alvarez, Cristian Cardona, John Koller, Peter Dille, Nick Schilbe, Vlad Ciupitu, Camden Tayler, Ryan Eckert, Justin Beachler, Andrew Benagas, Jason Littrell, Cash Turner, Stanley Phan, Tim Cox, Leigh Davis, Mike Degler and, of course, Kimberly Brennan, who, despite my best efforts otherwise, is still hanging in there.